Industrial Histories of Britain Series—Associated Volume

THE BRITISH HOSIERY AND KNITWEAR INDUSTRY: ITS HISTORY AND ORGANISATION

INDUSTRIAL HISTORIES OF BRITAIN SERIES

General Editor: Professor W. E. Minchinton
Professor of Economic History
University of Exeter

BRITAIN'S RAILWAYS: AN INDUSTRIAL HISTORY

Harold Pollins
Tutor in Industrial Relations and Economics Ruskin College Oxford

In preparation

HISTORY OF AGRICULTURE

M. A. Havinden
Lecturer in Economic History University of Exeter

NON-FERROUS METAL INDUSTRIES

Roger Burt
Lecturer in Economic History University of Exeter

Industrial Histories of Britain Series—Associated Volume

THE BRITISH HOSIERY AND KNITWEAR INDUSTRY: ITS HISTORY AND ORGANISATION

by Professor F. A. WELLS

DAVID & CHARLES: Newton Abbot

ISBN 0 7153 5437 X

First published 1935
by GEORGE ALLEN & UNWIN LTD

Revised edition 1972
by DAVID & CHARLES (PUBLISHERS) LTD

Set in 11/12pt Plantin
and printed in Great Britain
by Bristol Typesetting Company Limited
for David & Charles (Publishers) Limited
South Devon House Newton Abbot Devon

CONTENTS

LIST OF ILLUSTRATIONS

PREFACE

The greater part of this work was first published in 1935 under the title *The British Hosiery Trade: its History and Organisation*. At that time hosiery ranked third among British textile manufactures and was growing rapidly, though it was still much smaller than the cotton and woollen and worsted industries. Now, with a total employment of 130,000 and an annual output exceeding £400 million, hosiery is comparable in size with the other two, both of which and particularly cotton have continued to decline. The present importance of the industry and its progress in technology and organisation in the past twenty years suggested the need for a revised edition of the original work.

As in the first edition, the study is in two parts. Part 1 deals with the history of the manufacture from Lee's invention in 1589 to its emergence as a factory industry in the latter part of the nineteenth century. Until that time framework knitting, as it was called, was carried on as a handicraft in homes and workshops. Other textile trades were among the first to be affected by the Industrial Revolution, and it is often assumed that in this country domestic industry was practically extinguished in the first half of the nineteenth century. Yet in hosiery we have a trade that has passed through an industrial revolution almost within living memory.

There is an element of romance in the origin of the hosiery industry and its history covers many changes of fortune. At times the condition of the framework knitters was about as bad as it could be, compelling the attention of government; and if little else resulted from the numerous inquiries of committees and commissions they at least provided a wealth of information for future students.

Besides the official reports and the records of the Framework Knitters' Company, there are fortunately two nineteenth-century histories written by men with an intimate knowledge of the industry. The first is Gravenor Henson's *Civil, Political and Mechanical History of the Framework Knitters*, published in 1831. This stops at 1780, for the intended second volume never appeared. Its chief value to the modern historian lies in its detailed account of technical developments. But its interest is by no means confined to this aspect; for Henson was an outstanding figure in local politics and his activities have attracted considerable attention from students of the early labour movement. The second work is Felkin's *History of the Machine-wrought Hosiery and Lace Manufactures*, 1867. This is particularly valuable for its statistical information, Felkin having continued the analysis of the trade begun by Blackner, himself a framework knitter, and included in his *History of Nottingham*, 1812. Apart from his painstaking, but somewhat inconclusive, researches regarding the early life of William Lee, Felkin contributes little to the history of the trade before his own lifetime, his account being based mainly on Henson's. The later inventions are, however, fully treated and illustrated and there are some interesting reminiscences drawn from his own experience. Both these works have recently been reprinted with valuable introductions by Dr S. D. Chapman, Pasold Lecturer in Textile History in the University of Nottingham.

There is a dearth of histories of individual firms in this industry and extensive inquiries about business archives have so far yielded little. The gap has, however, been partially filled by Charlotte Erickson's study, *British Industrialists, Steel and Hosiery, 1850–1950*, published in 1959, which traces the origins and careers of many Nottingham hosiery manufacturers. A more recent book, of a very different kind, is *Stockings for a Queen* by Milton and Anna Grass. Its sub-title, *The Life of William Lee, The Elizabethan Inventor*, is rather pretentious, for despite their extensive inquiries the authors are unable to add much to the meagre facts already known. They did, however, discover important evidence of Lee's sojourn in Rouen, to which reference is made in my first chapter. I am also indebted to Dr Chapman for kindly lending me his article, 'The Genesis of the Hosiery Industry', before its publication. This is based on an investigation of the wills and insurance inventories of hosiers in the seventeenth and eighteenth centuries and adds considerably to our knowledge of the industry in this period.

Part II has been completely rewritten and expanded. Here I am indebted to the research undertaken by Professor A. G. Pool and G. Llewellyn and published by Leicester University in three reports (1955–8). These, however, are limited in scope; for instance they do not include any study of labour conditions. Further, a survey made in the 1950s is now out of date in many respects, for important changes in the structure of the industry and its external relations have occurred in the past ten years.

These changes, as I have endeavoured to show, are part of a process which is transforming the whole textile and clothing group. The traditional trade divisions based on material or product are becoming blurred and even obliterated. Thus it is no longer proper to speak of the 'hosiery' industry. The industry has always produced many articles besides stockings and output is now more varied than ever before. The manufacture is better defined in terms of its characteristic process, and this has recently been recognised by converting the former National Hosiery Manufacturers' Federation into the Knitting Industries Federation, though the trade union retains a more conservative style as the National Union of Hosiery and Knitwear Workers. I have adopted the same nomenclature in my title as being the more familiar and in the text I use the name 'hosiery industry' partly for convenience but also because that is how the industry came to be known when framework knitting was superseded by power-driven machinery.

In conclusion, I must express my thanks to the many persons connected with the industry who have helped with information and advice. Some of these contacts extend over many years to the time when I was myself a member of the industry.

F. A. Wells
University of Nottingham

NOTE

The publishers much regret the death of Professor Wells just before this book appeared. With Mrs Wells, they are greatly indebted to his colleagues, Professor A. W. Coats and Dr S. D. Chapman of the University of Nottingham, for their assistance in the final stages of publication.

Part One :
Historical Development

CHAPTER 1

THE ORIGIN AND EARLY DEVELOPMENT OF THE INDUSTRY

The history of the British hosiery trade properly begins with the introduction of the art of hand knitting into this country. Just when this took place it is impossible to say; there seems to be no mention of knitting before the fifteenth century, but by Henry VII's time knitted caps were important enough to be included in a list of articles whose prices were regulated by Act of Parliament. In the early sixteenth century the manufacture of these goods extended rapidly; London alone had eight thousand workers engaged in its various branches, and there were places all over the country, including Leicester and Derby, where it was carried on.[1] Knitted stockings, however, were as yet unknown in England; indeed Adam Smith suggests that the art of making them was probably not known anywhere in Europe in the time of Edward IV, all hose being made of cloth cut to shape and seamed at the back. It seems likely that the new method originated in Spain; at all events, it was apparently that country which supplied the first knitted silk stockings worn in England. Dr Howell in his *History of the World* relates that 'King Henry VIII, that magnificent and expensive prince, wore ordinarily cloth hose, except there came from Spain, by great chance, a pair of silk stockings; for Spain very early abounded in silk. His son, King Edward VI, was presented with a pair of long Spanish silk stockings by his merchant, Sir Thomas Gresham, and the present was then taken much notice of'. It was not long before the imported article was successfully imitated here, for the same authority informs us that 'Queen Elizabeth, in the third year of her reign, was presented with a pair of black silk knit stockings by her silk woman, Mrs Montague, and thenceforth she never wore cloth ones any more'.[2] Others relate that 'one William Rider, an apprentice on London Bridge, seeing at the house of an Italian merchant a pair of knit worsted stockings from Mantua, made

15

with great skill a pair exactly like them, which he presented in the year 1564 to William Earl of Pembroke, and were the first of that kind worn in England'.[3]

From whatever source it may have come, knowledge of the art of knitting stockings quickly spread throughout the country. That considerable quantities were being made in Surrey in 1584 is evident from the report of a case in which two men were charged at Kingston with having dyed 1,000 dozens of knit hose with logwood.[4] Eleven years later Peck's Report on *New Draperies in the Countie of York* mentions the large output of knitted stockings in the North Riding; over a thousand were engaged in this work in and about Richmond and one hundred and twenty at Doncaster.[5] In 1774 Richmond still had a good trade in stockings and sailors' woollen caps, while Doncaster made knitted waistcoats and petticoats besides gloves and stockings.[6] Hand knitting was also important in Norfolk where, according to Defoe,[7] it was at one time worth five to ten thousand shillings a week; although the trade had dwindled by the beginning of the eighteenth century it revived later, the output of Norwich alone being computed at £60,000 a year in 1774.[8] In all the woollen districts stocking making was developed as a branch of the manufacture, and in many parts it survived as a handwork industry long after the introduction of the stocking frame. Postlethwayte, for instance, mentions Campden as 'famous for its manufacture of stockings'; Bruton, Shepton Mallet, and Evesham were also important; at Christchurch, 'a large and populous borough', the chief manufacture was stockings and gloves; the poor of Peterborough were constantly employed in weaving and knitting; the town of Bridgnorth was 'as famous as any other for the making of stockings'.

Knitting was also taken up extensively in Scotland; indeed, some authorities suggest that the art was practised there before it was introduced in England,[9] but whether that be true or not the flourishing industry of the Shetland and Orkney Islands may well have developed independently. The fine wool of the island sheep favoured the production of high-quality goods, and a considerable trade grew up between the natives and the Dutch fishermen in the seventeenth century.[10]

In Adam Smith's day more than a thousand pairs of Shetland stockings were imported annually into Leith, the price being fivepence to sevenpence a pair, though hose at a guinea a pair and upwards were also produced. At this time, however, the chief centre of the Scottish knitting industry was Aberdeen, where the trade had grown to the extent of 70,000 dozen pairs of stockings annually, worth on the average thirty shillings a dozen.[11] The stockings were chiefly exported to Holland and thence dispersed throughout Germany; in some years these shipments, together with those to London, amounted to £80,000 in value. The rise of this trade is the more remarkable in that little of the wool used was grown in the district, supplies being obtained mainly through Newcastle and London. But the cheap labour available was doubtless an important factor; rates were so low that the women and children employed in knitting could not make more than 2½d a day.[12]

The Shetland and Orkney knitters were independent producers growing their own wool or buying it from neighbours and selling the finished articles; it was not until about 1840, when the shawl trade became important, that the system of employment by merchant capitalists began to develop,[13] and even as late as 1908 the primitive organisation survived in the Shetlands.[14] In Aberdeen, however, capitalist control came much earlier. Down to the middle of the eighteenth century it was customary for the importers to sell the raw wool to the country people by whom it was combed, spun, and knitted; the goods were then sold in the local markets or to merchant exporters. According to Postlethwayte 'insufficiency and cheating in every degree was frequent' under this system, so that the importers were driven to undertake the combing in their own warehouses; the tops were then given out to spinners and knitters who worked under their direction.

Even today machinery has by no means completely ousted hand knitting which, apart from its private uses, is still an industry in parts of Scotland and Ireland; but it was the introduction of the stocking frame that laid the foundation of the modern hosiery trade. The inventions in textile machinery that introduced the new industrial era have tended to obscure the work of the genius who, two centuries earlier, without the guidance of any previous efforts produced this prodigy of complicated and delicate mechanism. Not the least remarkable fact about the invention is that it seems to have been unprompted by any urgent demand. It is true that the price of knitted stockings was very high at the time,[15] but they were but recently introduced and there must have

B

been ample supplies of labour to meet the demands of what was as yet a comparatively restricted market. There is possibly some truth in the story that Lee was driven to his task by disappointed love; but it may well be that he turned to mechanical experiments merely as a relief from the tedium of a country parsonage, for like Cartwright, the power-loom inventor, Lee was a clergyman.

Unfortunately little is known of Lee's early life. Thoroton, the seventeenth-century historian, merely informs us that 'at Calverton was born William Lee, Master of Arts in Cambridge and heir to a pretty freehold here; who, seeing a woman knit, invented a loom to knit, in which he and his brother James performed and exercised before Queen Elizabeth'.[16] Calverton is a village seven miles north of Nottingham in which hosiery manufacture is still carried on, but the birth of the industry's founder is not recorded in the church register, which dates only from 1568. Others give the neighbouring parish of Woodborough as the birthplace, but here again, although as at Calverton various members of the Lee family are recorded, none can be identified as William Lee the inventor. There is, however, a record of Lee's matriculation at Christ's College, Cambridge, in 1579, from which we may assume that he was born about 1560. His father was a substantial yeoman farmer; but when he died in 1607 his landed property passed to two of William's brothers; William, the eldest son, was left 'one ring of gold, in the value worth 20 shillings, in full discharge of his filial portion'.[17] By this time he was absorbed in the exploitation of his invention and had long since left Calverton; but he could have spent some years there after graduating from Cambridge, and although direct evidence is lacking there seems no reason to doubt the traditional story that he was a curate in his native village at the time when his invention was made.

For technical details of the invention we have to rely on information derived from apprentices trained by Lee and his youngest brother James and passed on to successive generations of framework knitters. They can be verified by reference to surviving examples of early frames which, although embodying improvements, as described by Henson,[18] still demonstrate the original principle. Lee must have realised almost at the outset the futility of trying to produce work in circular form, as when a stocking is knitted on pins; a frame-knitted stocking would have to be made flat and afterwards seamed. This was a disadvantage in one way, but it meant that a frame-knitted stocking or other garment could be shaped or 'fashioned' by varying the number of loops in a course of knitting. Lee thus established the principle on which all frame-knitted hose were made for some two hundred years. He also saw that he must have one needle for each loop. The needles were set horizontally in a bar and in between were the sinkers which manipulated the thread laid across the needles. A remarkable feature of the invention was the needle itself. It took the form of a spring hook which opened to receive the thread presented by the sinker and was then closed by pressing the barb into a slot cut in the needle shank, so that the fabric could be pushed forward over the needle hooks. The making of these needles, especially for fine-gauge work, must have tested the cleverest craftsmen. The larger parts of the mechanism were made of wrought iron and fixed in a heavy wood frame, with a seat for the operative and three pedals. Two of the pedals worked the sinkers, laying the thread and forming the loops first from one side then from the other. The loops were brought under the needle hooks by pulling the sinkers forward; then the third pedal was used to bring down the presser bar and the fabric was pushed over the closed needle hooks, thus completing a course of knitting. The first machine, with eight needles to the inch, could make only the coarsest kind of work.

Elated with his success, Lee determined, if possible, to secure protection for the invention and financial assistance under the State patent policy begun in 1561. In the first twenty years of the new system thirteen patents had been granted for mechanical inventions and Lee's claim seemed eminently worthy of recognition.[19] He was fortunate in securing powerful influence at court through Lord Hunsdon,[20] a kinsman of Elizabeth, who, it is said, was so impressed with the machine that he arranged for his son to be taught the art of framework knitting in return for a guarantee of support for the invention.[21] When the frame was demonstrated before the Queen, however, she professed disappointment at the coarseness of the work and further declared that she could not grant a monopoly for a machine which would deprive so many of her subjects of their employment. There seemed to be better hope of obtaining a patent for a machine to make silk hose, since this would not have such serious effects on the hand industry. Moreover, a finer-gauge frame was likely to be much more profitable, for the difference in speed as compared with hand work would be far greater.

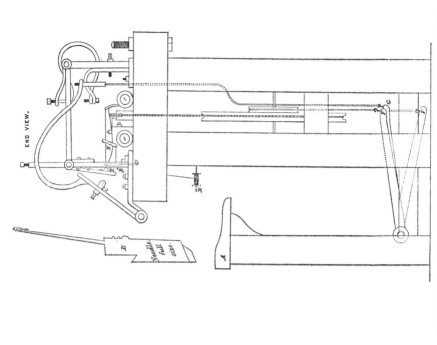

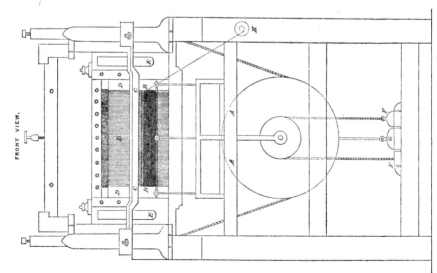

Line drawing of a stocking frame, from W. Felkin, *History of the Machine-Wrought Hosiery and Lace Manufactures* (1867)

Accordingly Lee set to work to make a finer-gauge frame, presumably with Hunsdon's financial backing. He eventually produced one with twenty needles to the inch and over a period of some ten years nine frames were built on this model. But Hunsdon died in 1596 and there was now little hope of securing a patent. There was even a danger that the frame might be prohibited. Opposition to labour-saving machines increased in the latter part of Elizabeth's reign and under James I prohibitions were imposed. Although the framework knitters claimed that theirs was a new art, the frame was always suspect as likely to cause unemployment among hand knitters.[22]

Being thus discouraged, Lee decided to seek his fortune in France. After many years of religious strife and political upheaval, France, the most populous country in Europe, was now united under the enlightened leadership of Henry IV. Following the Edict of Nantes in 1598, the harassing of Protestants, which had driven so many skilled and enterprising people abroad, especially to England, had ceased. It was the King's policy to encourage manufactures and skilled crafts, silk working being especially favoured. Hospitality and financial backing were offered to foreign inventors and artisans. Thus when Lee received an invitation to set up in France 'he embraced the seeming fair opportunity and went himself, taking his brother and nine workmen and as many frames to Roan [Rouen] in Normandy, where he wrought with great applause'.[23]

The provisions for the establishment of the French enterprise are fully set out in a contract between William Lee and Pierre de Caux for 'a company to manufacture stockings of silk and of wool'.[24] Mention is made of four machines already delivered and of Lee's obligation to supply another four, together with six skilled workers from England, so that manufacture could begin by 26 March 1610. Further, Lee 'the inventor and chief executive of the manufacture' undertook to train French apprentices in the building, maintenance and operation of the frames, whereby the original nucleus should be expanded to forty machines as speedily as possible. On the other hand, de Caux and his associates promised to pay Lee, by instalments, 2,500 livres for the frames already delivered and a bonus to his two mechanics. They were also to finance the construction of further frames and to provide working capital for wages, rent and materials. Every three months there was to be 'an accounting of what had taken place, handled sold &

distributed,' the profit to be shared equally among five or six associates, including Lee.

It is evident from the wording of the contract that its preparation had begun early in 1610, or perhaps in the previous year. However, despite de Caux's promise to have it ratified within two months, the date on which it was 'acknowledged before the Tabelliones [notaries] of Rouen' is 10 February 1611. In the meantime, only two months after the enterprise was due to begin, a disastrous event had taken place. Henry IV was assassinated. His death and the subsequent dismissal of Sully, the leading statesman of his reign, brought to an end the brief period of religious toleration and state encouragement to immigrants introducing new industries.

The political uncertainty so created is reflected in Lee's contract with de Caux. It contains various clauses designed to safeguard the interests of the inventor and his English associates, and it is significant that some of its provisions were evidently added after the original draft had been prepared. Besides the risk of commercial failure there was now the possibility that the French shareholders, as Huguenots, might be prevented from continuing in business. Thus, in case of such default, Lee and his apprentices were 'free to depart from this country, without being held responsible for making any restitution for any of the money they may have received from the sums specified above; nor to contribute to the sending back of himself and his apprentices'. Alternatively, Lee should be entirely free to manufacture on his own account if he wished. As a further safeguard, de Caux and his associates undertook to secure letters of French citizenship for Lee and his mechanics.

How long the company survived, and whether it succumbed to trade depression or to political pressure imposed on its promoters, we do not know. It is established that Lee went to Paris, presumably in the hope of getting his privileges confirmed, and that he died there, worn out by his efforts and the disappointments of twenty years. After Lee's death his brother James managed to bring back eight frames and all but two of the English workmen to London where they set up in Old Street Square.[25] Here they were at least free from religious persecution, but the state of the new industry was still precarious. One group of framework knitters, 'after fruitless experiments here,' had recently gone over to Venice[26] and the returning emigrants must have found it difficult to re-establish themselves. James Lee did not attempt to settle in London; after a short time he sold his machines and returned to Nottinghamshire, where he joined Aston, a former apprentice of William Lee, who had, in the meantime, effected important improvements which made it possible to build frames at less than half the former cost.[27]

There were now two branches of the manufacture, one centred in London and the other in Nottinghamshire; but despite the initial difficulties it was the former that developed most in the early years. The framework knitters found their most profitable employment in the production of high-quality fancy goods, like silk hose and waistcoats, the market for which was naturally found in the capital, the centre of fashion. It was to London that foreign buyers came and 'the best artisans of the manufactory' it was said, 'bend their endeavours all they can to the foreign vent'.[28] The market for imported silk was also in London, and when, at the end of the seventeenth century, the Huguenot silk workers, who had settled at Canterbury, migrated to London and established their industry at Spitalfields in the midst of the framework knitters, a further fillip was given to the trade.

On the other hand, Nottingham had an advantage in the production of worsted hosiery. The sheep of Sherwood Forest were of a peculiar breed, 'small in size, but covered with a fleece having the wool of the longest filaments or staple and of a fineness equal to any in Europe'.[29] When the industry spread into the neighbouring county of Leicester proximity to raw material was again an important factor. Defoe tells us that the Leicester and Lincoln sheep had the largest fleeces of any in England, yielding wool of the longest stable and finest quality in the whole island, some few places excepted.[30]

The comparatively slow growth of the framework-knitting industry during the seventeenth century was doubtless due to the nature of its trade. Although the frame greatly increased the speed of knitting, it was costly to build and maintain and it required a skilled man to work it. But hand knitting was done by women and children, supplying the needs of their own families or, if they worked for wages, poorly paid. It was in fine-gauge knitting, using silk and fine worsted yarns, that the frame found its most profitable employment, and the early framework knitters preferred to concentrate on this lucrative but limited trade rather than develop the market for cheap goods. Henson estimates[31] that in 1664, when the trade was incorporated, there would be four or five hundred frames in London itself, chiefly in the parish of St Luke, Middlesex, and in the neighbourhood of Norton Folgate and Shoreditch. As at that time two persons commonly wrought in one frame, the number of workers would probably be about 800. In addition there were some 50 frames at Berkhamsted in Hertfordshire, and Chesham and Tring in Buckinghamshire, with a few at Godalming and Farnham in Surrey, and at Odiham in Hampshire. Nottingham and its neighbourhood had more than a hundred frames and Leicestershire about half that number, while a few, not more than ten, had been introduced in Dublin. In all, there would be about 650 machines and 1,200 framework knitters, of whom three-fifths were employed in silk, making stockings and pieces for trousers, breeches, and waistcoats. Besides those actually working frames, however, there were, as the petition of 1655 points out, many 'merchants, hosiers, dyers, winders, throwsters, sizers, seamsters, trimmers, wire drawers, needle-makers, smiths, joyners, turners, and other assistants' all drawing profit from the industry.

About this time efforts were being made to encourage the establishment of framework knitting, along with other industries, in Scotland. But despite the privileges offered in the Acts of 1661 and 1663,[32] it was not until twenty years later that the first stocking frames were introduced. An interesting account of the experiment is contained in the minute books of the New Mills Cloth Manufactory.[33] This company was founded by a group of Edinburgh merchants and shopkeepers in 1681, with an Englishman, Sir James Stanfield, at its head, the workers being drawn from Yorkshire and the West of England. Beginning with the coarsest cloths, production was at length extended to superfine woollens, and in 1682 it is recorded that 'the managers made due agreement with Sir James Stanfield for foure silk stocken frames for which they are to pay 2,000 marks'.[34] In all, seven frames were acquired, including some brought by a master stockinger from London, one Edward Pike. The names of the other framework knitters, Francis Perry, John Godson, and Burton, suggest that they were also English. Doubtless they were an independent set of men, fully conscious of their value as pioneers of a new art, and there seems to have been some difficulty in arranging contracts. In the end it was agreed to pay 2s 6d per pair of hose, with an addition of 10d for every ounce above three; and when striped stockings were introduced a settlement at 4s 7d was approved.

The records of buying and giving out silk at a few pounds at a time show that production was never on a large scale, and there is evidence of fluctuations in demand for the various articles made. In 1684 worsted stockings were tried, but orders were not satisfactory, and next year it was decided that 'noe more worsted stockens be made unless fyne worsted can be had, but that they work upon silk gloves and plain marbled silk stockens, long unstriped, and women's silk stockens'. Four years later orders were given that 'the silk frames be rouped [sold at auction] unless a letter arrive with hopes to dispose of them in London'. The last heard of them is in the minute of October 1688, noting an agreement with a framesmith to repair 'the wholl seven frames and make them compleat for sixtie pund sterling'.

It was many years before any further attempt was made to set up framework knitting in Scotland. According to Bremner there was a strong prejudice against the frame and no one would venture to introduce it. There is, however, a record of an Edinburgh hosier with a shop of twelve frames in 1739 and a few years later a group of merchants in Glasgow were running a framework knitters' shop.[35] Then in 1771 Bailie John Hardie introduced four frames at Hawick. This eventually became the chief centre of the trade in Scotland; but progress was slow and twenty years later there were still only twelve frames producing in the year 3,505 pairs of lambs' wool and 594 pairs of cotton and worsted hose and giving employment to 14 men and 51 women. There were a few frames scattered about in other places, but it was not until the early nineteenth century that the trade became fairly established in Scotland.[36]

The main reason for the tardy development of framework knitting in Scotland was the lack of demand for machine-wrought goods in a country where the art of hand knitting was so universally practised. Frame-knitted articles would have to be very cheap to compete. Considering the cost of frames, their upkeep and the wages paid, expenses at New Mills appear to have been high, so that only fine-gauge silk work was worthwhile and Scotland had no particular advantages in this trade. A century later, when frames were cheaper and framework knitters more numerous, it could still be said that in Scotland stockings were 'knit much cheaper than they could be anywhere upon the loom, being the work of servants and labourers who derived the principal part of their subsistence from some other employment'.[37]

Several attempts to introduce framework knitting in foreign countries are recorded in the petition of 1655, but in every case the enterprise had failed. Of the two men left in France after James Lee's return, one had died and the other, after forty years, was still working the frame on the old principle, without Aston's improvements, and was 'so far short of the perfection of his trade [as used here], that of him, or what can be done by him, or his means, the petitioners [were] in no fear'. Foreigners were apparently ever on the lookout for workmen who could be induced to emigrate. In one case

> a Venetian Ambassador gave £500 for a remnant of time of one Henry Mead, then an apprentice to this trade, and conveyed him with his frame from London to Venice, where, although his work and the manner of it were awhile admired and endeavoured to be imitated, yet as soon as necessity for reparation of his frame and instruments happened, for want of artificers experienced in such work and of ability in him to direct them, the work prospered not in his management, so that, his bought time of service being expired, affection for his native country brought him home again to England. After his departure the Venetians grew disheartened and, impatient of making vain trials, they sent his disordered frame and some of their own imitation to be sold in London at a very low valuation.

The failure of the Venetians, then among the finest smiths in Europe, is a significant tribute to the genius of Lee and the skill of the English mechanics.

A similar result attended an attempt, a few years later, to establish the industry in Holland. Abraham Jones, who had 'by underhand courses and insinuations, and not by servitude as an apprentice, gotten both the mystery and the skillful practice thereof', and so had attracted the 'jealous notice' of the trade, decided to remove with a few others to Amsterdam.

> There, taking some Dutch unto him as servants, he erected frames and wrought for the space of two or three years, until the infection of the plague seized upon him and his whole family. His frames also (as things unprofitable to them that could not find out their right use without an able teacher) were sent to London to sell at slight rates.

Hence the petitioners are able to declare that 'in spite of continued efforts for the fifty years last past, the trade is still an art peculiar to our nation; and to the nimble spirits of the French, the fertile wits of the Italians, and the industrious inclination of the Dutch, a concealed mystery unto this day'.

CHAPTER 2

THE FRAMEWORK KNITTERS' COMPANY

The framework knitting industry began at a time when the evolution of industrial organisation had reached an interesting stage. All through the sixteenth century there had been developing within the trade companies a struggle between the commercial interests, as represented by the merchant class, and the industrial interests of the small masters, a parallel to the earlier conflict between masters and journeymen in the craft guild. It was out of this struggle that the Stuart corporations of small masters emerged.[1] The position of the framework knitters, however, was rather different from that of the older trades in which the company was an established institution. Theirs was a new craft and its members were apparently independent of any existing body. Indeed, there does not appear to have been a hosiers' guild in London, though probably they were attached to the drapers as at Chester.[2] It would seem that the hosiers arose out of the draper class who, before the introduction of framework knitting, not only sold but manufactured hose, to which branch the tailors had formerly laid claim.[3] Doubtless some of the hosiers, as men possessing capital, were among the pioneers of the new industry, which could be developed only by people of substance owing to the costliness of frames and materials; at all events it is significant that in later years the larger manufacturers were always known as hosiers. According to Henson the trade was originally carried on by two sorts of employers: one, the hosiers who made their own goods and kept retail shops; the other, those who made and sold them either to their connections, by taking orders, or to retail hosiers.[4] It seems fairly certain that at this stage there was no clear distinction between a trading and an industrial class, while the small scope of the trade and the necessity for close contact between producer and consumer were further factors inimical to the differentiation of functions.[5]

As the trade expanded the class of master stockingers grew in importance, but in the first forty years of the industry's existence in London they had apparently no regular association of their own, nor were they attached in a body to any other institution. Being 'dispersed among divers Companies of London and elsewhere' they had not 'that form of government as [was] necessary and advantageous to the Art and Mystery of Framework Knitting';[6] and in particular they had no legal sanction for regulating apprenticeship in the trade, since framework knitting was unknown at the time of the Statute of Artificers (1563) and therefore could not be included in it. In 1655 the stocking-makers felt that they had become sufficiently numerous to justify a petition to Cromwell for a charter of incorporation, whereby this deficiency could be remedied.[7]

According to mercantilist ideas framework knitting seemed to have special claims for protection. As the petitioners pointed out, it was an entirely new art invented in England and, unlike other manufactures which had been granted privileges, there was a possibility of reserving it for this country. Further, the trade imported raw silk at cheap rates and exported it in the form of manufactured goods 'at the utmost extent of value, the vent thereof being more foreign than domestic'. But the policy of the interregnum period was rather unfavourable to the regulation of industry and trade by corporations,[8] and the petition was examined with a good deal of caution, being first referred to the Lord Mayor and Court of Aldermen of London and then to the Attorney-General who was asked to consider whether the particulars desired were repugnant to the laws.[9]

It was only after a delay of two years that the request was granted and the framework knitters received a charter of incorporation under the Great Seal, dated 13 June 1657.[10] Unlike the subsequent charter of Charles II, this applied only to London and the district within four miles of the City. It named the master and assistants, the latter appointed for life and with power to elect their successors, who had 'full power to ordain, constitute, appoint, and set down such reasonable acts and ordinances' as were thought necessary for the government of the trade. The company might charge 12d a quarter to all freemen and 'foreigners' exercising the trade, and such other reasonable sums as the master and wardens thought fit for defraying necessary expenses. Power was given to enforce the Statute of 1563 as fully as if the trade had been incorporated before it; none was to exercise the art unless he had served a seven years' apprenticeship, and no aliens were to be taken apprentice. Finally the letters patent were to be taken as good and sufficient in law and to be construed in all Courts of Record 'most beneficially and largely for the advantage of the master, wardens and assistants'.

Before the bylaws could be legally operated, however, it was necessary, under an Act of 19 Henry VII, to get them signed by the Lord Chancellor and Chief Justices, and a year later we find the framework knitters complaining of the difficulty of securing their sanction. In the meantime frames were being made for export, which meant that other nations would 'get our trade, make goods worse, and sell them at under rates'. For instance, an Italian merchant had bespoken thirty or forty frames for speedy export at the high price of £80 each and several were already delivered. The petitioners therefore begged that all such frames be seized by the customs officials and detained until the bylaws be passed.[11] After further delay an Order in Council was made (14 June 1659) for customs officers not to permit export of frames till the pleasure of Parliament should be known.

With the restoration of the monarchy in 1660 Cromwell's charter became void, but the framework knitters lost no time in applying for a new one. In their petitions of 1660 and 1661 they complain that the ruin of the trade by imperfect frames and unmerchantable wares, and the carrying over of their machines beyond the seas, threaten to bring them to beggary; and they ask for powers to correct these abuses.[12] The Council of Trade reported favourably on the application. They recommended, however, that the application of the charter should be restricted to the same area as before, though if there were any considerable number of framework knitters in any other part of the kingdom they might be incorporated under like privileges. Another of their recommendations is especially interesting in view of the conflicts that arose later: 'None should be compelled to be of the corporation or under its government, but left to the free use of their trade'.[13] As will be seen, neither of these limitations appears in the charter which was granted in 1664.

By the Royal Charter of 1664, the framework knitters became a body politic and corporate under the title of 'The Master, Wardens, Assistants and Society of the Company of Framework Knitters of our cities of London and Westminster and our Kingdom of England and Dominion of Wales,'[14] having the right to hold property not exceeding £100 yearly and able to sue and be sued at law. The master, wardens, and assistants might make such regulations as they thought proper for the government of the society, for the reformation of abuses, or preventing fraudulent work, and might inflict and levy all fines by distress and otherwise.

The charter provided that all persons exercising the art of framework knitting should within six months present themselves before the officials and be sworn members of the craft, any who neglected this duty to be fined £5 for every week of default. It declared that henceforth none should be admitted to the trade unless he had served a seven years' apprenticeship to an accredited member. It empowered the company's deputies to examine any work and destroy what was 'bad and deceitful', and also to seize any frames destined for export. Finally, it authorised the making of bylaws, subject to the approval of the Lord Chancellor and Chief Justices, by a small body of men, named in the charter, appointed for life, and with power to name their successors.

How far the promoters of the company were truly representative of the industry, or what class they represented, it is difficult to say. According to Henson, 'the charter by no means gave satisfaction to the body of framework knitters; they complained that it was got up by a junta in London and they never very cordially fell in with its provisions'.[15] That there was some opposition to Cromwell's grant of incorporation is evident from two documents preserved among the State Papers of 1660.[16] A petition from William Savill, gentleman, and John Chettle, engineer, declared that the charter was obtained by some twenty of the silk stocking weavers 'upon recital of their great service for Oliver Cromwell'. These had ruined the trade and tradesmen by imperfect frames and the making of wares unmerchantable and most deceitful, so that the art was like to be lost here and carried into foreign parts where the artists might hope for encouragement. The petitioners ask that the corporation may be made void and that they, who have much improved the art, may be empowered to correct all abuses; and their application is supported by forty-seven other persons who are ready to substantiate the complaints upon oath.

It is clear, however, that there is no question about the principle of regulation; all that appears is a struggle of rival interests for control of the trade. Both sides made the same complaints, but it was the petition of the company that eventually succeeded.[17] Some of the charter's provisions, particularly the apprenticeship regulations, would doubtless meet the wishes of the London stockingers, jealous of their status as skilled craftsmen, and afraid lest the industry they had built up should pass elsewhere. On the other hand, restrictions on labour were not to the interest of the masters; but it should be noted that the bylaws gave certain advantages in this respect to the wealthier members. No ordinary member might keep more than one apprentice until he had been free of the company for four years, then he might keep two; but liverymen, who paid a fee of £10 on election, were allowed three apprentices. Prevention of the export of frames suited all but the enterprising few, usually backed by foreign agents and merchants, who were prepared to undertake such transactions; and this aim was diligently pursued by the company in the first thirty years of its existence. Again, the masters producing best-quality work and the superior workmen would both be interested in the prohibition of 'fraudulent' goods. Thus it seems likely that there would be fairly general support for the charter at first. But as the trade expanded the manufacturer and journeyman classes became more sharply distinguished, this leading to a cleavage of interests, while the company itself ceased to represent either, having got into the hands of people who used it as an instrument for self-aggrandisement rather than for promoting the good of the trade. In the conflicts of the eighteenth century, which we have now to describe, the position becomes clearer.

The company apparently soon waxed prosperous, and ostentatious display was made with 'a gilt barge rowed by twenty watermen accompanied by a numerous band of music and adorned with magnificent flags having the arms of the Company emblazoned'. A splendid carriage was bought for the master and wardens, others were hired for the clerk and assistants, while beadle and deputies turned out in liveries covered with gold lace. A hall was built in Redcross Street, and it is said that they scarcely ever met upon business but they had a sumptuous feast prepared.[18]

It was not long, however, before complaints were heard from the poorer members whose fees contributed to this expensive pomp. In 1693 the company petitioned the House of Commons for a Bill to regulate abuses in the trade. They complained of the continued export of frames and the production of fraudulent

page 33 *A framework knitter at work*

page 34   *The interior of a framework knitters' shop*

goods, several members having lately 'got into the way of making slight work to undersell the rest contrary to the by-laws' whereby the trade had fallen into great discredit. This was quickly followed by a counter-petition from the framework knitters in and about Nottingham alleging that the company's exactions were unreasonable and asking for relief. 'The Master and Wardens of their Company living constantly in London have by their many by-laws imposed severe penalties on the petitioners, compelling them to come to London for their freedoms, choosing petitioners for their Stewards when they pleased, which office is only expensive, and laying great fines for refusal to serve therein,[19] so that by their by-laws they raise about £200 per annum amongst the petitioners who have no manner of benefit thereby; they therefore pray for relief and that the money so raised may be applied to set the poor of their trade in the county, who are very numerous, to work'.[20]

Similar complaints were made a few years later in a petition purporting to come from the framework knitters of Nottingham, Derby, and Leicester. The master and wardens, it was alleged, were making bylaws and orders contrary to the law that were very vexatious to the country stockingers. 'For instance they compel every apprentice when out of his time to go to London, though above a hundred miles from thence, to take out his freedom, and many other exactions are imposed on the Petitioners to the great decay of the trade'.[21]

Of these first recorded disputes nothing further is heard, but early in the eighteenth century conflicts of a more serious nature arose which clearly indicate the growing divergence of interests within the trade. Encouraged either by deliberate slackness or mere lethargy on the part of the company flagrant breaches of the apprenticeship regulations had been allowed to go on unchecked even in London, until the position became intolerable to the journeymen stockingers. Many found themselves deprived of employment in the overcrowded state of the trade, and about the year 1710 they decided to take the law into their own hands in a manner that became only too familiar in later years. Henson gives a detailed account of the incident though he admits uncertainty as to the exact date.[22] The outbreak began with an attack on one Nicholson of Old Street Square, who kept twelve apprentices. Forcing their way into his house, the mob beat the master and his apprentices, smashed the frames and threw them out of the windows. 'They then proceeded in a body, joined by the silk

C

weavers and others, to Twister's Alley, Bunhill Row, where they broke another shop of frames. Frame breaking continued all that and the next two nights in the parishes of St Luke, Cripplegate and Shoreditch until nearly a hundred frames were destroyed; and what is very remarkable none was apprehended or punished for the offences'.

After this the masters who remained in London agreed to abide by the rules of the trade as to the taking of apprentices, but others set the company at defiance and, fearing the vengeance of the workers, removed to Nottingham and other places. Among these was one Fellows, who is said to have had at one time forty-nine apprentices, many of whom were parish children.[23] Thus a fillip was given to the migratory movement which eventually deprived London of its position as the leading centre of the trade.

The unregulated increase in the number of apprentices also began that overcrowding of the industry which later became such a chronic evil. In the provinces many of the masters contrived to carry on almost entirely with the labour of apprentices who, when they came of age, were invariably discharged to make room for other learners. The men so displaced wandered about seeking work, which they were often driven to accept at low prices to the detriment of journeymen who were members of the company and paid fees and quarterage. Although the company's deputies continued to hold their courts at Nottingham, Leicester, Hinckley, and Derby for the admission of freemen and binding of appren-tices,[24] their position was becoming increasingly difficult. Occa-sionally the serving of writs would be sufficient to secure the sub-mission of offenders,[25] but many were openly defiant. In 1725 the Nottingham deputies reported a combination two hundred strong against the company at Southwell; there was talk of obtain-ing an injunction against the master and wardens, while others threatened to call the company to account for the money they had been receiving all this time. The deputies began to feel 'not a little uneasy' and in their next letter to the master, dated 26 July, they express themselves very definitely. 'We desire a positive answer what you design to do in this case,' they write, 'and not only an answer but to make it a court or no court without the least delay, and not for one part to pay their money to it and another never come there'.[26] At the end of the year the Leicester-shire deputies report that there has been no business at their last three courts, adding a reminder to the clerk that the expenses of their 'long and dirty journeys' have not yet been met.[27]

It became clear that if the company were not to relinquish all control of the trade in the Midlands some prosecutions of offenders must be undertaken. Mere threats might cower a harassed journeyman or a small master into submission, but the weightier weapon of the law was required for the larger employers expanding their businesses and growing rich on cheap labour. A case was apparently in progress during the summer of 1725 against one Blacknall of Calverton;[28] but the master and wardens were so dilatory in the matter that in March of the following year they were bluntly informed that unless the prosecution went forward all business at Nottingham was at an end.[29] At length, on 28 May 1726, the case was brought to trial in London before Lord Chief Justice Eyre. The charter was read, but owing to a mistake in one of the names of the court of assistants the company were non-suited. At the same time the charter and bylaws were declared to be good and reasonable and the judge recommended the defendant to submit.[30] A few weeks later the Nottingham deputies reported that Blacknall's two sons had been admitted.

During the next few years hardly any business was done at the Nottingham court[31] and meetings at other places ceased altogether. In January 1728 the deputies at Nottingham, Hinckley, Mount Sorrell, Mansfield, and Derby were informed that the company intended to apply to Parliament for a Bill for the better execution of the powers granted by the charter. Counsel was of opinion that they had not sufficient powers for the regulation and good government of the trade and, in particular, that they could not proceed under the Elizabethan Statute of Artificers because framework knitting was not a trade then; there appeared, therefore, to be reasonable grounds for applying to Parliament. But funds were not forthcoming, and eighteen months later, when the Nottingham deputies complain of continued irregularities, the London officers retort that they have not assisted the company in preparing their case. 'If this continues,' they write, 'you must expect our court will think no more about it.'[32] Finally, the deputies agree to help in raising a subscription, though they apparently have doubts as to the success of the proposed application. The reply of the London court is reassuring: 'It will not be the first time that our charter hath appeared there and stood the test of a parliamentary inquiry, and we are not at all moved at any attempt that may be made to disannull our charter.'[33] Nevertheless nothing more is heard of the matter.

Something had to be done to revive the flagging enthusiasm of the deputies, however, and despite this uncertainty as to the legal validity of their bylaws the company determined to risk another lawsuit. On 19 April 1729, a letter was sent to the former representative at Leicester informing him of the court's resolution 'to try a point with respect to compelling persons exercising the trade and keeping workshops to be admitted, and first to begin with some unadmitted member in Leicester'. They desire that the deputy will fix on some responsible person who has served his apprenticeship to an admitted member but now carries on the trade without being himself admitted. No prosecution appears to have resulted on this occasion, but a similar request was sent to Nottingham, and in the following year an action was begun against a Nottingham master named Cartwright, for breach of the apprenticeship regulations.

The Cartwright case marks a definite turning-point in the history of the Framework Knitters' Company. Hitherto it had been assumed that the company had power to compel anyone exercising the trade to apply for his freedom and to bind his apprentices; and, indeed, that anyone who had not served a regular apprenticeship and been duly admitted might be prevented from following the trade. The charter, it will be remembered, is quite definite on these points; and although the Blacknall case failed it was only on some technical irregularity.

The company, as we have seen, had begun to have doubts as to the extent of their legal powers, but the invalidity of the bylaws had yet to be proved. The Nottingham deputies had their doubts, too; it appeared that their opponents had resolved to bind an apprentice and then to bring actions against the treasurer for taking fees in excess of the amounts permitted by law. They ask the London court to indemnify their treasurer and also to say if they must bind Cartwright's boy, if requested at the next court, and insist on charges.[34] The officers reply that not only Cartwright's fee but also a fine of forty shillings for the offence should be insisted on as an example to others.

Cartwright was summoned to the Nottingham court but apparently did not appear, and the next we hear of the case is in a letter from London, dated 25 February 1731, giving an account of a trial which had taken place there on the previous day. The charter had been approved by both judges and the whole court, and the bylaws were found to be properly signed yet they were not allowed to pass for good proof in court and the company were thereby non-suited. 'But don't be discouraged,' the letter continued, 'if our by-laws are not allowed very few charters in the City of London will be of much effect. We intend to have consultation not only in respect to the defence of your suit but also of reviving the suit against Cartwright; if we have any encouragement we shall have a hearing before the Chief Justice in the King's Bench.'

At the end of the year the master informs the Nottingham deputies that 'the court are now framing a new set of by-laws for the doing of which we had the express direction of the judges before whom the Cartwright case was tried.' They must be patient, for the bylaws had lately been condemned in so public a manner that they could not hope for success against offenders until they had been rectified.[35] But the patience of the deputies was at last exhausted. Their letters had gone unanswered and it appeared that the London court were negotiating with their opponents behind their backs. Finally they had considered 'whether it were proper to hold courts any longer to take and exact money from such few poor honest neighbours as wish well to the court whilst almost all others refuse to obey any summons and bid open defiance to the court'; they had therefore decided not to act as deputies after the next court day.[36] When the new bylaws were sent for their approval a few months later they replied that the regulations would involve members tying themselves up still more, while trespassers would be at liberty to take the bread out of their mouths.[37] The master points out, however, that the authority of Parliament would be required to make the bylaws applicable to all in the trade;[38] this they intend to apply for, the deputies can be sure that the court have it as much at heart as they, but first it is necessary to repair the breach made by the late Cartwright trials.[39]

This marks the end of the first phase in the company's relations with the trade in the Midlands; from 1732 to 1745 there were no deputies at Nottingham and the trade was entirely free. In view of the growing hostility to the pretensions of trade corporations, not only in Parliament but among the country gentry and parish officers, it is highly improbable that an application by the company for increased powers would have been successful. But in the meantime the officials in London had had other schemes on hand which may explain the seeming indifference with which the appeals of their deputies were so often treated. The year 1720 was a time of wild speculation which saw the South Sea Bubble and a host of other more or less fantastic projects for rapid fortune-making foisted on a credulous public.[40] In this burst of misguided enterprise the framework knitters also played a part. Despite their extravagance the company had accumulated a fund of over £10,000, and as the charter only allowed them to hold property of £100 yearly value it seemed desirable to find some means whereby the fund might be disposed of to advantage. Accordingly it was resolved that a joint stock company be formed to carry on the trade in silk and worsted stockings.[41]

The scheme was floated at a meeting of the court of assistants on 7 June 1720, when it was ordered that a company be formed with a capital of £2,000,000.[42] The books were to be laid open at the Hall and subscriptions taken at the rate of 25s for each £1,000 of stock, while Mr Pocklington, the promoter, was given the privilege of subscribing for what sum he thought fit, not being more than £10,000 without paying any deposit for the same. The next week members of the court were given each £1,000 stock as a bonus, and on 18 June it was resolved that all the undivided stock should be equally divided among the projectors without their paying any deposit and that the receipts for stock should be given in such names as they each should nominate. By this time subscriptions amounting to some £1,800 in cash had come in, and so elated were the committee that they voted Pocklington 200 guineas out of the subscription money 'for his trouble and invention' and a piece of plate, value 10 guineas, to Mr Warden Austin 'for his extraordinary trouble'. At the same time all warehousemen belonging to the court of assistants were invited to bring in their goods to be purchased.

Before long, however, the subscribers, who were 'exceedingly numerous,' began to have doubts as to the legality of the scheme. An Act had recently been passed prohibiting the formation of companies with transferable shares unless they obtained incorporation by charter from the Crown or by Act of Parliament.[43] Legal opinion was sought, and it appeared that to be safe the framework knitters ought to apply to Parliament for an Act to enable them to trade as a joint stock company; but Pocklington held out such hopes that it was resolved at a meeting of the general committee to carry on the trade as far as possible with safety and also to apply to Parliament. The company's credit was still good, for early in the following year a bond for £1,000 on which £12 10s had been paid was sold in 'Change-alley for 15 guineas.[44]

For several years the company persevered in manufacturing and selling goods with varied success. According to Henson the journeymen of London, Godalming, Odiham, and Oakingham received handsome wages while their masters made high profits.[45] But the company had no monopoly, and what finally killed the scheme was the increasing competition from the provinces. The country masters with their cheap labour were easily able to undersell those who worked for the company, and in 1730 the framework knitters were forced to abandon their undertaking. It was resolved that the venture had been for the good of the trade and that whatever balance remained should belong to the company.

For twelve years after this the company lay dormant; their funds and energies were exhausted and practically nothing was done to regulate the trade. They were forced to let the Hall in Redcross Street and resort to a tavern for their meetings, and when an order was made for the livery to take part in the procession on Lord Mayor's day it had to be repealed on account of the state of the company's debt.[46] In an effort to increase membership it was decided in 1742 to give a guinea to anyone who would bring a member to purchase a freedom.[47]

The revival of the company after this period of quiescence is difficult to explain. It may be, as Henson says, that the rapid decline of the London trade and the dissatisfaction of the older journeymen roused them to action;[48] or perhaps it was mainly a desire to raise funds and regain their former prestige among the City corporations. But whatever the cause the year 1745 saw the beginning of a determined effort to reassert their control of the trade. On 3 January the court of assistants met at the White Hart Tavern in Bishopsgate and approved a code of thirty-one bylaws which, after certain alterations, were confirmed and signed by the Chancellor and Chief Justices on 22 May 1745. As Blackner says, the sanction of the new bylaws shows that the validity of the charter was still unshaken;[49] but it is certainly surprising that so little difficulty should have been experienced in obtaining confirmation, in view of the company's previous reverses in the courts.

In the main the bylaws of 1745 confirm the powers granted

by the charter, and are practically a repetition of the earlier code.[50] As hitherto, the officers are to be elected by the court of assistants who shall, as often as they think fit, admit such members as are free of the City and of the livery to be assistants, any refusing to serve to forfeit £10. Deputies are to be elected 'to rule and govern all persons exercising the trade of framework knitting within each district'. Dinners are to be provided, as of old, for the master, wardens, and assistants, and the usual penalties exacted from stewards who decline the honour of entertaining them. The apprenticeship regulations are reaffirmed,[51] though nothing is said this time about limitation of numbers. No one is to engage in the trade unless admitted a member of the company, and every master must give proof of his skill before being allowed as a 'workhouse keeper'. The fee for admittance is fixed at 15s, and in addition every master must pay 6d a quarter and every journeyman 3d. For every apprentice bound the charge is 9s, and a workhouse keeper submitting his proof piece must pay 13s.

Armed with these powers the company were theoretically in as strong a position as ever; but it is incredible that they could ever have supposed it possible, in the condition in which the trade now stood, to enforce such a code of regulations. The hosiers and masters who profited by the employment of cheap labour were naturally opposed to regulation; those workers who had come into the trade without serving a regular apprenticeship were afraid of being deprived of employment; while the older craftsmen were in most cases too poor to pay the fees demanded.

When deputies were appointed at Nottingham in 1745 they refused to act, and though a court was eventually established it achieved nothing.[52] Entries in the Court Book show numerous orders and threats of prosecution against framework knitters in London and, according to Henson, many non-members were induced to join.[53] In 1750 the master and wardens were directed to go to Godalming; no court had been held there since 1734, and the only members were a few old men who had long ceased to have any communication with the company; they now refused to pay quarterage.[54] A visit to Towcester the following year for the purpose of binding apprentices and admitting members was more successful,[55] and the company received such encouraging support at Reading, Odiham, Oakingham, and Berkhamsted that it was resolved to proceed against the defaulting members at Godalming.[56] Writs were served, but the framework knitters, encouraged by the gentry and other ratepayers who were afraid lest the trade should be driven from their district, determined to defend the action and, if necessary, petition Parliament. This so alarmed the company, who had already had to borrow £50 for the expense of the case, that they decided to suspend action on the pretence that certain proofs were lacking.[57]

The company now made a further effort at Nottingham. On 27 August 1752, a notice appeared in the *Nottingham Journal* that all journeymen would be admitted on payment of 5s, and on 14 October it was announced in the same paper that a court would be held on the 26th at the Crown Inn, Long Row. 'No quarterage will be asked of poor men, many of whom, though not old, are scarce able to get bread, it being thought sufficient to call on those who keep frames and apprentices. Then let us immediately agree to be of one mind, for this general good,' the appeal concluded, 'and heartily join with one voice to proclaim the Court our Protector! And no more Colts.'[58]

But the deputies had misgivings. One of their letters complains that 'the employers and shopkeepers that are got into the hose business are incessantly at work to give the towns and country a bad opinion of the Court'; and though there was said to be 'a good disposition among the journeymen to be admitted,' it was felt that some of the principals from London might come down to encourage them.[59] On 27 January 1753, the Nottingham court report that they have suspended meetings, there being no prospect of any business until a suit against some unadmitted framework knitter had been undertaken; they are, however, willing to resume as soon as the company's affairs take a happy turn.

The implied hope was speedily extinguished, for the opposition which had been simmering so long now boiled over at all points. On 15 February, the House of Commons received a petition from 'several persons employed in framework knitting in the town of Nottingham' complaining that the company's bylaws were against all reason and contrary to general liberty. This was quickly followed by petitions from London, from Godalming, Guildford, and other places in Surrey, from Mansfield and from the town and county of Leicester, while the company replied with a plea that further regulations were necessary to restore the credit of the manufacture which of late years had much decreased, and asking for a hearing to refute the charges made against them.[60]

It is interesting to review the opposing forces. The only

supporters of the company are a group of Nottingham stockingers, presumably the remnant of those who had faithfully upheld
the court in the old days, who declare that they want the bylaws,
and especially the apprenticeship regulations, to be more strictly
enforced. But even in Nottingham these were not representative,
for the first petition, already quoted, comes from workers who
find themselves allied, in opposition, with 'freeholders and tradesmen of divers occupations in the town and county'. In the same
way the Surrey workers meet on common ground with the gentry
and other ratepayers, while in London the hosiers and framework
knitters have joined forces. The Mansfield petition comes osten-
sibly from the workers themselves, though the account of how the
manufacture has 'flourished and increased there in recent years'
while free from restriction suggests that the employers may also
have had a hand in it. That from Leicester is couched in similar
terms and has apparently been promoted by the manufacturers.
This unity of interests is, of course, more apparent than real. The
employers' reasons for opposing the company were obvious
enough, but the tradesmen and large ratepayers had a different
motive; they were anxious for the prosperity of the workers,
which meant greater purchasing power and low poor rates, yet
were alarmed lest restrictions that could not be universally
enforced should drive trade from their district and increase the
burden of the unemployed. The almost unanimous opposition of
the workers is not difficult to understand in the light of the company's record. To the workers it must have appeared that this
elusive body in London was interested in them mainly as a source
from which the coffers might be replenished. After making every
possible allowance—and it must be granted that failure to
control the trade by a fixed code of regulations was inevitable
under the changing conditions—one is driven to the conclusion
that they were right.

All these points emerged in the parliamentary inquiry of 1753.[61]
The storm of protest aroused by the attempt to enforce the
new bylaws quickly resulted in the appointment of a House of
Commons Committee which made a thorough examination of
the company's records and took evidence from persons connected
with the trade. The evidence from the first source was damaging
enough, and it was endorsed by most of the witnesses. The
deputies had never been known to apply any money for the
benefit of the trade, never refused the freedom to anyone who was

willing to pay for it, and never asked for the proof piece when apprentices were bound, though they took care to get the fee. It appeared that the sole reason for putting the bylaws into execution was to raise money; and as to preventing frauds in the manufacture, the deputies themselves were among the worst offenders.[62]

Several cases of extortionate demands were brought to light. When the officials visited Godalming in 1751, a number of poor stockingers had been mulcted of arrears of quarterage for the six years during which the new bylaws had been nominally in force. Others had refused to pay, and one Henry Moore, who had been admitted twenty-four years earlier for fear that he would not be allowed to work and who had just had to sell his goods to pay rent, was actually proceeded against; fortunately sympathetic neighbours had come to his support. The company had threatened to trouble everyone who should presume to carry on the business of framework knitting without being admitted, and several small masters had thought it expedient to join. James Grahame of Sunbury, for instance, declared that he knew nothing of the trade, but had bought two frames with the intention of employing a workman who should teach his son; yet he did not think it proper to use them until he was free of the company, so he therefore became a member and had his son bound apprentice to him, paying altogether 15s.

The only representatives of the trade to appear in support of the company were some witnesses from Nottingham, who contended that the deputies were appointed for the good of the trade and that the company's rules tended to increase the manufacture rather than restrain it. The company themselves were represented by Matthews, who had been clerk from 1728 to 1742. During all this time he had never known them guilty of one hard act; eight or ten actions had been brought but not above one tried, the rest being discontinued on submission or on account of the poverty of the defendant. Asked if the company took measures to improve the trade he declared that in London they used to examine work and detect frauds; he believed this was true of the country also, and he himself had attended their searches at Godalming; this vigilance made persons cautious as to what goods they manufactured.

The weight of evidence against the company—and perhaps the most damaging was that abstracted from their own records—could have only one result. The committee found that the oppos-

ing petitioners had fully proved their allegations. They resolved
that the bylaws were injurious and vexatious to manufacturers
and tended to the discouragement and decay of the industry. The
powers granted by the charter were hurtful to the trade and
tended to a monopoly, and in their opinion the bylaws were
illegal and contrary to the liberty of the subject. These resolutions,
with the exception of the last, were endorsed by the House. Clearly
the bylaws could not be declared illegal when they had been
recently confirmed by the highest authority, in accordance with the
law. Evidently it was not thought worth while to repeal them; the
company's power was dead and they were left, as it were, with the
unburied corpse. But was it really dead or only in a state of
coma? Many years later the depressed stockingers did succeed
in producing some stirrings of life, and it was not until the early
nineteenth century that the last hope was abandoned.

CHAPTER 3

LOCALISATION IN THE MIDLANDS

The concentration of the hosiery manufacture in the three Midland counties of Nottingham, Leicester, and Derby, dates from the first half of the eighteenth century. As we have seen, there had already been some dispersion of frames before the trade was incorporated, and of the new centres Nottingham was the most important. Powerful influences now began to force a more decided movement in this direction. In the first place there was the desire of the larger employers to escape from the power of the chartered company which, although nominally extending over the whole country, was necessarily much more real in the metropolis where it was backed by the prestige of the City Corporation. Secondly, the nature of the trade was changing; instead of being confined to luxury articles it was extending to the production of plain goods made of worsted and cotton, which, being more standardised and less susceptible to fashion changes, could be manufactured almost anywhere. Thirdly, the new trade offered vast possibilities of expansion, but cheap labour was essential to secure this market. There would be few homes of the humbler sort where hand knitting for family needs was not carried on as a spare-time occupation; in Cumberland, for instance, stockings were almost invariably knitted at home at the end of the eighteenth century, the wool being bought at 8d a pound and spun by members of the family. Indeed, in the country north of the Trent, almost every article of dress worn by farmers, manufacturers, and labourers was made at home.[1] Manufactured goods would have to be very cheap to induce these people to buy them; the need for cheap labour was therefore the chief factor in drawing the hosiery manufacture away from London.[2]

Given the accidental circumstance of its origin in Nottinghamshire, it was perhaps natural that the industry should gravitate there when the advantages of concentration in London declined. But there was also the factor of proximity to raw materials. This, and the fact that a considerable manufacture of hand-knitted goods was already established in the district, seem to have been the main reasons for the rise of framework knitting in Leicestershire. The first frame seen in that county was set up at Hinckley in 1640 by William Iliffe, who is said to have paid £60 for it, and kept it working day and night with the help of an apprentice.[3] Although the enterprise, within its limits, appears to have been successful, there was no further development until thirty years later, when Nicholas Alsop of Northampton began business as a framework knitter in Leicester.[4]

The tardiness of progress during these early years was mainly due to the opposition of the hand knitters. 'So great was the prejudice of the lower orders to hose wrought in a frame, on account of the knitters, that when the business was about to be established we are told that frames were set up in cellars and other secret places where they were worked by night as well as day.'[5] Within the first half of the eighteenth century, however, development was rapid. When Defoe visited the district, about 1724, he remarked on the 'multitudes of people' employed in stocking weaving; 'almost the whole county seemed to be employed in it,' he says.[6] By 1750 the number of frames in Leicester itself had grown to about a thousand, with a weekly production of 1,000 dozen pairs of worsted hose for home consumption.[7]

It was during the same period that the industry became important at Nottingham. The town had only 2 master stockingers in 1641, but in a list of trades for 1739 they number 50, together with 14 framesmiths, 12 needle-makers, 8 frame setters-up, 3 dyers, and 3 wool-combers who also employed frames.[8] Deering's estimate of 1751 puts the number of frames in the county at over 3,000, some 1,200 of which were in Nottingham itself. Besides the 3,000 knitters employed on the frames there was a considerable number of winders, sizers, seamers, wool-combers, frame-smiths, setters-up, sinker-makers, and needle-makers, giving a total of over 4,000 workers dependent on the industry.

For the country as a whole we have Henson's statement of the distribution of frames in 1727,[9] which may be conveniently summarised as follows:

South			Midlands		
London	...	...	2,500	Leicester	...	...	500
Surrey	...	...	600	Nottingham	...	...	400
Towcester	...	...	150	In villages of Leicester,		
Odiham	...	...		Nottingham, and		
			100	Derby	...	...	3,750
Reading	...	...				
			3,350				4,650

The tendency to concentrate in the Midlands is already apparent, but London is still important. Nearly the whole of the bespoke trade, which included about half the silk branch, remained there, enjoying not only the advantage of ready access to the market, but also to supplies of raw material, for the bulk of the silk imported into the country came to London. Moreover, the silk weaving at Spitalfields made a good deal of waste in the winding, warping, and reeding processes; this was spun into knitting yarn, and in addition there were always large quantities of embezzled silk on sale, the dyers contriving to abstract it in boiling out the gum, while substituting other ingredients to make up the weight.[10] Cheap materials helped the London hosiers to undersell their competitors at Nottingham, and so long as the bespoke trade continued to be important they were in a favourable position; but towards the middle of the century fashion changes caused a decline in this branch, between 1730 and 1750 some 800 frames being transferred from London to Nottingham,[11] and when Deering wrote, what remained of the London manufacture did 'hardly deserve the name of trade'.[12]

An important factor contributing to the rise of the silk hosiery manufacture in the Midlands, and particularly in the Derby district, was the establishment of Lombe's silk-throwing mill. Tradition tells how in 1716 John Lombe made a journey to Leghorn and at great peril obtained drawings of the machines in use there. In the following year several silk-throwing machines were set up at Derby, but the development of the enterprise was left to Thomas Lombe, his brother dying soon after his return to England. Obtaining a patent in 1718 for fourteen years, Thomas Lombe erected his factory, the first in England, on an island in the Derwent.[13] It seems probable that in choosing this district Lombe had an eye on the stocking manufacture, for the local weaving trade had not yet begun, and the button-working trade of Macclesfield could not constitute more than a minor attraction.[14] The selection of Derby in preference to Nottingham seems to be accounted for by the better facilities for power. As one writer puts it, 'he preferred swift Derwent to sluggish Trent'. Derby thus became the centre for the manufacture of silk hosiery as Leicester tended to specialise in worsted and Nottingham in cotton. This specialisation was never very rigid, being largely a matter of emphasis, but it remained fairly marked until comparatively recent times.

The connection between machine cotton spinning and the Nottingham hosiery trade is still more important. According to Henson the first pair of cotton stockings made in England were produced at Nottingham in 1730.[15] A considerable manufacture of cotton fustians had been carried on in Lancashire for more than a century,[16] but the yarn used was utterly unfit for knitting, being irregularly spun with weak places and big lumps which could not be looped on the needles. Stockings made from it 'had a wretched appearance and would not wash or wear'. Yarn of suitable fineness and uniformity could only be obtained from India, but even then the framework knitters of London, where it was first introduced, refused to work it because of its stubbornness. Finally a supply was sent to Nottingham, where a stockinger named Draper, of Bellar Gate, undertook to use it in a twenty-gauge silk frame; it was so fine that four threads had to be doubled for the leg and five for the heel.[17] The success of this experiment started a new branch of the hosiery trade, cotton stockings gained in popularity on account of their extreme whiteness and were actually preferred to silk.

Thus a fresh stimulus was given to the Nottingham manufacture to the detriment of London; but the Midland hosiers did not long remain unchallenged. The spinners of the West of England woollen district had been used to short staple wool, and when turned on to cotton they were able to produce a yarn which, though coarser than the Indian, could be worked on the knitting frame. This provided material for the manufacture that had grown up at Tewkesbury; but, instead of the four or five threads of fine cotton, only a double twist of this coarse yarn was used, producing goods much inferior in quality though similar in appearance.[18] The Nottingham hosiers now found themselves completely undersold, but their efforts to get similar yarn spun in their neighbour-

page 51 *A modern multi-feed interload machine. The defects of earlier multi-feed machines have been overcome by a positive feed mechanism which effectively controls the supply of thread to the knitting needles (see p 174)*

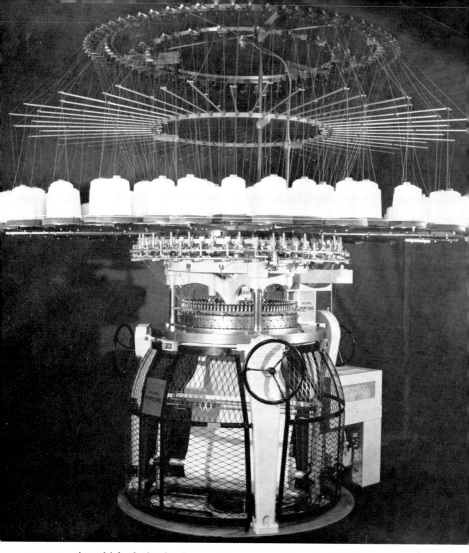

page 52 *A multi-feed circular frame. Like most modern circular frames this uses latch needles. Wide machines make plain and patterned fabric in the piece for the cut-and-sewn trade. Narrower frames may make simple garments in tubular form (see p 180)*

hood were vain, for the women in the Midlands had only known long wool and could not be brought to spin a thread bearing the least resemblance to Indian cotton.

> Undersold and losing their trade likewise by the Tewkesbury frauds and their apprentices becoming a dead weight upon them, the Nottingham manufacturers half resolved again to court the assistance of the Company to check the evil, but shame forbade that, and having no alternative they applied to Parliament for protection. This application was made in the most secret manner, unknown to the workmen.[19]

The result was a measure passed 'with uncommon secrecy and celerity' in 1766,[20] requiring manufacturers to mark all goods with eyelet holes corresponding to the number of threads in the yarn, but 'it is doubtful,' says Henson, 'whether any person has ever been convicted under its provisions; even if it had been properly worded it wanted an authorised body to enforce it'.

The real obstacle, however, was the lack of adequate supplies of suitable yarn; so long as this continued, no great expansion of the cotton hosiery trade was possible. It may be said, therefore, that the growth of this branch in the last decades of the eighteenth century was entirely due to the inventions in spinning machinery. The details of these inventions have been too often described to need treatment here; our main concern is to trace the connection, or rather interconnection, between the early experiments in cotton yarn spinning and the hosiery manufacture.

The first attempt at machine spinning of which we have definite knowledge is that of Lewis Paul, who patented his device for drawing out cotton by rollers in 1738.[21] If Henson's information be correct, Paul's first efforts, in 1734, were directed towards producing thread for the manufacture of cotton stockings in London, where he was born; and five years later he was in Nottingham experimenting with a machine to spin four threads at once. This apparently worked, 'but the product was inferior and higher in price than handspun'.[22] Although the account seems plausible enough it can hardly be accepted without confirmation, and according to Mantoux there is no evidence that Paul's machine was applied anywhere before 1740. When it was eventually set up it was in a small factory at Birmingham run by Paul and his partner Wyatt, while it is also known to have been used in at least one factory in London.[23]

D

As it is generally agreed that Paul and Wyatt's frame was not a practical success its possible connection with the hosiery manufacture is of no great importance. No doubt the idea of roller spinning would have been developed, as it was later by Arkwright, had the demand for yarn been such as to induce people to sink capital in the enterprise; but it was not until about 1760 that the demand for more and better-quality yarn grew really insistent. Various abortive attempts to spin by machinery were made at Nottingham between 1740 and 1767, resulting in some progress, though the yarn was still inferior to the West of England hand-spun.[24] At the same time similar experiments were going on in Lancashire and about 1764 the problem was partially solved by James Hargreaves, the Blackburn weaver, whose jenny, though based on the principle of the spinning wheel, produced several threads at once.

For a year or two, Hargreaves kept his invention to himself, using it to spin yarn at home, and even when, in 1767, a few machines were made for sale, they were still not patented. Restricted as his activities were, however, it was not long before the inventor suffered from the attentions of the machine smashers who broke into his house and destroyed his frames. Such persecution and the difficulties of coming to terms with the Lancashire manufacturers drove Hargreaves to seek refuge in Nottingham. Here again he had difficulty in getting support owing to the failures of previous inventors, but eventually capital was supplied by Thomas James. A small mill was built in Hockley and the firm began to supply the local hosiers with cotton yarn spun on jennies of sixteen or more spindles.[25] In 1770 the apparatus was patented, and in the next few years a large number of jennies were sold to other spinners and to hosiers,[26] for since the jenny was worked by hand and could be set up anywhere it was not difficult for hosiers with large requirements to produce their own yarn. Hargreaves's business was only moderately successful however; his invention was pirated, 'a coalition of hosiers and others engaged in spinning' was ranged against him, and he shrank from the expensive contest that would be necessary to enforce his claims.[27] When the case was eventually tried the courts held that the jenny had been used in industry before it was patented and the rights were therefore declared to have lapsed.

An even more important event in the development of the cotton hosiery trade was the migration of Richard Arkwright to Nottingham in 1768. The merits of Arkwright's claim to the invention of roller spinning do not concern us here; in any case the idea was not new, though whether Arkwright or Hayes, whose invention the former is said to have appropriated, was acquainted with Paul's specification is doubtful. Whatever Arkwright, the Preston barber, may have lacked in mechanical genius, he certainly possessed extraordinary ability for the profitable exploitation of ideas; and it was to him, more than to any other individual, that the practical success of the new methods of spinning was due.

With the outbreak of machine smashing in the Blackburn district Arkwright thought it expedient to leave Lancashire,[28] but there were special reasons which induced him to migrate to Nottingham. The difficulty of obtaining supplies of good-quality yarn for the hosiery manufacture was well known; there were capitalists in the district willing to assist new inventions; and there had grown up with the framework knitting industry a class of skilled mechanics such as were generally difficult to obtain at a time when engineering, as we know it, was still in its infancy. Arkwright was not long in securing the interest of the Wright brothers, the local bankers, but at the end of a year they grew alarmed at the risk involved and withdrew their support.[29] They, however, introduced him to Samuel Need, 'the leading Nottingham hosier,' who became Arkwright's partner, built him a small mill near that of Hargreaves, and enabled him to patent his roller spinning machine.[30] But the yarn was 'of wretched quality,' full of thick places and apparently much inferior to that spun on the jenny, though this was by no means good, being knitted with difficulty owing to its bumps and burrs. Need, who is said to have expended £1,200 on the enterprise, grew impatient, but success was eventually attained by fluting the rollers.

The next stage in Arkwright's progress is marked by his removal to the neighbouring county of Derby. Unlike the jenny, the roller spinning machinery was from the first worked by power. But the horses which were the only source available at Nottingham proved too expensive for use on a large scale, so that water power was essential if the manufacture was to be developed.[31] The vast possibilities of machine spinning had been recognised by Jedediah Strutt, of Derby, with whom Need was associated in the production of rib stockings, and it was with Strutt's help that Arkwright now began to erect his mills in the Derbyshire dales where there was water power in abundance. Strutt was in many ways an ideal partner for the pioneer of the new industry. Originally a farmer, but with a taste for learning and mechanical pursuits, he became interested in the hosiery trade through his brother-in-law, a hosier of Derby, who suggested to him the need for a device to make ribbed fabric on the stocking-frame. All the ingenuity of the framework knitters and mechanics had so far failed to produce anything satisfactory; but where they had failed the farmer succeeded, after much labour and expense, in making the most notable addition to Lee's frame since its invention. The apparatus consisted of a separate set of needles which operated vertically and in between the original horizontal needles, taking the loops from the latter and reversing them so as to make a rib stitch. Having taken out patents in 1758 and 1759, Strutt and his partner began the new manufacture at Derby where it brought them considerable wealth.[32]

Strutt therefore was able to bring skill, capital, and enterprise to the furtherance of Arkwright's schemes. During their partnership, which lasted till 1781, two mills were built at Cromford and a third at Masson, employing altogether 1,150 people, while Belper, where three large factories were set up, grew from a mere village to a town second only to Derby itself.[33] In a few years large quantities of excellent yarn or twist were being produced, yet the proprietors found great difficulty in introducing it into public use. 'A very heavy and valuable stock, in consequence of these difficulties lay upon their hands, and they were necessarily driven to attempt the manufacture of the yarn themselves.' Their first trial was in weaving it into stockings, but although this succeeded Arkwright himself did not develop the hosiery branch, possibly because it could not easily be adapted to the factory system in which his genius found its peculiar expression. Instead he turned to the manufacture of calico.[34]

With the adaptation of the steam engine for driving machinery the lack of water power was no longer an obstacle to the rise of cotton mills in Nottinghamshire. The first steam-driven mill in England was set up at Papplewick in 1785;[35] seven years later Denison's mill, with 3,024 spindles and 300 workers, opened in Nottingham;[36] and by 1815 there were eight cotton mills in Nottingham, three at Mansfield, six at Papplewick and Linby, two at Newark, and a doze more at Worksop, Retford, Southwell, and other places in the county.[37] These supplied the hosiery and the newly developed lace trades and also produced cotton twist for Manchester.

By this time, however, cotton spinning was gravitating towards the main centre of the industry in Lancashire. After much litigation Arkwright's patents were cancelled in 1785 and his methods came into more general use. Crompton's mule, brought out in 1779, was a Lancashire invention, and, in the great development of fine spinning which followed, Lancashire's humid climate was an incomparable advantage. Finally, Cartwright's power loom, patented in 1785, though not extensively used until much later, laid the foundations of an ever increasing demand for yarn. These and other factors, such as facilities for import and export, contributed to strengthen the localisation of the cotton industry in Lancashire and to weaken its position in other centres; but in 1836 there were still eight mills in the Mansfield district and eight more in Derbyshire, with altogether about 4,450 workers, supplying yarn for cotton hosiery.[38]

The expansion of the hosiery trade following the introduction of the new methods of spinning is comparable to the effect produced by artificial silk in our own day. 'Cotton stockings have become very general for summer wear,' says a contemporary observer, 'and have gained ground very much upon silk stockings, which are too thin for our climate and too expensive for common wear for people of middling circumstances.'[39] It is not known what quantity of cotton was used in the hosiery manufacture before 1770, but it must have been very small. In 1787, however, it was estimated that 1,500,000lb were consumed, and by 1836 the annual amount was over three times as great.[40] Silk hosiery had always been expensive and the price of wool was increasing with the growing shortage of supply;[41] on the other hand, cotton was enormously cheapened by the new processes.[42] Wide markets were opened up for cotton hosiery both at home and abroad, and by 1815 the plain cotton hose branch employed the greatest number of frames in the trade.[43]

The Leicester trade, being mostly in worsted hosiery, was not at first affected by the new spinning processes. Some of Hargreaves's jennies had been introduced by Coltman, a Leicester hosier, and Gardiner relates how, in 1780, he assisted in knocking them to pieces for firewood in consequence of their having been superseded by Arkwright's invention.[44] It was not long, however, before the roller principle was applied to worsted spinning. Hitherto, all yarn used in the trade had been spun on the wheel after the combed tops had been laid by for twelve months to toughen in oil. The new process not only enabled many threads to be spun at once, but also eliminated this waiting period, for the wool could be spun as soon as combed. Brookhouse, the inventor, made his first successful experiments at Melton Mowbray in 1788 and immediately offered the rights to Coltman and Whetstone, two of the largest worsted manufacturers in Leicester, who took him into partnership. But the Leicester people were no better disposed towards this innovation than they had been to the stocking frame a hundred years before.[45] The workers feared unemployment if the use of the spinning machine became general; so threatening was the opposition that the machine was removed to Harborough for greater safety, but the mob, 'encouraged by the superior class,' followed and destroyed it, bringing the fragments back in triumph to Leicester. They then attempted to pull down the houses of Coltman and Whetstone, and the riot was not quelled without bloodshed.[46]

After this none dared to use the new process in Leicester; but it was developed elsewhere, and for many years Leicester manufacturers were obliged to send to Worcestershire, Yorkshire, and even Aberdeen for much of their worsted yarn. Not until about 1830 did the lost industry begin to return. In the meantime Brookhouse himself had made a fortune with his machinery at Warwick.[47]

Despite this handicap the Leicester trade continued to expand. Whereas formerly it had consisted mainly in coarse hosiery, great quantities of fine goods were now being made for the home and foreign markets, and manufacturers rapidly accumulated large fortunes.[48] Blackner's analysis of 1812 gives the number of frames in the town and county as 11,183, while Nottingham had 9,285.[49] Derbyshire came next with 4,700 frames, and apart from Scotland, which had 1,449, the only other district of importance was Gloucester, with 970. The southern counties where the trade had formerly flourished now contained only 267 frames all told,[50] and the rest of England about 760. For Ireland, the return was 976 frames, but with the establishment of free trade between that country and Great Britain in 1823, 'the greater part of the frames employed in the Dublin hosiery manufacture were thrown idle and sold as scrap iron'.[51]

As these figures indicate, the process of localisation in the

Midland counties was now completed. With the concentration of the manufacture there and the changing nature of the trade, methods of distribution changed too. In Deering's time nearly all the Nottingham hosiers traded direct with London, but when production was no longer for a specialised market and the home trade was increasing relatively to the export, manufacturers began to distribute goods themselves. Hosiers would travel the country on horseback, laden with their wares, and generally continued on their journeys until all were sold.[52] None ventured to make much for stock in those days, but by 1777 the bigger manufacturers had begun to keep large quantities of goods on hand for the more convenient dispatch of orders.[53] Riders were employed to transact business in the remoter parts, being often away for eight months of the year; orders were given on sample and the goods sent out by packhorse. Gardiner's father, who was placed as a young man with Chamberlain & Burgess, the largest stocking-makers in Leicester, used to relate how the carrier would bring a string of eight or ten horses to the warehouse to be loaded with goods for Lancashire and Yorkshire. In this way Leicester goods were carried to all parts of the country.[54]

London, however, retained its importance as the main commercial centre of the trade. Midlands hosiers often apprenticed their sons to London merchants and family connections were common. Some eventually became London merchants on their own account. The outstanding case was that of the Morley brothers, who, like many others in the trade, had combined the business of hosiery with farming near Nottingham. Towards the end of the eighteenth century John Morley established a warehouse in London for distributing the firm's goods, which developed into a general wholesale house.[55] Another important example of a merchanting enterprise originating in the Midlands is that started by Nathaniel Corah of Leicester. He too came of farming stock and had been apprenticed to a framesmith. His first business venture in that line failed, but in 1815 he began to trade in knitted goods collected in Leicester and sold, not in London, but in Birmingham, where he had been working in a gun factory. In the following years the Corahs, while steadily expanding as manufacturers in Leicester, opened warehouses in Birmingham, London, Leeds, Glasgow, Manchester, Liverpool, Newcastle and Cardiff, which continued until 1927 when a change in marketing policy brought a gradual closure.[56]

CHAPTER 4

THE CAPITALIST DOMESTIC SYSTEM IN THE FRAMEWORK KNITTING INDUSTRY

A study of the later stages in the struggle between the company and the employers, and particularly the evidence taken by the committee on the bylaws, brings out the growing differentiation of classes and cleavage of interests within the industry. On the one hand we have the entrepreneurs and middlemen opposing the company in its attempts to regulate entry into the trade and determine the kind and quality of the work produced. As business men rather than craftsmen, interested in profit-making rather than in the general welfare of the trade, their aim was to get cheap labour, and of this there was always an abundant supply. Again, unrestricted entry into the trade increased competition among the journeymen and brought down wages. The hosiers, too, wanted freedom to produce the kinds of goods demanded by the market in the way that afforded the biggest profit, and resented the company's claim to search for and confiscate articles which the officials considered fraudulently made. On the other hand, we have the journeymen stockingers and smaller masters intent on maintaining their status as skilled craftsmen and hoping to sustain the value of their labour by limiting its supply and by preventing what they called 'fraudulent' methods of production. To them the company was the symbol of protection, and after that body itself had sunk into impotence they were untiring in their efforts, by petitions to Parliament, to get some of its regulations reimposed.

It seems probable, for reasons already indicated, that the framework knitting industry was established on a capitalist basis at its very inception. The high cost of frames and the value of the raw material made it essentially a trade for the capitalist undertaker. Indeed, the independent craftsman may have been far less common in domestic industry of the seventeenth century than is often supposed, even in trades where the cost of equipment and materials was not so great. In 1615 a large part of the woollen industry was in the hands of rich clothiers who employed spinsters, weavers, and tuckers 'all at the lowest rate for wages'.[1] Professor Daniels concludes that similar conditions probably obtained also in the cotton industry in the seventeenth century. 'The popular view is that in Lancashire up to the coming of the factory in the latter years of the eighteenth century the majority of work people were more or less independent producers who usually bought their materials and, after working them into cloth, sold it to traders. That this was not generally the case is certain, and that it obtained as a general rule in the previous century is seriously open to question.'[2]

In the framework knitting industry independent workers are mentioned in only one instance, and that is in the account of the cotton hose trade at Tewkesbury, where it was the custom in 1779 for the hosiers to sell the material outright to the stockingers and buy back the finished product. But they were independent in name only, for the system only afforded further opportunities to the capitalist oppressor. The men were 'in a starving condition and obliged to submit to the masters for terms'. 'The masters of Tewkesbury,' they complained, 'compel the men to buy materials and make stockings which they afterwards purchase of them and sometimes throw them upon the hands of the workman. The men are compelled to buy cotton wool from the masters and sell it to spinners and then purchase thread from the spinners; they give 2s 4d a pound for best cotton which does not cost the master 1s 6d a pound'.[3]

At the end of the eighteenth century there were, broadly speaking, two types of relationship between worker and manufacturer; some framework knitters worked direct to the hosier and others to masters or middlemen. As late as 1750 it was apparently the general custom to work direct, for the fifty manufacturers who employed frames at Nottingham were 'commonly called putters-out'. Subsequently this term came to signify a person engaged by the hosier to distribute work, but the putters-out of Deering's time were essentially independent entrepreneurs since they all traded directly with London.[4]

There were several factors that contributed to the survival of the older relationship. Hosiers contended that they got the work done better to their liking and were able to execute orders more promptly where the workers were under their supervision, which was particularly important in the higher quality trade and in the production of fancy goods where fashion changes were frequent and new lines were being continually introduced. There was also less chance of material being lost where it passed through fewer hands. On the other hand, it was often inconvenient for the hosier to deal with large numbers of people bringing in work and taking out yarn from the warehouse. In the numerous inquiries into the condition of the industry we find also frequent complaints from the stockingers of time wasted in this way. The following statement is typical: 'The worsted for the week is given out by the hosier, who lets frames and employs, every Monday morning. Stockingers go for it about eleven and get it home about twelve or one, then some has to be damped and wound. They begin work about two on Monday and finish at two on Saturday to take the work back to the hosier. It must be in by four; sometimes they have to wait till six as all the work is weighed. At some warehouses the workers have to wait most of the day.'[5]

The employment of middlemen was therefore a convenience both for hosiers and workers, and as framework knitters became more numerous and the trade spread into the country districts this class assumed an ever growing importance accompanied by increasing independence. But the precise position of the middleman is often difficult to determine. Sometimes he acted simply as an agent between employer and worker and received a fixed commission for taking-in, the amount being deducted from the worker's earnings. In some cases the master stockinger who worked at the frame and employed a few journeymen and apprentices in his workshop undertook this function; in others he dealt through a middleman in the same way as the stockinger working at home. We find the term 'master' used in several different senses; often it indicated a person little removed in economic status from the ordinary journeyman, except that he let standing room for a few frames in his house or workshop, or it might mean a more or less independent entrepreneur owning many frames and distributing work over a wide area. Indeed the fact that people in this category are occasionally called 'undertakers' suggests that a distinction was recognised.

In many ways the putting-out system favoured the undertaker class and enabled persons who were enterprising, and perhaps not over scrupulous, to rise to positions of some importance in the industry. The middleman, who seldom worked for one hosier, but often represented six or eight, received yarn with orders to get certain goods made and he generally distributed the work as he pleased, sometimes giving out direct to journeyman stockingers and sometimes to small masters who, in their turn, shared it among their workers. He was often free to make his own bargain with the stockinger, in which case he and not the hosier was the actual employer. But even where he was supposed to be merely an agent paying fixed prices for work his position might be little different, for hosiers seldom troubled to inquire what price the worker actually received, and the putter-out could squeeze an extra profit by getting work done at cheap rates.

In a rather different position from the undertakers were the bagmen or bag-hosiers. These were a class of small manufacturers found mostly in the villages, who, besides putting out work, sometimes had frames on their own premises. They occasionally made for the warehouses, but usually finished the goods themselves and sold them to the small shopkeepers and hawkers. The bagmen bought raw materials where they could, a good deal being obtained from stockingers who had embezzled yarn given out to them.[6] Most of the abuses of the trade were attributed to this class: 'That reptile race,' as a pamphleteer calls them, 'who have wriggled themselves into the business and who, with a mixture of cruelty and rapacity, at once snatch bread from the mouth of the worker and fair profits from the hands of the regular and honest manufacturer.'[7] The superior workman only restorted to them in bad times when work was unobtainable elsewhere.

If the system of distributing work was complicated, that of frame letting is equally difficult to elucidate. The practice of letting out machines on hire was not peculiar to the hosiery trade. For instance, in the sixteenth century we find the weavers complaining that the wealthy clothiers were ingrossing looms and letting them out at unreasonable rents; and by an Act of 1555, it was ordained that no person should possess more than one loom, nor directly or indirectly take any manner of profit by letting looms.[8] As late as 1844 the ribbon, tape, and smallware weavers paid loom rent in some places.[9] But in no other industry did the rent system become so characteristic and universal as in that of framework knitting.

We have seen that in the textile industries capitalist control was fairly general when framework knitting became established.

It implied that the craftsman was no longer responsible for buying materials and selling the product; but in most cases he still owned the instruments of production. In the hosiery trade, capitalism went a stage further. The stocking frame, with its numerous parts and delicate mechanism, was a costlier machine to buy and to maintain than the hand loom; judging by the transactions described elsewhere the price of a frame in the early days could hardly have been less than £50 or £60, which was a considerable sum in the seventeenth century and beyond the means of most small craftsmen. Here was evidently an opening for the employment of capital, and as the industry expanded some entrepreneurs became owners of frames on quite a large scale. But this does not explain the practice of charging the worker for the use of the machines. It seems probable that the explanation of the system of making capital cost a direct charge on the worker is to be found in the fact that the owner needed some safeguard to ensure an adequate return on his capital. Where machines were not under direct supervision they might be used to make work for other employers.

Whatever its origin, frame renting began quite early in the history of the hosiery trade, as is shown by the following extract from the bylaws of the Framework Knitters' Company drawn up in 1663: 'Be it ordained that noe person being a member of the said Societie shall take to hire for his own or for another's use any frame from any person or persons other than such as are lawfull members of the said Societie on pain of forfeiting 12d a week for every frame so hired.' But although this regulation was included in the rules approved by the Chancellor and two judges, it is not to be found in the charter itself, which suggests that the practice was not yet recognised to any great extent. The clause is repeated in the new regulations of 1745, and the petition from Nottingham protesting against the regulations complained of this attempt to monopolise the lending of frames for hire.[10] Evidently it was now becoming more usual for stockingers to hire their frames. Thirty years later hiring seems to be the general practice in all districts, as is revealed by the Report of the Committee on the Petitions from Framework Knitters in Nottinghamshire, Leicestershire, Derbyshire, Godalming, Tewkesbury, Northamptonshire, London, and Worcester.[11] By the end of the century the stockinger owning his frame was rare.

The extension of the frame renting system is to be explained partly by the increasing poverty of the stockingers, though not entirely, for second-hand frames could be bought very cheaply at times.[12] A Tewkesbury framework knitter, examined by the House of Commons committee in 1779, put the value of the frame for which he paid 1s 6d a week at £6 or £7, while a London worker declared that some frames lately sold at £12 10s were now let at 4s a week. With rents so high one might suppose that every stockinger who could manage to save or borrow a few pounds would have taken advantage of these low prices to secure a frame of his own. Many machines were, in fact, acquired through the frame clubs whose members made monthly payments and were from time to time allotted sums for purchasing frames; but their owners mostly found that their resources were inadequate to maintain the frames in repair and they were forced, after a time, to let them go.[13]

But apart from the lack of capital there were other circumstances that militated against independent ownership; even if the worker acquired a frame of his own he was still dependent on the capitalist for the supply of work, and was, in fact, more in the power of the hosier or middleman than the worker who hired his frame. He must find work to keep his machine, especially if he had borrowed money to buy it, and there were unscrupulous masters who would take advantage of this circumstance to force down the price of work. At Nottingham it was said, masters would not employ a man without his taking a frame; or, if a man used his own frame he was charged half-rent. In times of depression the 'independent' stockinger was always the first to suffer. Hosiers with frames out on hire took care to keep them as well supplied with work as possible, so that the operatives might be able to pay their rent. The independent man got what was left.[14]

As time went on, the frame rent system became more and more an instrument of oppression, and abuses were encouraged by the methods of collection which were part of the complex organisation of the framework knitting industry that developed during the eighteenth century. Wherever employment and payment for work was indirect so was the payment of frame rent. If the stockinger worked direct to the hosier he paid his rent direct, but if he worked for a middleman or for a small master stockinger the latter deducted the rent from earnings and in turn paid rent to the hosier from whom he probably hired in bulk at so much a year.[15] Part of the middleman's profit was derived from this system of sub-letting frames, for it was customary to charge the stockinger a higher rent than that paid to the actual frame owner. From the hosier's point of view the extra rent obtained by the middleman could be regarded as a cost of collecting.

There were also many private persons who had invested in a number of frames and were prepared to let them out in bulk to anyone who could find work for them. Provided that the owners got an adequate return on their capital, the putter-out might make as much more as he was able to exact from those who worked the machines. This view of rent as a payment for finding work was often taken by the stockingers themselves, although normally the master was already paid for his services as a go-between by his commission for taking-in. Sometimes it happened that the stockinger was unable to get work from the master who supplied his frame and was driven to seek it elsewhere. Here was a fresh opportunity for exploitation, for the new master might refuse to give him work unless he agreed to make a payment in lieu of frame rent.[16] It is true that the worker might give up his old frame and take another, but it was not easy, after having spent years working one machine, to adapt oneself to the peculiarities of another. Workers found that it often took three or four months to get used to a different frame.[17]

An appreciation of this fact throws much light on the perplexing economics of frame rent. All inquiries failed to discover any principle upon which the amount deducted for rent could be said to be based. As the commissioner reported in 1845: 'The amount of deduction is regulated by no fixed rule or principle whatever; it is not dependent on the value of the frame, upon the money earned, or the extent of the work made; it has differed in amount at different times and now does so at different places; the youthful learner or apprentice pays the same rent from his scanty earnings as the most expert and skilful workman.'[18]

One might suppose that with the continued increase of frames and their decline in cost, rents would have shown a tendency to fall. But it would appear from the frequent complaints of the stockingers and the evidence adduced from time to time that there was a considerable increase between 1780 and 1840. It is difficult to make any precise statement because of the variety of frames and the diversity of charges for frames of the same kind. For the ordinary narrow frame, however, ninepence seems to have been the usual rent about 1780. In the evidence for later years, nine-pence is very rare, a shilling and fifteen pence being the most frequent charges, while the wide frames introduced early in the nineteenth century let at much higher rents.

The hosiers contended that the shilling rent charged in 1845 did not yield as much profit as did ninepence at one time, as the frames wore out sooner with the use of the harder machine-spun yarn and the greater carelessness of the operatives.[19] There may have been something in this, but it was only by taking advantage of the workers' position in a period of trade depression that the frame owners had been able to force up rents. Asked why competition did not lower rents, a witness before the 1812 committee stated that attempts made when trade was good sometimes succeeded, but even then there were great variations, some making only 7 per cent on the capital outlay, and others as much as 20 per cent.[20]

To some manufacturers the profit from the hire of frames was more important than that from the product.[21] It was undoubtedly more certain; if the stockinger did any work at all he was bound to pay his rent, since it was deducted from his earnings, and even when he was totally unemployed rent would often be demanded unless he gave up the frame altogether. Failure to pay rent might even lead to imprisonment, as in the case of a man brought before the Leicester Bench in 1836. The defendant was charged with neglect of work, not having worked up the yarn given out to him, and was also in arrears with his rent. He said he was willing to give up the frames, but could give no security for arrears of rent and was sentenced to six weeks' hard labour.[22]

Frame rent, though one of the chief items, was not the only deduction from the stockinger's earnings. Before being sent to the warehouse the hose, which were made flat on the frame, had to be seamed; if the knitter worked at home, this would usually be done by his family as would also the winding for the frame; but if he worked for a small master, in his workshop, and the seaming was put out, the cost would be deducted from his earnings. Charges were also made for frame standing and for taking in work in cases where the small master acted as agent for his journeymen. The amount of the various items is shown in the following list which is dated November 1811.[23]

					s.	d.	s.	d.
Average weekly produce of ten frames, each				...			13	3¼
Weekly deductions								
Seaming	...	...	...	...	I	I		
Needles	...	...	...	...		3		
Oil	...	...	...	...		½		
Candles	...	...	...	...		3		
Coals	...	...	...	...		1½		
Frame standing ...	...	...	...		3		
Expenses taking in work ...	...	...	I	0		
(will be more if he goes in person)								
Frame rent	...	...	...	...	I	0		
							4	0
Clear Earnings	...	...	...	...			9	3¼

Such charges as these are now recognised as expenses of production for which the employer and not the worker is directly responsible; they are properly regarded as items which, together with wages, bear a direct relation to the price of the product. The whole system of frame renting, for instance, appears fundamentally wrong in the light of modern ideas of costing. The rent included interest on the capital laid out in buying the frame, cost of upkeep, and depreciation charges, yet it bore no relation to any of these items. Indeed, it had the characteristics of a true economic rent, though, as with all rents, custom played a large part in determining its amount.

In a domestic industry where the workers were scattered and under no direct supervision it was inevitable that wages should be paid on a piece basis. This was the rule in the framework knitting industry and the system is still general in the modern hosiery trade. The variety of articles made on the frame was very extensive and throughout the eighteenth century was constantly being added to as people realised the many uses to which the knitted fabric was suited. Work could be made in many different qualities according to the material used and the gauge of the frame, while mechanical improvements enabled fancy patterns to be introduced. Thus the industry came to include a very wide range of goods, and in a trade so dependent on fashion some items were always changing. The price system on which the stockingers were paid was, therefore, bound to be exceedingly complex; but it grew up on a customary basis, being adjusted from time to time as occasion required. An attempt had been made in the Framework Knitters' Bill of 1779 to get wages regulated by law, but it only came to be realised how complicated the whole wage system was when a proposal was made in 1812 to compel hosiers to exhibit in their warehouses printed schedules of the prices paid for work.

The essence of the proposed schedules, which were to be agreed to by both sides, was that they showed the worker beforehand the price he would receive for his work and the basis upon which that price was calculated. For instance, the price of silk stockings would be reckoned according to quality, length, number of needles used, number of courses to the inch, number of narrowings in the calf, etc, the price of ornament, if any, being added. In measuring an elastic fabric like hosiery it seemed fairest to take the number of courses in a given length; but it was obviously impossible to count them by hand, so it was proposed that a device called a rack should be attached to each frame to count the courses automatically. The evidence given before the select committee appointed to consider the petitions, if it did nothing else, at least brought out the complexity of the wage system in the industry. Hosiers contended that it was impossible to draw up a rigid schedule of prices on the basis suggested because no two frames made work exactly alike and the stockinger had to use his own discretion in deciding how many needles were required for a given width. The stockingers argued that schedules had been agreed to before, but the hosiers now opposed anything in the nature of a written agreement. When work was given out, they said, there was no contract that it should be paid for at a certain price, the worker only knew that he had made similar goods before at a customary price and it seemed that he could be fairly sure of getting the same price again, that was all.

But apart from the uncertainty of prices there was always the question as to whether work brought in was up to the standard required by the hosier. A hose might be too small or too slack or perhaps soiled, for white silk was easily damaged in this way. The hosier would then make a deduction from the usual price. Doubtless this was justified where there had been obvious negligence on the part of the worker, but it is easy to see how the practice of abatements could be turned into an instrument for reducing prices, and there were many complaints of alleged unjust deductions.[24] It is true that the worker had the right of appeal to a magistrate in any dispute about the price of work; but the points at issue were usually so technical that magistrates who knew nothing about the trade were loath to intervene, while

E

those who happened to be hosiers declined to do so. This remedy, therefore, was not very effective. There were also disputes about the amount that should be allowed for waste. The yarn was given out by weight, and when work was taken in it was again weighed; it was often contended that insufficient allowance was made for waste in winding, and it was even alleged that some hosiers gave out their silk damp, so that when the goods were weighed they showed a deficiency.[25]

It is clear that the methods of paying wages had a direct bearing on their amount; but the general issue, as we have seen, was mainly governed by the conditions of entry to the trade; when these relaxed the stockinger was at the mercy of competitive forces. Yet although the regulation of the number of apprentices broke down early in the eighteenth century an apprenticeship system of some sort was still in existence a hundred years later. The records show that the Framework Knitters' Company themselves continued to bind apprentices all through this period; but in most cases, and always in the case of parish children, the function was performed by the local magistrates.

If apprenticeship survived, however, it was in a debased form. Originally the system was designed to provide a sound industrial training, but in the absence of restriction on numbers it became more and more a method of securing cheap labour. The apprentice began on the frame at about the age of ten, and when he became fairly adept was set a weekly stint, that is, he had to produce for his master, say, six pairs of hose. In addition to the stint which provided for his board and lodging, he might make perhaps two shillings a week for himself. But that depended on what sort of a master he had. The Mayor of Leicester, trying a framework knitter's parish apprentice charged with neglecting work, described the system as 'legalised slavery'; in this case the boy was required to earn for his master thirteen shillings a week,[26] which at that time, in 1836, was as much as any man could earn working overtime. In another case the mayor declared that where complaints against parish apprentices were well founded they would be sent to prison, but at the same time the magistrates were their protectors and were determined that bad masters should be punished too.[27]

Although outdoor apprenticeship became increasingly common during the eighteenth century,[28] up to about 1800 it seems to have been the general rule in the framework knitting industry for both parish and ordinary apprentices to live with their masters. But with the increasing cost of food and the relatively low prices of work, masters now began to find that they could not maintain their apprentices and preferred to make the parents a small allowance—perhaps two shillings a week in the first year and rising by sixpence for each succeeding year of the term—to enable the boys to live at home.[29] Parish children could not be dealt with in this way and were forced to work long hours in order to earn their keep, unless subsidised by the Poor Law authorities.

The decay of the apprenticeship system, like the growth of frame renting is evidence of the extension of capitalist control. Many of the capitalists, as we have seen, were small men with a semi-independent status, whose incomes might be part commission and part profit. Some had doubtless risen from the journeyman class, others were shopkeepers who had branched out into the hosiery business, while a large number had begun like Jedediah Strutt and the Morleys as farmers and often retained their former occupation. This combination was particularly common in Leicestershire: 'the farmer is a stocking manufacturer and employs the poor in spinning,' says Eden in his reference to the county.[30] Examples were to be found in Derbyshire, too. The *Nottingham Journal* of 21 May 1768 announced that Messrs Barber & Raynor, hosiers, of Loscoe, were disposing of their property on retirement from business. It included fifty frames at work in the neighbourhood and a convenient dwelling house with good warehouse, orchard, barns, stables, and upwards of seventy acres of rich enclosed land all in their occupation.

Among the true entrepreneurs some firms of considerable size emerged. In 1753, the three principal hosiers in Nottingham and one at Godalming had 100 frames each;[31] sixty years later Thomas Hayne of Nottingham was reported to have £24,000 invested in frames, another hosier employed 300 workers, and a third paid £200 a week in wages.[32] According to Felkin, there were in 1824 several manufacturers employing over 1,000 frames each, mostly their own property,[33] while in 1845, I. & R. Morley owned 1,700 frames and employed 1,000 more besides.[34] Ward, Brettle, and Ward, of Belper, said to be the largest hosiery makers in the world, had 400 silk and 2,500 cotton hose frames with an output of 100,000 dozens yearly.[35] Measured by the number of workers employed the size of some of these undertakings is scarcely exceeded in the modern hosiery trade.

CHAPTER 5

FLUCTUATIONS IN PROSPERITY:
1696-1819

In contrast with the previous slow development of the framework knitting industry, the early part of the eighteenth century was a period of rapid expansion especially in the East Midlands. This was partly due to the extension of the trade into cheaper lines; but the growth of exports was an important factor. It was fostered by the vigilance of the company in controlling the export of frames and so preserving something of a monopoly for English manufacturers. Instances have already been given of the numerous attempts to establish framework knitting abroad, and these continued after the incorporation of the trade, in spite of Charles II's proclamation.[1] In 1686 a new proclamation was issued ordering that no frames should be bought, sold, or moved without notifying the company, while customs officers must search for and seize all frames destined for export; offenders were to be treated with the utmost severity of the law.[2] Even this was not sufficient, however, as was shown by the company's petitions of 1693 and 1696.[3] Both emphasise the great encouragement given to the export trade in woollen goods by the continued improvements in framework knitting. But the export of frames must be stopped if this country was to retain its monopoly in the art, and the company found difficulty in enforcing the regulations for want of a penalty. The second appeal was successful in remedying this deficiency, for by the Acts 7 and 8 Wm III, c 20, the export of frames was forbidden under a penalty of £40 and forfeiture of the machines, anyone failing to inform the company of the sale or removal of frames to be fined £5.

Another measure of protection, of benefit to the English trade in particular, was obtained in 1688. There had been a serious leakage of frames and workers to Ireland where the company's charter did not operate, and there was a possibility of competition from manufacturers using cheap apprentice labour. However, some of the trade in Dublin, induced, it is believed, by the English company,[4] applied for a grant enabling them to regulate the industry on similar lines, and received a charter from James II, dated 11 July 1688, incorporating them as the Guild of Knitters, Hosiers, and Stocking Makers. Although seven years later the Irish House of Commons resolved that the grant was 'a monopoly, illegal and a grievance',[5] there is evidence that the guild continued to exercise considerable power, for in 1726 we find the London company requesting them to trace an absconded apprentice who is reported to be working as a journeyman in Dublin, adding that they will always be willing to oblige on a like occasion. The Dublin company reply that they have discovered the man and are then asked to prevent him working and to send him back to serve the rest of his term.[6] However, in spite of these apparently amicable relations the export of frames to Ireland was forbidden.[7]

According to Henson, the Act of 1696 completely prevented the exportation of stocking frames, with the result that the French, Spaniards and Italians continued to build machines on the seventeenth-century model, all later improvements being unknown to them till the beginning of the nineteenth century.[8] This probably exaggerates the effectiveness of control, for much depended on the vigilance and power of the Framework Knitters' Company, and the influence of this body, as we have seen, was destined to decline. In any case it was impossible to inhibit entirely the spread of knowledge by way of industrial espionage, the smuggling of machine parts or the emigration of craftsmen. Diffusion was, however, a gradual process and for the time being the English maintained their technical supremacy.

This was evident in the growth of exports. In the four years 1699–1702 exports of woollen hose alone amounted to nearly 400,000 dozen pairs, of which Portugal took over 76,000 dozens.[9] It was a precarious business, always liable to be interrupted by war or by changes in commercial policy.[10] Nor was the home market any too certain, depending so largely on the fashionable demand. The War of the Spanish Succession depressed both home and foreign trade; but the end of Anne's reign saw a distinct recovery and there followed a period of fair prosperity. Earnings throughout the industry averaged 10s 6d a week in the country and 15s in London; in 1714 Nottingham stockingers were said to earn 10s 6d working only four days a week, plain silk hands earned 2s 6d to 3s 6d a day, while those on embroidered work could make as much as 5s.[11] With meat $1\frac{1}{2}$d a pound and bread 14d a stone these wages afforded a comfortable livelihood. The fact that the Framework Knitters' Company had accumulated a fund of £10,000 by 1720 is further evidence of the prosperity of the trade, although some of this had been subscribed by outsiders joining the company to secure the advantages to which membership of such a body gave title.

But as time went on this stability was undermined, partly by the pressure of foreign competition and still more by the erosion of the company's power to regulate the trade. The chief competitor abroad was France. Here the industry had languished after the failure of Lee's enterprise, but its possibilities were recognised by Colbert with his policy of fostering skilled crafts under state regulation. His representative secured drawings of the stocking frame in London and about 1660 an establishment was set up near Paris for building frames and training operatives. Eventually France came to have far more frames than Britain. Before the end of the seventeenth century the country had become largely self-sufficient in knitted goods; our French exports were only 8,638 dozens in 1685.

The first complaints of worsening trade in the eighteenth century came from the woollen branch, which began to suffer, allegedly, from the relaxation of regulations governing the export of raw wool. In 1738 we find the hosiers and framework knitters associated with the wool combers and spinners of Leicester in a petition complaining of the decay of the manufacture and praying Parliament for relief.[12] Six years later a petition from Nottingham complains of the high cost of carrying goods to foreign markets, declaring that 'the stocking weaving already lies under great hardship by reason that the French make up their goods in a much slighter manner than we do and, of course, sell them at a much lower price, so that it is impossible for us to go to foreign markets upon an equal footing'.[13] The suggestion is that French goods were inferior, but this was not necessarily the case. For some time the Nottingham hosiers had been making finer and finer stockings, apparently to economise silk which cost 1s 9d to 2s an ounce, and in 1745 one Joseph Stocks, reputed to be the best workman in the trade, produced a pair weighing no more than $1\frac{3}{4}$oz. But it so happened that fine hose became fashionable, keen rivalry sprang up between Lyons and Nottingham, and in the end it had to be admitted that the French goods were the finest ever seen.[14]

So far it was only competition in foreign markets that had to be faced; but later French and Italian goods began to find their way into the home market, with disastrous results to the silk branch, according to the petition of 1765 from the hosiers, framework knitters, and dealers in silk stockings, gloves, and mitts in Nottingham and district. 'This very valuable branch of inland trade has gone to decay and been almost totally ruined,' they complain, 'whereby many hundreds of industrious families have been and are now reduced to very great hardships, poverty, and distress.'[15] The petitioners believe this to be due to the large quantities of foreign silk stockings, gloves, and mitts clandestinely imported. They were able to prove their case to the satisfaction of Parliament, for an Act was immediately passed prohibiting the import of silk stockings, and in the following year a London dealer in hosiery reported that he had had 'a full supply of goods of a better manufacture than before the prohibition, and that the trade had been brisker'.[16] According to Henson, however, the manufacturers themselves were largely to blame for the decline, having filled their shops with apprentices who made goods of the most wretched description. French silk hose were preferred in London even at 2s more a pair, and they were driving the English completely out of foreign markets. 'So great was the aversion of the public to Nottingham wrought goods that for over twenty years after the passing of this Act the workmen were instructed to work in eyelet holes in the welts the word "Paris".'[17]

Though manufacturers might complain of their difficulties the workers were in far worse case. If manufacturers were losing their monopoly in the trade, skilled workers had long since lost theirs. Manufacturers might appeal to Parliament for protection with the assurance of a sympathetic hearing, but now that the company had collapsed the workers had no protection whatever against the flood of cheap labour which was continually forcing down their standards. It must be admitted, of course, that in the commoner branches, which now formed the bulk of the trade, framework knitting was no more than a semi-skilled occupation, and some deterioration of standards might be expected. It is doubtful, indeed, if a seven-year apprenticeship had ever been really necessary in this craft.[18] But apprenticeship regulations did tend to ensure that the supply of labour was adjusted to long-period rather than to short-period conditions. As it was, an interval of brisk trade saw hordes of workers drawn into the industry, many of them parish children apprenticed by the overseers, who were prepared to pay perhaps £5 to any master who would take a pauper off their hands.[19] Even when trade was good this cheap labour kept wages from rising, and when slack times came the worker, if he could get work at all, was forced to accept even lower rates.

The ominous phrase, 'as poor as a stockinger', began to be heard as early as 1740,[20] and the parliamentary inquiry of 1753 revealed the poverty into which so many had fallen. A Godalming master reported, for instance, that three of his men, good workers who had served their apprenticeship, had to apply to the parish to eke out their wages.[21] Even the London journeymen, the best paid in the trade, could seldom make more than 9s or 10s a week in 1747, though the trade was said to be 'abundantly profitable' to their masters.[22] In pleasant contrast is Gardiner's idyllic picture of the Leicester stockingers, though it must be remembered that he was writing a hundred years later.

> Then every stocking-maker had his frame at home, and his wife and daughters had their spinning wheels. Scattered through the country, these artisans in summer left their frames and wheels to assist in getting in the harvest, after which they returned to their usual employ and thus had constant work throughout the year. A flatness of trade was never known. Surplus goods were laid by to meet seasons as they came round. The population of Leicester at that time was not more than 10,000. Situated in the centre of an agricultural district, provisions were cheap, which enabled the steady and industrious to lead easy and comfortable lives.[23]

But whatever conditions may have been at the middle of the century they grew far worse during the next twenty-five years, and at length, in 1778, the framework knitters in all districts petitioned Parliament for a Bill to regulate wages in the industry. The petitioners declared that notwithstanding their utmost care and industry they were not capable of providing for themselves and their families the common necessaries of life, not only because of the small wages paid, but also on account of frame rent and other incidental charges. In evidence before the committee appointed to consider the petitions[24] it was stated that wages had been declining since 1757; men who twenty years before earned 2s 1d a day could now make no more than 1s 7d, out of which they must pay frame rent and charges for winding, seaming, needles, and candles. Earnings varied according to the kind of work and the efficiency of the worker, but in Nottingham a good man could not make more than 4s 6d a week clear on coarse worsted. There were many women and children in this branch and some could earn nearly as much as the men. In the Leicester glove trade the average workman earned about 5s a week clear, while on silk work wages were higher, being about 6s 6d a week at Godalming and Derby and sometimes as much as 9s in London. For these meagre earnings the stockinger had to work thirteen to fifteen hours a day, though half a day was lost if he took his work to the warehouse. While wages had fallen the price of food had risen by about one-third, and many men with families found it impossible to make ends meet even when fully employed. At Godalming a good workman with two children could not live by his trade and many were receiving relief from the parish.

The stockingers' demands were moderate enough, they asked for no more than 1s 6d or 2s a week advance; but the hosiers of Nottingham and Derby grew alarmed at the proposal to regulate wages by Act of Parliament and sent up a counter petition. In a trade with such a wide range of products and so susceptible to fashion changes, and where there were such great differences of skill among the workers, it was impossible, they said, to fix wages by legislation. Any advance in wages would mean a loss of trade, especially in foreign markets,[25] and the workers, through unemployment, would be worse off than before. These arguments proved sufficiently convincing and the motion to bring in a Bill was defeated.

In the following year the Nottingham stockingers, threatened with still further reductions, made a fresh appeal to Parliament which was followed, as before, by petitions from other districts. The workers in the Midlands had strengthened their position by gaining the support of local members of Parliament, and it seemed that this second effort might be more successful. This time the petitioners, in renewing their complaints about low wages, alleged certain frauds and abuses[26] which discredited the manufacture and handicapped the fair trader who was willing to pay better prices. The hosiers again retorted with a counter petition, while the workers of Towcester found that they had been induced to sign their petition by the persuasion of 'artful and designing men' and now felt convinced that the Bill would be 'destructive to the manufacture and ruinous to themselves and families'. However, the House gave leave for the introduction of a Bill to regulate the framework knitting industry and prevent frauds and abuses. This passed the second reading, but was amended in committee and on the motion for the third reading was ordered 'to be read this day two months', which was equivalent to rejection.[27]

The events which followed this second disappointment are described elsewhere. Methods of terrorism might wring concessions from employers and scotch the decline in wages, but under existing conditions in the industry only a revival of trade could bring permanent improvement. This seems to have begun with the close of the war with the American Colonies, which had severely affected some branches of the hosiery trade.[28] The treaty with France of 1786, under which moderate duties were substituted for the former prohibitions on English textiles and other goods,[29] also brought a great increase in trade, while at home the demand for fancy goods revived. As a result wages improved and a list of prices agreed to in 1787 was fairly well maintained in the Midlands for the next twenty years, during which earnings on plain cotton and worsted work averaged 10s to 12s a week, and on silk 10s to 14s, subject to the usual deductions.[30] In the long years of misery that began soon after the opening of the nineteenth century the framework knitters were wont to look back to this period as almost to a golden age.

The prosperity of these years may be ascribed partly to the remarkable outburst of mechanical invention that marked the later decades of the eighteenth century. Ever in search of some novelty with which to tempt a capricious public, ingenious stockingers continued their experiments throughout the depression. Though prizes were few, and even the successful often failed to hold their gains, there was never a lack of eager competitors. The results were seen in a series of inventions which, while leaving the essential principle of the frame unchanged, added greatly to the range of articles that it could be made to produce.[31] In 1764 a device for making eyelet hole fabric was patented, and the first step taken towards a much more important achievement nearly twenty years later when point net was produced on the stocking frame. Velvet pile fabric and figured lace web came out in 1767 and 1769, followed by knotted work and twilled or plaited hose in 1776. An invention of a different kind, patented about the same time, was the warp machine which, uniting the principles of the loom and stocking frame, was superior to either in the range of patterns which it made possible. It was still further improved in 1791 by the introduction of Dawson's wheels which made the working of the pattern automatic.

While the demand lasted, the manufacture of fancy goods was extremely profitable; high prices were obtained, and workers earned the reward of their skill with wages of 18s to 30s a week. Although some articles, such as silk velvet and brocade pieces and fancy silk vest webs, went out of fashion with the change to more sombre dress towards the end of the century, there were still seventeen or eighteen different kinds of hose worn in 1800. Then the demand for plaited, embroidered, and warp-vandyked hose began to decline. By 1810 fancy silk mitts and gloves, which employed 600 or 700 frames, had gone out of use, as had also cotton spider net which had required 1,500 frames, with 400 in Nottingham.[32] These changes threw a large number of machines back on to plain work, so that the trade in all three branches of wool, silk, and cotton soon began to show signs of distress.

The overcrowded state of the industry now became apparent. In addition to the old frames which had been working for perhaps fifty years or more, many new machines had been built in the prosperous years of the late eighteenth century. With the rise in rents frames became a profitable investment, and all sorts of people with no other interest in the trade laid out capital in this way. It was the growing emphasis on profit from frames rather than from the actual manufacture that led to the vicious practice of spreading work, which became one of the main grievances of the framework knitters. Rent was usually charged whether the frame was working or not, but there was obviously a limit to this; when work was scarce, therefore, it would be spread over as many stockingers as possible, so that each earned at least enough to pay the rent of his frame, which was, of course, deducted from his wages before he received them. Some employers even contended that frame rent was an advantage in ensuring that what work there was should be distributed as widely as possible; but actually, besides throwing the burden of trade depression almost entirely on the worker, it tended to perpetuate the overcrowding of the industry.

As the quantity of machinery had increased so had the number of workers. Besides the general tendency for children to follow their parents' occupation, unregulated apprenticeship brought more and more learners into the trade. In prosperous times framework knitting offered attractions to people in other occupations, and farm workers and domestic servants who had saved a little money and wished for a more independent life would pay £5 to £10 to learn the craft. It was very common, too, for a gentleman's servant, who had saved £150 or £200, to learn the business and then set up with a few frames as a small master.[33]

By 1812 conditions in the Nottingham trade had become so intolerable that the workers decided on an appeal to Parliament similar to that which had failed in 1779. In evidence before the committee[34] appointed to examine their case the petitioners repeated the complaints about overcrowding and excessive frame rents, but their chief grievance was against the introduction of what they called 'fraudulent work'. Since the decline in trade, manufacturers of both lace and hosiery, in the endeavour to find work for their machines, had taken to making cheap and spurious goods which, it was said, brought the trade into disrepute and made the position worse. The chief complaint was against 'cut-up' work, that is, stockings cut out of a straight piece of fabric and seamed. The genuine wrought or full-fashioned hose was shaped on the frame as it was made, the narrowing being done by reducing the number of loops with each course; thus a selvedged edge was produced the loops of which were joined together in seaming, so that even if the seam gave way the fabric did not suffer. But a stocking shaped with the scissors had no selvedge, and when once the seam was burst there was nothing to prevent the fabric unroving from the rough edge. Naturally cut-ups could be turned out at a much faster rate than fashioned hosiery and with far less skill.

As the committee remarked in their report, it was 'singular that the grievance most complained of 150 years ago should in the present improved state of the trade be the same grievance which is now most complained of; for it appears by the evidence that all the witnesses attribute the decay of the trade more to the making of fraudulent and bad articles than to the war or to any other cause'. It was also singular, they said, that there should be no parliamentary regulations for this important trade except the Tewkesbury Act of 1766, though this might be owing to the fact that the charter was still in existence.

It is worth noting, as showing the changing attitude towards state intervention in such matters, that the framework knitters in their evidence about low wages 'never expressed a wish or expectation that Parliament would meddle with wages paid to workmen in any branch of trade; on the contrary they admitted that it could not be done, and that trade must always be left to find its own level'. But they did ask for regulations that should give the worker a fair deal. They asked that employers should be made to hang up schedules of prices for each kind of goods, subject to change at a week's notice, and that this schedule should state definitely the charge for frame rent. 'Such a provision,' said the committee, 'would take off one of the great objections made by the workmen on this head, that frame rent is not governed by any known rule, but is constantly fluctuating and depending upon the will and caprice of each particular master, and therefore that it is arbitrary and oppressive.'

Another grievance connected with wages was the growing practice of paying in goods instead of money. This, of course, was no new complaint; as long ago as Edward IV's reign truck had been prohibited, and under George I and George II Acts were passed which expressly said that workers should be paid in money and not in goods, the first named specifically including the framework knitting industry. But in spite of legislation the practice became prevalent in periods of bad trade when men were glad to get work from anybody on almost any conditions, though it seems to have been confined to small masters and bag hosiers, particularly in the villages.

A typical case was described by a witness from Sutton-in-Ashfield, Nottinghamshire. One of the employers there was not only a hosier, but a grocer, miller, mercer, and clothier as well; in his various capacities he dealt in an interesting assortment of goods including shoes, clogs, herrings, vegetables, bacon, cheese, meal, malt, and other things, with which he was in the habit of paying his workmen.[35] Another witness related how he got work from a bag hosier for three of his frames, because he could get none elsewhere, and had to take payment in groceries. 'At one time,' he said, 'I had a reckoning of about £3 10s. and I had received soap, candles, and a number of different things to the amount of that except a few pence, and he was unwilling to give me that and recommended me some herrings to make up the rest of the money.'[36] The witness had, in turn, to pay these goods to his workmen. This bagman was said to be paying a hundred people in Sutton in this way; truck was so common there that one person was known to have paid half a pound of tenpenny sugar and a penny to have a tooth drawn, while the sexton had been paid in sugar and tea for digging a grave.

In the face of these grievances the committee decided that some regulation was necessary, and in June 1812 the House gave permission to introduce a Bill 'for preventing frauds and abuses in the framework knitting manufacture and in the payment of persons employed therein'.

Up to now the hosiers had taken little active interest in the proceedings,[37] though one or two said that they saw little to object to in the proposals. When the full import of the Bill was realised, however, the manufacturers became alarmed and immediately requested an opportunity of stating their case; so the inquiry was resumed. The manufacturers were practically unanimous in opposing the proposed schedules of prices, repeating the same arguments as had prevailed in 1779. But on the subject of fraudulent goods, opinion was divided. Some agreed with the workers that the production of inferior goods was ruining the trade and was the main cause of the depression, while those who were making these goods claimed the right to produce whatever the market required and contended that such a policy was for the good of the trade.

For instance, considerable quantities of cotton caps made of single thread yarn were exported to the Peninsula and Mediterranean countries, the trade having recently been won from Germany; 10,000 dozens were made in 1811, one manufacturer alone exporting nearly £4,000 worth. Being of single cotton the caps were not only cheaper but, it was said, better for the purpose; they were softer than if made of double thread yarn, and were actually preferred by buyers.[38] Yet the Bill would prohibit such articles, and in this case the trade would simply revert to Germany. There was also an important trade in cotton gloves with Canada and the United States. Since these had been made on the cut-up principle cost of production had been reduced from 12s to 5s 9d a dozen, with a corresponding reduction in selling price. Thus the demand had considerably increased, and if cut-up gloves were prohibited hundreds would be thrown out of work.[39]

It appeared from this evidence that the introduction of cut-ups, so far from lessening demand, had actually increased it in some markets. Although, as the difference in cost of production shows, less labour and less skill were required in making these articles, the extension of demand might in normal times have absorbed all the labour available. But the European war had put an end to the continental trade, except that to the Mediterranean, and the war with America, which broke out in 1812, closed that market too.[40] The hosiers attributed the depression mainly to the war which, besides closing foreign markets, restricted purchasing power at home by heavy taxation. Considering the extent to which the industry was dependent on foreign trade, the export of Nottingham hosiery being estimated at three-quarters of the home consumption,[41] one can hardly agree with those representatives of the framework knitters who laid all the emphasis on 'fraudulent' manufacture and refused to admit that the war was an important cause of the depression.

After hearing the manufacturers' evidence the committee issued a second report in July 1812, in which they felt called upon to state that a considerable difference had taken place in their opinion as to the propriety of enacting several of the provisions in the Bill. They nevertheless recommended that it should be passed as an experimental measure to expire in three years unless renewed by Parliament.

The Bill now came up for its third reading in a House certainly not unsympathetic towards the cause of the framework knitters, but rather bewildered as to the best course to take in view of their committee's change of front. Its chief opponent was Joseph Hume, who showed in a long speech[42] that he, at any rate, had no doubt about the matter. All previous attempts to regulate the hosiery manufacture had broken down, and it was easy to see that in the present instance the prohibition of certain classes of goods might check the expansion of trade on profitable lines and prevent innovations that were genuine improvements.[43] The only province where legislation was indisputably necessary was in preventing deliberate frauds on the purchasing public, but this could be secured by a mere extension of the Tewkesbury Act requiring manufacturers to mark all goods according to the process or the material used. Hume even argued against the truck clauses, with a conviction that seems incredible to anyone acquainted with actual conditions in the trade.[44]

The House of Commons passed the Bill in an amended form, but in the Lords there was more opposition. The Earl of Lauderdale could not conceive a more monstrous principle of legislation than that embodied in the Bill, and the Earl of Liverpool entirely concurred, although he was satisfied with the goodness of the motives which actuated the very respectable individual who introduced this Bill in the other House. Viscount Sidmouth felt himself compelled by his public duty to give his direct negative to the principle which it sought to establish, which he considered most mischievous in its tendency and consequences, and he trusted in God that no such principle would be again attempted to be introduced in any Bill brought up to that House.[45] After such earnest entreaty their lordships could do no other than reject the obnoxious measure.

After 1815 conditions in the hosiery trade became even worse; for now the depression spread to the woollen branch in which Leicester was chiefly engaged. During the war a good deal of machinery had been employed in supplying the army and navy with worsted webbing, but the peace brought a great reduction in this demand. At the same time another 1,500 frames were put on to worsted pieces owing to the failure of the trade in warp plain and ribbed cotton pieces which had been used in very large quantities since 1800 for making pantaloons. Wages on this work had been 25 to 30 per cent above those for plain goods, but as the fashion changed the price fell from 2s 6d to 8d a yard, and by 1816 they had almost ceased to be made. Then common ribbed trouser pieces and German ribbed pieces went out of fashion, in spite of price cutting which brought down earnings from 2s 7d a yard in 1809 to 4d a yard in 1819.[46] In the meantime the manufacture of point net, which had thrived in Nottingham up to 1815, had been ruined 'by constant striving after cheapness'.[47]

Nottingham manufacturers in the cotton branch petitioned Parliament on the subject of cut-up work in 1818, but were advised that nothing could be done for fear of foreign competition. This did not deter those in the Leicester trade, and in the following year a joint petition was sent from manufacturers and workers in the worsted branch. So acute were the privations of the Leicester stockingers, as disclosed in this petition, that once more a committee was appointed to take evidence and report.[48] The inquiry showed that wages had fallen from about 14s a week in 1815 to a present average of 7s for a full week's work of fifteen hours a day. It was customary for all members of the family able to earn anything at all to contribute to the family income, but even then many with young children found it impossible to maintain them without relief from the parish, while others, to avoid this, had sold frames and household effects. As a typical instance, in the parish of St Margaret's, Leicester, there were 61 stockingers who with their dependents made a total of 300 persons, all receiving regular relief; their average earnings when fully employed did not exceed 6s 6d a week. The burden of the poor rate had increased enormously in the hosiery districts, and the action of the gentlemen of the town and county who subscribed towards the expenses of the petition may not have been entirely disinterested.[49]

As with the cotton branch, it was contended that the depression in employment and in wages was mainly due to the introduction of cut-up goods. There was also another kind of hose now being made which was inferior to the cut-up variety. In this article the leg was not even shaped with scissors; it was seamed straight, like a tube, and then stretched on a leg board and steamed, which process gave it the appearance of a fashioned stocking, though when washed the fabric reverted to its original form. These goods, it was said, were even more fraudulent than cut-ups, since the deception did not become apparent until the stocking was washed. The method had been introduced to obviate the waste involved in cutting hose from the piece, the saving being much more important in wool than in cotton, especially now that wool had so increased in price.

The makers of woollen hosiery believed that they had a much better case for the prohibition of cut-ups than had those in the cotton branch, because they were not, like the latter, driven by foreign competition to produce cheap goods. There was little foreign competition in woollen hosiery, since foreigners found it difficult to procure the long staple wool required for worsted yarn. It therefore rested with the British manufacturers themselves to decide whether they should produce none but fashioned goods, and though the majority were in favour of prohibition an Act was necessary to enforce the rule throughout the trade, for if some continued to put irregularly made goods on the market competition would force the rest to follow.

The committee was satisfied that the deteriorated condition of the workmen was, in a considerable degree, owing to the introduction of the article complained of. But one can hardly agree with the emphasis placed upon this point. We have seen that the depression in the woollen branch began with the decreased demand for certain goods, and the cut-ups seem to have been

F

introduced with the object of expanding the market and finding
work for the idle frames. It was admitted that the increase in
foreign trade had been mainly due to the irregularly made articles,
though at the same time the demand for fashioned goods had
declined.[50] Another factor to be taken into account was the rise
in the price of wool from 13d and 15d a pound in 1812 to 24d in
1819,[51] and a manufacturer declared that the high price of yarn
'would prevent, in great measure, the export trade, if wages had
not been reduced'. Asked if a reduction in wages would not therefore have been necessary in any case, he replied that before the
introduction of cut-ups they had always been able to raise the
selling price in accordance with the cost of raw material. It is
hardly necessary to observe that though the elasticity of demand
might permit this to some extent, the policy could not be carried
far without seriously curtailing sales. Indeed, it seems to have
been the inability to sell at remunerative prices all the goods the
industry was capable of producing that led to the introduction of
a cheaper article. But even then cut-ups and straight hose could be
made so much faster than fashioned goods that though the demand
did expand it was still not great enough to absorb the potential
supply. In these circumstances price-cutting was inevitable.

It was admitted that workers making the inferior goods earned
rather more than those on fashioned work—perhaps ninepence
or a shilling a week, it was said; but the prohibition of cut-ups
was expected to raise earnings on fashioned work. Behind this
argument, however, was the quite unjustifiable assumption that
people who had bought cut-ups would be willing to pay much
higher prices for fashioned goods. Failing this there were,
theoretically, two alternatives: either a section of the workers
earning relatively high wages and the rest unemployed, or low
wages all round. Under the keenly competitive conditions in the
industry, both among manufacturers and workers, there is little
doubt which alternative would have prevailed.

There can be no question that the workers seriously weakened
their case by placing such emphasis on the prohibition of inferior
goods. The demand for the prevention of abuses in the payment
of wages was reasonable enough; its satisfaction, while removing
long-standing grievances, would have brought definite, if
restricted, improvement. But the clamour against cut-ups was
really beside the point; their introduction was an effect, not a
cause, of the decline in the better-class trade. It is clear that

the ideal of a well-ordered trade, meeting a steady demand for the wares of its skilled producers, and secure in its monopoly of skill, had long since ceased to have any real meaning. The restricted channels had been opened; when the tide of prosperity flowed there was work for all, and shoals of newcomers drifted in; but the ebb left everybody floundering and scrambling for what little trade remained. It would have been impossible at this stage to reverse the tendencies that had been gaining force during a hundred years of expansion. It is indeed remarkable that the stockingers' claims should have been so strongly supported in Parliament, for, as in 1812, the House of Commons gave a favourable verdict, and in the Lords the Bill was only lost by two votes. Whether the measure, if it had become law, could have been made effective, is another matter; what is significant is that a measure involving such drastic restriction on freedom of enterprise should have got so far. There was still a strong feeling in the legislature that government shirked responsibility when it left industry to 'find its own level' under the pressure of economic forces, and if the arguments for non-intervention finally prevailed it was due as much to a sense of impotence as to positive conviction that this was in all circumstances the right policy.

CHAPTER 6

FRAMEWORK KNITTERS' UNIONS

In Chapter Two we traced the history of the Framework Knitters' Company down to 1753, and we saw that in the crisis of that year the main support for the chartered body, such as it was, came from the journeymen stockingers of Nottingham. However unwillingly, the company had become in fact an incipient trade union; and if the general support of the workers at that time was lacking, it was due to resentment against unreasonable exactions without any return rather than opposition to a policy of regulation. The evidence of poverty-stricken workers, mulcted of fees by grasping officials, proved a very useful weapon in the hands of the employer class, whose motives in destroying the company's power were, of course, very different from those of the workers with whom they made temporary alliance. The unreality of the alliance soon became evident. As time went on, the company came to be regarded by the workers with something like reverence, its misdeeds were forgotten, and in retrospect it was always associated with the prosperity of the early days.

Thus it was natural that the framework knitters should turn, in the depression of the later eighteenth century, to the one body that seemed to offer hope of protection.[1] In 1776 they began to form associations in the various centres of the trade with the object of inducing workers to take up their freedom and of opposing non-apprenticed stockingers. 'So powerful did they become in Nottingham,' says Henson, 'that they had complete control over the return of members of Parliament.' Support was obtained from the London company, and at the election, in 1778, of Abel Smith, son of the well-known local banker, the whole association marched in procession, accompanied by Reynolds, the company's clerk, and two assistants, while representatives attended from Leicester, Derby, London, and most of the other districts, affording a display of strength 'exceeding anything then known in the Midland counties'.[2] The comprehensive character of the movement is shown by the fact that when the trade decided to appeal to Parliament petitions were sent simultaneously from Nottingham, Leicester, Derby, London, Northampton, and Gloucester. In the meantime the Nottingham hosiers had formed a counter-association with a local lawyer named Turner as secretary; but, 'though very desirous of submitting evidence against the Bill, not one of them had the courage to venture his person, property, and character against the general odium of the working classes.'[3]

On the defeat of the first Bill the framework knitters, far from being discouraged, immediately began a fresh effort in which they looked to the company for support. Hallam, of the Nottingham committee, had arranged for the clerk to come down on 4 May 1778, to enrol members, but it turned out that Reynolds had business in Ireland and his visit was postponed. Three months later he had still failed to appear, and Hallam, complaining that the committee had been 'shamefully neglected', arranged for a meeting of the Amicable Association of Framework Knitters on the racecourse ground. There it was decided to petition Parliament for a Bill, not to raise wages, but to fix them at the highest rate then paid; subscriptions of 3s 1d a frame were to be raised to defray expenses. Still it was thought that the support of the company was desirable, and Hallam undertook a journey to London at his own expense to investigate the position; he was met by a representative of the London stockingers and together they went to interview the clerk. It appeared that the company were willing to enrol the journeymen, but of course they must have their fees; freedoms could not be sold for less than 5s each, which would include 2s for stamp, 2s for the clerk, and 1s for the beadle. 'Allowing only 12,000 to require to be entered,' says Hallam in his letter to the trade,[4] 'it will require £1,800 to be raised to pay the clerk and beadle; but where it is to be obtained I know not in the present state of trade.' In the end it was agreed to give Reynolds £50 and Simmons the beadle £20, in return for their promise to come to Nottingham with two assistants and enrol members at half price for the next three months.

From the point of view of Hallam, with his visions of thousands of potential members, the response to these efforts was not encouraging; though it was sufficiently remunerative to the company. Between 25 September and 2 October, 134 were enrolled in Nottingham, Abel Smith among them, and others at

Derby and Leicester; while in the following year 45 were admitted
in London.[5] Beyond taking their money, however, the company
appear to have done nothing whatever to further the cause of the
framework knitters. Nor is this apathy surprising when the List
of Liverymen is examined. In 1789 the only representatives of the
trade in a total membership of 97 were 14 hosiers, 3 stocking
makers, and 1 stocking trimmer; the rest were brokers, merchants,
drapers, victuallers, gentlemen, and so on; of the few members
outside London only three lived in Nottingham.[6]

It was at this stage, when preparations for the second appeal
to Parliament were in full swing, that certain of the Nottingham
hosiers took the extraordinary step of reducing the rate of silk
stockings 25 per cent. No move could have been better calculated
to exacerbate the general indignation. A second meeting on the
racecourse was attended not only by framework knitters, but by
people of all classes and it was resolved to begin a general public
subscription to finance the parliamentary campaign. 'Every engine
was instantly employed to raise money. Butchers solicited from
their customers,[7] landlords from their guests, and many respectable people went voluntarily to collect; every street, lane, and
highway, as well as each village, had its collector, and almost
every inhabitant was in motion.' A happy issue for the 'most
glorious cause' was confidently anticipated.[8]

The final result we already know. The Bill passed its second
reading by only one vote, and when it came up for the third,
Need, the Nottingham hosier, had made sure of matters, according
to Henson, by suing for the support of the venal Cornish
members. News of the Bill's rejection reached Nottingham two
days later, on 10 June, which happened to be a holiday. In a few
hours all was in ferment, and the great Market Place filled with
malcontents. At nightfall the orgy of destruction began with
attacks on the houses of Need, Lawyer Turner, and other culprits,
and an attempt was made to fire Need's cotton mill. The Riot Act
was read and the military turned out, but were repeatedly out-
manoeuvred by the mob. Sunday brought a cessation of violence,
but next day crowds of country stockingers poured into the town
and the campaign was renewed with machine-smashing and more
destruction of houses and furniture. On the Tuesday a five-hours'
parley with the hosiers broke up in disorder. No work was done
for the remainder of the week. Finally the magistrates, who had
enrolled three hundred special constables, announced that 'the

vigilance of justice should be exerted with the utmost severity', and the hosiers were persuaded to issue a conciliatory statement. This promised to remove every oppression if the rioters would desist and allow friendly negotiations with the framework knitters' committee; the hosiers intended to bring all in the trade up to a fair price, not the highest but the best generally paid.

In the proceedings which followed these disorders the authorities showed creditable leniency. As Henson says, 'the magistrates in town and country seemed to regard the outrages more as unruly freaks of children than as crimes of desperate and wicked men; the hosiers also seemed to have a great share of humanity, if blended with selfishness.' Some of the committee and several other persons were arrested, but most got off with small fines, while John Peck, who was charged with wounding W. C. Sherbrooke, Esq, JP, with a stone, was liberated on asking pardon of that gentleman in court. Pilkington, Wright, and Herring, as members of the workers' committee, would have been treated with more severity, but the grand jury failed to bring in a Bill of indictment for conspiracy. Caleb Herring, however, seems to have been pursued with peculiar vindictiveness; hounded by the press gangs and prevented by the masters from following his trade, he was finally compelled to flee the country.

It is not difficult to account for the failure of the framework knitters in this first attempt at combination on the grand scale; indeed the wonder is that it achieved so much. As it was, the organisation of the petitions and the promotion of the two Bills were eloquent of the ability and untiring energy of the leaders, the determination of their followers, and the generosity of the public. The aloofness of the chartered company, still regarded by the workers as the official mouthpiece of the trade, stands out in contrast; but probably the cause suffered little by the loss of an advocate so severely trounced twenty-five years before and not likely to be in favour with a Parliament now still more antagonistic to a policy of regulation. It is to be noted that the combination was not one to raise wages by strike, the point being emphasised by Mr Robert Smith, the member for Nottingham, in supporting the Bill.[9] The framework knitters, he said, came submissively to the legislature with a humble plea for protection. When that plea failed and the hosiers announced their intention of opposing all regulation by charter or Act of Parliament,[10] there was still no suggestion of using the strike weapon.

Fear of the law and the exhaustion of funds and energies were doubtless a sufficient deterrent on this occasion; but the main obstacle, which appears again and again in the history of the trade union movement among the stockingers, was the impossibility of adequately organising the scattered workers. Even for the purpose of organising a parliamentary campaign the framework knitters' committee, as described by Henson, looks cumbersome enough, consisting as it did of two chairmen, one from the workers and the other from the hosiers favourable to the fixing of wages, two representatives of the company, two each for the master stockingers, the Nottingham journeymen, and the country workers, together with members from Leicester, London, and other places who attended occasionally. To imagine such a body attempting to enforce highly complicated lists of prices in an already overcrowded industry, and with the strike threat as their only sanction, is to realise the sheer impossibility of the task.

The revival of trade and the comparative prosperity of the next twenty-five years brought a lull in trade union activity among the framework knitters. As is shown by advertisements in the local press, members of different branches would meet from time to time to discuss prices with their employers, but for the most part they were content to accept, with due gratitude, such share of the benefits as fell to them. Probably the modern tactics of strikes on a rising market were not even thought of by these pioneers of trade unionism; it was only when goaded by intolerable poverty that they took action, and then it was usually with the object of getting some existing regulations reimposed. This policy appears once more in the early nineteenth-century campaign for the enforcement of the apprenticeship rules. The Webbs cite several cases brought by artisans between 1810 and 1812 with a view to putting into force the Statute of Apprentices;[11] but the framework knitters' effort came somewhat earlier, and their case was different since it rested not upon statute law but upon the company's charter and bylaws.

The first move is indicated by a letter of 17 October 1805,[12] in which the workers of Nottingham, Derby, and Leicester complained to the company of the many oppressions they suffered through the illegal practices of unfair tradesmen who kept as many as ten apprentices and would teach adults for a small premium. They desired to be under the company's protection and offered to pay £20 per annum for each court deputed to act for the company's authority. A committee was appointed to consider this, and it was resolved that at the expense of the applicants the clerk should examine the charter and bylaws, take the opinion of counsel, and propose a case.[13] A year later deputies from Nottingham and Leicester were invited to attend the court and hear the committee's report. It appeared that 'a deputation, as far as was legal and not injurious to the trade, and under the control of the court, was all that was required'; whereupon eleven members were approved and, having paid ten shillings each to the company, were appointed as deputies for Nottingham, Leicester, Hinckley, Mansfield, and Loughborough.[14] Early in the following year six deputies were admitted for Derbyshire and two for Gloucestershire and Worcestershire.[15]

For more than twelve months past the framework knitters in the Midlands had been raising funds with the intention of bringing a case against some master for breach of the apprenticeship regulations, and had selected a hosier named Payne, of Burbage in Leicestershire, for prosecution.[16] This case was now in progress, and the company, doubtless encouraged by the acquisition of 62 new members at £1 11s 6d each in Leicester and another 66 at 10s each in the county, resolved to give 'all reasonable assistance'.[17] They were not prepared to risk any money, however, for when in the following year the Payne case was brought to London, the workers' association, which had already spent a good deal in local litigation, was called upon to place the sum of £440 at the disposal of the master and wardens who were superintending the prosecution.[18]

The final hearing took place in the King's Bench division on 13 February 1809, before Lord Mansfield, Payne being charged with following the business of framework knitting and teaching others without having served a legal apprenticeship. The result was similar to that of the Cartwright case in 1731. Although the company's charter was found in point of law to be as good as other charters of like description, its application must be restricted to matters concerning the internal government of the company, such as choosing officials and spending money which members might think well to contribute, provided such money were not applied to purposes contrary to the statute law of the land.[19]

This episode marks the final withdrawal of the Framework Knitters' Company from the scene of conflict in which it had played so inglorious a part. For many years it had been mainly occupied in the laudable if rather humdrum business of administering its various charities, and was dragged from its seclusion with reluctance; now it settled down to the honourable retirement of a City livery company.[20] As for the deputies and the unfortunate stockingers who had put their trust in the law, they were doubtless glad to have returned to them the balance of their £440, amounting to £191 19s 10d.[21]

While these costly and futile proceedings dragged on, the tide of prosperity in the Nottingham trade had rapidly ebbed, and the only legal means of action now lay in a fresh appeal to Parliament; this, as we have seen, was made in 1812. But the framework knitters had learned to employ more direct methods on occasion; among them were desperate men, convinced that only by taking the law into their own hands could better conditions be secured, and these were the dominant influence during the next few years. The Luddites, as they were called, were no mere hooligans bent on the indiscriminate destruction of property,[22] for except in a few cases where mistakes were made, only frames employed on spurious work or belonging to hosiers who paid low prices were broken, and it was claimed that the Framework Knitters' Charter authorised such actions.[23]

The story of the Nottingham Luddites and their counterparts in Lancashire and Yorkshire is too well known to need detailed treatment here;[24] but their activities are so interwoven with the more legitimate manifestations of trade unionism in the hosiery trade as to be inseparable from its general history. The contemporary view of government, which regarded any combined activity of the workers, whatever its real origin, as part of a gigantic conspiracy to overthrow the established order, might be absurd; but it is certainly difficult, so far as the framework knitters are concerned, to determine to what extent their trade societies and leaders were implicated in the militant policy of frame breaking. On the part of the great body of the workers and some of the small masters there was undoubtedly connivance, but the whole business was so cleverly managed and protected by the loyalty of the workers, who refused to divulge any information, that the actual organisation was never unearthed.[25]

Much interest centres in the somewhat enigmatical character of Gravenor Henson. 'It is not too much to say,' writes Felkin, 'that there was no trade combination in the three Midland counties during the first forty years of this century with which

Henson was not acquainted both as to their leaders and designs, and in due time their operations.'[26] At this time still in his early thirties, 'a sensible fellow and very fond of talking',[27] he is revealed in his later writings as a man of remarkable ability and learning, while contemporary evidence records his unflagging zeal in the cause of his fellow-workmen. Yet his real part in the movement remains something of a mystery. It is probably true, as Henson himself contended, that he acted as a moderating in-fluence;[28] on the other hand, there are reports which, if believed, would suggest identity with the elusive Ned Ludd himself. Frame breaking was supposed to be under the direction of the framework knitters' executive committee with Henson as its full-time leader; he was known to be connected with many 'desperate ruffians' believed to be frame breakers;[29] he had been heard to speak favourably of Luddism. Worse still, he became engaged in 'treason-able practices against His Majesty'; the Nottingham magistrates had no hesitation in giving affidavit to that effect.[30] As the chief instigator of the Hampden Clubs he corresponded with the dis-affected in other parts of the country, and the 'plan for a general and simultaneous tumult was in great measure laid by him'.[31] One informant said he thought Henson 'equal to the perpetration of anything Robespierre ever committed'. The evidence can only be given for what it is worth, since nothing was ever proved; but the man who could inspire such rumours was clearly a remarkable character.

The first case of frame breaking occurred early in March 1811. At a conference with some of the Nottingham hosiers it had been agreed 'to give the men unabated wages provided they would join in bringing up the under-paying masters to the same standard and put down cut-up work'.[32] Thus encouraged the men set about the task, but persuasion failed, and at length threats were put into execution. Men came from all parts of the county and assem-bled in Nottingham Market Place; the appearance of the military prevented any acts of violence in the town, but that night sixty-three frames were smashed at Arnold and two hundred more at various places during the next three weeks.[33] All through the year the outrages continued, until about eight hundred frames were destroyed and the intimidated employers were disposed to come to terms.[34] Felkin relates how as a youth of seventeen he was required by his employers to convey the information that if their frames, numbering about three thousand, were spared, one shilling a dozen advance would be paid the following Saturday and be continued whether others paid it or not.

> It was a dreary afternoon with heavy rain and winter sleet. He rode hard, and at Basford, Bulwell, Eastwood, Heanor, Ilkeston, Smalley, Sawley, Kegworth, Gotham, and Ruddington, delivered to their head framework knitters the joyful news of the offered advance. It prevented, for that night, the marauding parties employing themselves; these frames had undoubtedly been doomed as belonging to one of the most influential houses in the trade. The promise was faithfully performed; not one of their frames was injured, and no further fears were excited as to the safety of their property.[35]

There were fresh outbreaks in 1812, sixty-eight frames being destroyed in the first fortnight in Nottingham and places round about;[36] the trouble seemed to be spreading into the adjoining counties, and the Duke of Newcastle suggested a declaration of martial law.[37] But the energetic measures of the magistrates, assisted by military force, were having their effect, and at the March assizes in Nottingham four frame breakers were sentenced to fourteen and three to seven years' transportation. In the same month, an Act was passed making frame breaking and destruction of goods a capital offence, and requiring all persons on whose premises such occurrences took place to report immediately to the police.

In August, Coldham, the town clerk, reported 'all quiet' in Nottingham. The workers' funds were exhausted by the parliamentary campaigns, and what unions still survived were merely small local bodies.[38] But this comparative inactivity did not last long, for towards the end of the year elaborate plans were being made for organising the trade, not merely in the Midland counties, but throughout the kingdom. The new union appeared under the innocuous title of 'A Society for obtaining Parliamentary Relief and the Encouragement of Mechanics in the Improvement of Mechanism,'[39] and contemplated a federation of small local societies linked together in the country districts by central committees and by general central committees in Nottingham, Derby, Leicester, Glasgow, and Dublin. An annual conference was to be held in each of the three Midland towns with one deputy from each central committee in the area, and every third year a national conference attended by a delegate from each central committee in the kingdom.

At the first conference,[40] held in Nottingham in the spring of 1814, it was reported that thirty-three societies had been formed in Nottinghamshire, eleven in Derbyshire, ten in Leicestershire, one at Godalming, and one in London. The main object of the organisation, as revealed in the resolutions of the delegates, was the relief of unemployment. Houses of call were to be established under the control of each society 'for better convenience and for information of taking and letting of frames, and for obtaining more certain employ for members'; but masters who were members might take or refuse journeymen sent from a house of call without giving cause. All money was to be paid into a central fund for the assistance of men travelling in search of work and for the relief of old age and infirmity; members teaching the trade to anyone but their apprentices to forfeit all benefits.

It is difficult to see what could be objected to in such proposals. Coldham himself confesses in his letter of 20 February, that he 'can form no judgment how far by their constitution they violate the law',[41] and the Nottingham magistrates' clerk did not see that they came under any existing law. But the suppression of the society was imperative, for the terror impressed on the minds of masters by the existence of such a 'desperate conspiracy' had placed them in a state of almost unqualified submission to the demands of their workmen who dictated their own terms.[42] The first step was taken at a 'very numerous' meeting of hosiers held at the Police Office Tavern in Nottingham on 22 May, where a liberal subscription was set on foot, and a secret committee appointed consisting of 'gentlemen of the greatest respectability'; they were fortunate in securing the services of the energetic town clerk in the capacity of secretary. The intention was to employ some 'confidential person' who would become a member of the society and provide information, but it could only be on the distinct understanding that he should not be called as a witness, and this obviously increased the difficulty of proving a case. In the meantime the resourceful Coldham suggested to Sidmouth that the disbandment of the local militia might enable the hosiers better to counteract the formidable combination; the more there were wanting work, the more difficult for the framework knitters' committee.[43]

It was not long before the workers' society laid itself open to prosecution. In any case it was illegal as a corresponding society, and the Procurator Fiscal of Dumfries discovered the letters sent by the Nottingham stockingers urging the formation of branches of the union in Scotland;[44] but the weapon ultimately used was the Combination Act. Ever since April the society had been engaged in a struggle to raise wages in the silk hose branch and was opposed by a combination of hosiers who had resolved, at a 'large and respectable meeting in London, to pursue every legal means to break up the workers' union'.[45] Efforts were directed against Messrs Rays, a large Nottingham firm, who were particularly vulnerable because they mainly employed independent frames. The society urged its members not to work for Rays unless they advanced prices, and offered to maintain them on its own work, with the result that a number of master stockingers and between two and three hundred journeymen withdrew their labour. Rays wanted to give in, but the secret committee and the rest of the hosiers were opposed to such a display of weakness, and after some wrangling it was decided to summon some of Rays's master hands in the name of the firm, but really under the direction of Coldham's committee. The charge was 'neglect of work', and it was hoped that the masters 'would be induced as one man to step forward and put an end to this nefarious combination'; one declared that they could end the strike, if they chose, by forcing their journeymen to work to orders; but it appeared that the majority of the masters 'were devoted to the combination and had committed themselves beyond power of retracting'. However, the committee had also taken up some of Rays's journeymen, and these gave information implicating three of their leaders. When the men's committee met on the night of 5 July they were pounced on by sixteen constables who seized all their books and papers and arrested two of the members. These, with a third culprit, were convicted two days later of 'receiving money for illegal purposes', but as this was the first case in Nottingham under the Combination Act, it was not thought politic to push the conviction to the full extent, and they were sentenced to a month's hard labour.[46]

The secret committee had waited until it appeared, from efforts that were being made to collect funds, that the men's resources were exhausted. An examination of the accounts, which were duly sent up to the Home Office, shows that over £900 was paid out between 25 April and 4 July 1814; mention is also made of money lent to finance the manufacture of silk hose, which, according to Coldham, had been the main support of their exchequer and had enabled them to produce a considerable quantity of goods for sale in London.

This experiment of the workers in manufacturing on their own account was the forerunner of a more ambitious scheme which developed three years later, when it was resolved to set up a market on the Huddersfield weavers' model. They estimated that £200 would be sufficient to begin with, and plans were submitted to gentlemen willing to subscribe, a committee being appointed to act under the gentlemen proprietors and receive communications from the trade as to the number of frames likely to be employed; a subscription of one penny a week was to be paid on each frame, and within a very short time eight hundred had been entered.[47]

It was thought that when the market was advertised in the leading commercial centres, merchants would resort to Nottingham insead of buying in London, with advantage to the town and also to themselves, for where goods were made on independent frames the hosier's profit would be eliminated. The workers too would benefit by the exclusion of the bag hosiers and middlemen; they would always know the price of work when it was sold in the open market; moreover, those not dependent on the hosiers for frames would have the alternative of working for the market if dissatisfied with their earnings. On the other hand, as one correspondent pointed out, most of the stockingers had no frame of their own and could not even afford to buy materials; it would be necessary to establish frame clubs and societies for supplying yarn on a co-operative basis if the scheme were to have any wide support.

Early in the next year the mart was opened at premises in Clumber Street; more than twenty commercial societies had been formed in Nottinghamshire and Derbyshire and it was expected that production would soon increase to £10,000 a week in value. But in spite of all efforts production was never more than £1,000 worth in a week, in fact demand exceeded supply; moreover, the committee complained that they had received no more than promises of subscriptions and that their salaries of £1 a week had not yet been paid. On 5 March the *Monitor* expressed regret at the backwardness of the trade in paying the weekly contributions for the development of the scheme, and that is the last we hear of it.

The venture in co-operative production provides yet another illustration of the unfailing vigour and resource of the framework knitters' leaders. Repelled at one point by the economic and political forces of oppression they were ever willing to resume the struggle on some other front. It was the same in Scotland. On two occasions the Hawick stockingers combined against their masters, in 1816 to resist a reduction of 4s a week in wages and in 1818 for a seven weeks' strike to restore the old rates. Both efforts failed and some arrests were made, but the men were let out on bail after a time and nothing more was done.[48] The workers then appealed to the justices to regulate wages and the magistrates acknowledged their grievances; they were of opinion, however, 'that any interference on their part would not only be vain and nugatory, but might even eventually operate to the prejudice of the petitioners themselves'. Although the law gave them the power to regulate wages it did not command them to do so. In making this reply the justices paid a tribute to the meritorious conduct of the operatives who had submitted for a long period to many hard privations in a most peaceable and becoming manner, and they could not help indulging a hope that by perseverance in a similar line of conduct for a short time matters in the natural course of things might operate a favourable change, or the wisdom of government might interpose to remove the cause of the evils complained of.[49]

But matters, so far from improving, got worse, for wages were again reduced 15 per cent. The framework knitters now resolved on a fresh expedient and, following the example of Gravenor Henson in 1811,[50] they brought a case against the hosiers for combining to reduce wages. It was obvious that the employers had some mutual agreement, for when a reduction came it took place throughout the trade on the same day; indeed, they had been seen to meet frequently of an evening, ten or twelve of them, and adjourn to a tavern, though the nature of their business there could only be inferred. The Procurator Fiscal undertook the prosecution and the workers proved their case; nevertheless the defendants were all discharged.[51] This was in 1819; three years later two-thirds of the hosiers proposed a further reduction of 10 per cent and locked out their men for twenty-eight weeks; wives and families were supported by public subscriptions and the framework knitters of Edinburgh, Dumfries, and Carlisle sent contributions of sixpence or a shilling a week to aid the struggle. In 1824 the men of Hawick were keeping up wages as best they could 'without making any noise or trouble about it'; they paid

3d a week into a small fund which allowed 7s out-of-work pay.[52]

Meanwhile the struggle in the Midlands continued. The break-up of the Society for obtaining Parliamentary Relief was followed, not unnaturally, by a recrudescence of frame smashing culminating in an attack on Heathcoat's lace factory at Loughborough on the night of 28 June 1816, when £6,000 worth of damage was done. One man was caught and eventually hanged for his part in this affair, but the rest were not discovered until the following year when, as a result of information given by their accomplices, a number of the chief Luddites were arrested; of these six were executed and three transported for life. In Henson's opinion it was the executions which caused the final disappearance of Luddism; altogether about a thousand stocking frames and eighty lace machines had been destroyed since 1811, and during the height of the terror wages had been raised about 2s a dozen, only to relapse as soon as the first wave had subsided.[53]

The next few years are a period of increasing distress and wearisome strife only relieved by the exhibition of public generosity on behalf of the framework knitters. Fear of the Combination Laws prevented the workers forming any permanent organisations, so that when statements were agreed upon it was impossible to keep all the masters to their bargain; indeed some of the employers told the men that prices could not be maintained unless they had 'something to trust to'.[54] In 1817, for instance, the Leicester stockingers managed 'with great difficulty' to get a statement of prices considered at a meeting of hosiers. The resolutions show that the feeling was not unsympathetic; they 'fully appreciate and highly lament the privations of the framework knitters arising from reductions of their wages, and they think the temperate and patient conduct of the framework knitters under the circumstances in which they have been placed entitles them to the highest credit and to the best exertions on their behalf'. The members 'pledge themselves individually and collectively to seize the first opportunity of making such advance of wages as fair competition with other houses in the trade will justify'; but they regret the 'utter impossibility of laying down any general arrangement by which an advance of wages or a uniformity of prices can be secured'.[55]

Ultimately, however, the manufacturers agreed to what they considered a fair scale of wages; but needless to say it was not long maintained. Scarcely a week elapsed before a member of the committee which had drawn up the statement departed from

G

it; this destroyed confidence and others began to fall away. 'The workers,' said one of their witnesses before the Committee on Artisans and Machinery, 'endeavoured to keep themselves united that they might know how the trade was going on and who was paying the price and who not; but such was the want of information in the county, the law being against us, that the combination entirely ceased and the manufacturers departed from their agreement to such a pitch that in 1818 we were in great distress and in 1819 worse.'

Usually it was the small manufacturers and bag hosiers who brought down wages. As the Rev Robert Hall says in his *Reply to Cobbett*:[56] 'a system is established by which an extensive trade in hosiery is conducted by persons of little or no capital; their bills weekly drawn on London are accepted, which is equivalent to a weekly supply of capital, and the inducement to afford this accommodation is the extreme low price of goods manufactured under statement.'[57] On the other hand, the bag hosiers had their defenders, like the writer who analyses the circumstances of the 1821 turnout;[58] he is satisfied as to the 'utter impossibility of maintaining a fixed rate of wages' and reiterates the 'economic truth' that supply must be regulated by demand. 'The framework knitters,' he says, 'complain of the bag hosiers who run down prices, but these are small manufacturers whose expenses being small, and who cannot wait for large returns, are content to sell goods at very moderate profits. Sometimes they rise to opulence, and no obstruction can be thrown in their way without infringing on the equal rights and liberties of Englishmen.'

On the whole it appears that the 'rights and liberties of Englishmen', when they happened to be employers, were sufficiently well cared for. Although the Combination Laws were not enforced so rigorously as is sometimes supposed, there were still occasional prosecutions,[59] and the workers knew that any attempt on their part to enforce uniformity of prices might lead to imprisonment. In other ways, however, they were more successful. One important factor in depressing wages was the practice of subsidising employment at the expense of the ratepayers; it had been adopted by the overseers as the simplest way of meeting their obligations to the poor, but such pauperising of labour was clearly unsound and was generally condemned by all classes. Accordingly, when the advance in wages was contemplated in 1817, the hosiers and their workers made representations to the Leicester overseers, who then resolved not to employ their poor in the manufacture of hosiery, except those compelled to live in the House, nor to give any help to persons travelling as agents for the disposal of hosiery, but to lend every assistance in their power to those out of work.[60]

It was hoped that the prohibition of cut-up articles would also help to check the decline in wages, but the rejection of the Bill in 1819 threw the workers back on their own resources. They had little organisation and no funds, but meetings were called and a general strike throughout the three counties was resolved upon. 'I believe there was never known in our country's history so general a turnout and so peaceably conducted,' said one observer.[61] When the strike began frames were delivered up to their owners, and in a short time 14,000 stockingers had ceased work. All classes, including some of the hosiers themselves, combined in support; in Leicestershire the public were particularly generous, and among the gentlemen who assisted in raising funds were the lord lieutenant, the members of Parliament, and most of the magistrates. Altogether about £800 was subscribed.

Eventually sixty-seven out of the ninety hosiers in Nottingham were induced to sign a statement raising the price for making stockings from 8s to 12s a dozen, but after nine weeks the workers' funds were exhausted and they were forced to return whether the increase was promised or not. Eight months later wages were as low as ever. In Leicester, however, the strikers were more successful, rates being advanced to the 1817 statement, which was maintained for two years.[62]

The general strike of 1821 was even more extensive than that of 1819; 'scarcely a dozen of hose was made in the three counties for two months,' says Felkin.[63] Again the old prices were restored, but it was only because accumulated stocks had been cleared and there was a brisk demand for goods; when trade returned to normal the usual price-cutting began. On this occasion the magistrates appear to have been less lenient, for four members of the framework knitters' committee were summoned at Nottingham for offences under the Combination Act. They contended that the money they had received was for the relief of distress and had been subscribed by the county gentry. But a handbill was produced reporting a meeting of the two-needle branch of framework knitters in the counties of Nottingham, Leicester, and Derby, at which it was resolved that hosiers refusing to pay the agreed price should be told to fetch their frames home. This was held to be an offence under the Act and the men were sentenced to three months' imprisonment. Fortunately, several gentlemen assisted to finance an appeal, which was successful in getting the conviction quashed.[64]

One experiment which did a good deal to relieve the privations of the Leicester stockingers in these years was the Friendly Society established by the Rev Robert Hall in 1819. Men in work were asked to pay 6d a week and women and youths 3d in return for an assurance of 6s and 3s a week respectively when unemployed; an eloquent appeal brought in supplementary contributions from the public, and the funds were managed by trustees.[65] Their first report dated 15 November 1820, showed that over £6,000 had been paid out in the year, of which the workers had contributed £4,400. Next year the situation grew desperate, 2,172 out of a total membership of 5,972 were unemployed, and £6,182 was paid out in the first three months; the trustees had to borrow £1,550, but a subsequent revival of trade enabled them to liquidate this out of workers' contributions. For nearly five years the society struggled on, but as the claimants increased so the subscribers diminished, and eventually the funds were exhausted. Altogether £16,182 passed through its hands, of which the public subscribed £3,000 and the parishes £2,500;[66] Hall claimed that wages were raised by one-third in the first two years of the society's existence, and there was a notable fall in the poor rate.[67] This was the most important enterprise of its kind, but the example of Leicester was followed with some success by Nottingham and other towns.[68]

In 1824 the framework knitters made their last great effort. When the strike began the Combination Laws were still in force, but there was 'a very general impression in the public mind that all such enactments are, if not useless, at least unequal in operation, unjust in principle, and pernicious in tendency'.[69] The dispute continued without interference for about four months, though according to Felkin there were 'great differences of opinion among the men as to policy'. In the end advances were secured in Nottingham and Leicester, but they were only paid for a few months, and the masters themselves formed a combination to resist further demands. There was little to fear; the means and even the will to fight were at last exhausted. The stockingers made no effort to keep up the contributions to their unions, and the memory of their sufferings in the long struggle made it impossible to organise a general strike again. A great outburst of trade union activity followed the repeal of the Combination Acts in 1824, but these pioneers of the movement played no part in it; not until the transition of the factory system, more than thirty years later, do we get the beginnings of effective organisation among the hosiery workers.

CHAPTER 7

A STAGNANT INDUSTRY

Among all the inquiries into industrial and social conditions instituted by the reformed Parliament, there are few that produced a more depressing report than that issued in 1845 by the commissioner on the framework knitters. The impression is that of utter stagnation; the stockingers and the manufacture generally seemed to have been left in the backwash of industrial progress. If the hand-loom weavers were in similar plight, it could at least be said that they were the victims of improvements in methods of production. No such mitigating circumstance appears in the case of the hosiery trade; the application of power was almost unknown, and the frame itself had remained practically unaltered for a hundred years or more.

When hosiery manufacturers talked of the factory system they simply meant the concentration of hand frames, perhaps wide machines making several hose at once, in large workshops; and although this had been done in some instances, as for example at Hawick,[1] they saw no reason for adopting the method generally. Division of labour was as complete with ten or twenty frames as with fifty or five hundred, they said, and although there might be advantages in better control over output and materials they were not sufficient to outweigh the extra cost involved. Moreover, the workers themselves were opposed to the factory system with its regular hours and strict discipline.[2] Several experiments which had been tried in the Midlands broke down for this reason, although one Leicester manufacturer who had fifty-five frames in a large workshop reported that he had more applications than he could fill.[3] But in this case the workers were mostly young girls; with the mass of the older workers, and especially the men, it seemed that their habits were 'so fixed now that it would be utterly impossible to establish a factory working under any sort of regulation as to hours'. All things considered, it seemed that the existing system was a manifestation of that 'natural order' in which men had been taught to believe. As one manufacturer put it: 'The fair inference is that the way in which a business settles and has been carried on in any locality for fifty years or more is under all circumstances the best way.'[4]

No doubt the inference was fair enough according to current doctrine; but the economic 'truth' might have received less emphasis had it not harmonised so happily with the interest of entrepreneurs. On the other hand, if the condition of the wage earners is any criterion by which to judge an industrial system, it is difficult to imagine anything worse than that which had developed in the hosiery trade. A mere average of earnings cannot be accepted without qualification, for as Felkin said, in evidence submitted to the commissioner,[5] 'the returns show a wide difference in the character of hosiers as to the rate of wages and treatment of hands; and of hands in the irregular working habits of many amongst them'. But in so far as one can speak of a 'level of wages' among the framework knitters, it is clear that it had remained practically stationary for about thirty years. It could not have fallen much lower; indeed, Cobbett refused to believe that it was so low in 1821; if it were true, they must all have been dead long ago, it was what the logicians called 'proving too much'.[6]

But if wages were no worse than they had been in 1812 and 1819 the people themselves had sunk lower. 'The condition of dwellings in the last seven or eight years has much deteriorated and many articles of furniture are gone,' says the commissioner's report.[7] 'This process is much slower in a depression than is usually supposed. In Arnold, where want of clothing is particularly specified, the rate of earnings is higher than in most places, yet the feeling of self-respect and honest pride in maintaining a decent exterior once having been broken down, it will be found that a better state of clothing or of household comforts bears no proportion to an advanced amount of earnings.' In Hinckley demoralisation was fearfully extending itself; hunger and distress were fast destroying all honesty in one sex and all chastity and decency in the other.[8] At Tewkesbury wages were exceedingly depressed and half the frames were idle. 'Such scenes of wretchedness as those I have witnessed this day,' says Felkin's correspondent, 'I never saw before, and hope never to see the like again.'[9]

There is abundant evidence of the deteriorated physical condition of the stockingers and their families. A Nottingham physician declared that he could always tell a stockinger by his appearance; 'there is a paleness and a certain degree of emaciation and thinness about them,' he said.[10] Their diet consisted mainly of bread and cheese, gruel and tea, while it was a common practice to drug infants with a preparation known as Godfrey's Cordial; a Nottingham chemist had known four children of one family die from its effects.[11]

One of the Factory Commissioners of 1833 gives an excellent description of working conditions at Leicester.

> We then went to the house of William Farmer. He has two shops. The one on the ground floor I entered. There were six frames; three on each side. The room measured in height 6 feet 8 inches, in length 13 feet, in breadth 10 feet 6 inches. The frames were wide ones turning off three or four stockings each at a time. They measured all alike, viz. 5 feet in length placed transversely with relation to the length of the room, height 5 feet, width 3 feet. It will be seen from the above proportions that little more than 6 inches were left for passage between two rows of frames. I got to the other end of the room with difficulty by stooping and moving sideways, where I found a little boy with a winding machine occupying the only space left by an irregularity in the wall. The men sat at their work back to back; there was just space for the necessary motion, but not without touching each other. The room was so close as almost to smother one. The shop above was of the same dimensions, containing also six frames. Of the men here at work most were sickly and emaciated. One of nineteen looked stout and well; he had been at it seven or eight years and said he had been lucky and lived well. This answer is universally given by the hale-looking stocking weaver who has been any considerable length of time in the trade. They are exceptions which seldom occur after the age of twenty.[12]

Illustrations could be multiplied, but these typical extracts from a mass of contemporary evidence show clearly enough that the condition of the framework knitters, as a body, could hardly have been worse. Let us look at the condition of the industry which provided their livelihood and see how far this state of things might be attributed to trade depression. Like other industries the hosiery trade suffered from the periodical crises of the time. That of 1825 was felt with particular severity, the unemployed machinery depreciated in value and outsiders who had invested in frames hastened to liquidate their capital; Felkin estimates that during the next seven years 15,000 frames changed hands at an average price of less than £5 each.[13] The crisis of 1837, which affected both England and the USA, also depressed trade, especially in the worsted branch which exported about one-tenth of its produce to America.[14] But it would be untrue to say that the hosiery trade was suffering from persistent depression. Judging by the following report the worsted branch appears to have enjoyed fairly steady prosperity:

> The worsted hosiery trade is not a speculative business, its annual demand is subject to little variation, its machinery has been stationary for the last twenty years, and is now even less in amount than at the conclusion of the war, while more stocks are required for the supply of numerous additional wholesale houses, new markets are opened and we have more consumers at home and abroad; there cannot therefore be any rational ground for alarm in this market.[15]

Although cotton hosiery from Saxony was said to have driven Nottingham goods out of the American market, the figures show that on the whole the exports of this branch were being well maintained.[16] Despite the removal of the prohibition on imports and the substitution of a 30 per cent duty in 1826, the silk trade had considerably increased.

The quantity of hosiery imported shows that foreign competition in the home market was negligible, and abroad Saxony was the only serious competitor. As for France—'with such frames and such workmen 'tis a perfect burlesque to talk of competition,' says a writer in 1839.[17] Some indication of the state of trade may also be gathered from the number of unemployed frames. According to Felkin's return there were 48,482 frames in the United Kingdom in 1844, and of these 5,830 were out of work;[18] not an unduly large proportion in view of the great variety of the trade.

The exports of hosiery, amounting to nearly one-sixth of the total produce, are a further indication of the general course of trade; the figures as given in the commissioner's report[19] are summarised in the table on page 110. Except in the case of silk the quantities of exports since 1833 compare favourably with those for the earlier period; but, as will be seen, there had been a great fall in values. This, however, does not necessarily indicate that the trade was less prosperous for manufacturers, being largely accounted for by reductions in the cost of materials; raw cotton, for instance, had been 1s 6d a pound in 1814, and was now about

$5\frac{1}{2}$d. It must be remembered, too, that many articles of inferior quality had been introduced, and that wages were now lower in some branches.

But if there is no evidence of an appreciable decline in the demand for British hosiery goods either at home or abroad, neither is there any sign of expansion; in fact, there was stagnation

BRITISH HOSIERY EXPORTS, 1814–43

| Years | Stockings | | Other Goods |
	Quantity	Value	Value
	COTTON		
	Dozen Pairs	£	£
1814–16 (av)	376,273	549,765	40,299
1834	399,885	168,583	11,161
1834–43 (av)	405,257	165,752	15,372
	SILK		
1814–16 (av)	56,592	209,128 (a)	
1834	24,618	51,734	23,891
1834–43 (av)	27,962	49,520	53,528
	WOOL		
1814–16 (av)	142,845	171,138	185,429
1834	173,063	92,286	22,932
1834–43 (av)	142,041	72,721	52,301

(a) Values not separated for these years.

here as there was in methods of production, the two circumstances being, of course, interconnected. At first sight it may seem difficult to reconcile this fixity of demand with the rapid increase in population and the expanding exports of the cotton and woollen industries, especially the former. There are several factors that help to explain it. Whatever the effect of growing population on demand, it had barely sufficed to offset the loss of the fancy trade due to fashion changes early in the century. Moreover, stockings and underclothing were articles that poor people economised in or made at home when prices of more essential commodities were high; it was an established maxim of the trade, said a manufacturer in 1840, that demand fluctuated with the price of provisions.[20] Although real wages were rising slowly the working-class standard of living was still too low for an increase in mere numbers to have much effect on a trade like that of hosiery. Abroad the prospects of increasing sales were still less favourable; the only large foreign market was in the United States, and that was being exploited by Saxony, which was said to export there some $1\frac{1}{2}$ million dozens of cotton hose and gloves annually.[21] For the rest, although framework knitting had not developed to any great extent except in Germany, heavy import duties made manufactured hosiery too expensive for the majority, and most of their requirements were hand knitted; it was said that in 1839 four-fifths of the worsted hosiery worn in France was made in this way.[22]

The disease from which the industry was suffering now becomes evident. While demand remained stationary productive capacity had increased. Felkin says that 'few new frames were made between 1810 and 1840',[23] but the figures hardly bear out his statement. According to his own estimate there were 48,482 frames in the United Kingdom in 1844, as against Blackner's return of 29,590 in 1812. The difference is too great to be accounted for by errors and omissions in calculation; but in any case whatever new frames were built would usually swell the total, for the 'carcase' of a stocking frame lasted indefinitely. Commenting on the production of redundant machinery, Felkin makes a plea for the diffusion of statistical information; if returns had been collected annually and transmitted to the Board of Trade they would have shown whether the public interests were being promoted as they ought to be by the operations of business, much capital might have been saved and the wages of the workpeople saved from fearful depression.[24]

There could be no doubt that the industry was over-crowded with workers. Even if their numbers had remained stationary the introduction of wide frames would have rendered some superfluous;[25] but there was 'a constant and manifest tendency' for numbers to increase.[26] Apart from the unemployed of other trades who drifted into framework knitting, there was the natural increase among the stockingers themselves. Although a Derby witness told the commissioner that he knew 'scarcely any framework knitters bringing up their children to the trade', and in some districts many of the boys went into the pits,[27] it was still the rule in most places for children to follow their parents' occupation. Felkin gives an instance of two stockingers, man and wife, whom he visited at Leicester in 1844; ten of their fifteen children had been put to the trade. 'They seemed to have the idea that having come of frame-

work-knitting stock they must for ever remain in that occupation.'[28] It might be thought that more children would have been
absorbed by the factories; but the framework knitters were loath
to send them, in spite of the higher earnings obtainable. A
Leicester stockinger declared that he would rather see his daughter
beg than go into a factory; they were 'complete hell-holes as to
morals', except in a few cases and there competition for entrance
was very keen.[29] That was in 1833, and although conditions had
been considerably improved since then by factory legislation, the
prejudice persisted. As for the chances of older persons getting
other employment, they seemed to be very small. Some were given
temporary work as stone breakers, but their fingers became set
and hard and they were handicapped on returning to their own
trade. Stockingers had not the strength for heavy manual work,
and no one would employ them as farm labourers; while if they
left the district in search of work their families would become a
burden on the parish.[30]

While admitting that the system of frame renting and deductions from wages was largely responsible for the excessive amount
of machinery and the practice of spreading work, the commissioner
was satisfied that the leading cause of the distress among the
framework knitters was 'the disproportion existing between the
supply of labour and the demand for it'.

> No permanent or general improvement in the condition of the
> framework knitters can be looked for, but by a diminution of
> their numbers proportionate to the demand for labour, or such
> an extension of the manufacture as would largely augment the
> amount of employment. The first of these means is in the
> exclusive control of the workmen themselves and can only be
> produced by abstinence from early or improvident marriages,
> or by bringing up their families to other occupations; results
> only to be expected from the slow operation of improved moral
> cultivation.

There is more than a suggestion of Malthusian influence in
the verdict, but it is difficult to see what other conclusion was
possible on the evidence. The workers contended that low wages
and unemployment were evils due to lack of protection for labour,
which could only be removed by legislative interference. Their
petition asked for 'a law empowering the Crown to appoint a
Commission in cases of dispute between employers and employed,
to fix and regulate wages and to make general regulations for the

guidance of masters and workmen'.[31] There was even a suggestion of reviving the provisions of the charter, though the Leicester stockingers dissented from this resolution, says Felkin,[32] on the ground that it was 'behind the age and impossible of execution'; nevertheless, it appears in the petition. Yet there was some justification for the view that in the existing condition of the trade higher rates could only be enforced at the cost of creating more unemployment. We know now that the usual effect of compulsory wage regulation is to force manufacturers to adopt improved methods, and to prevent competition driving rates below a minimum standard. But no one believed that any improvement was possible in the manufacture of hosiery, and even the effort to cheapen production by making several hose at once was bitterly opposed by the workers, who asked Parliament to restrain the practice. As for checking competition, it was assumed that the workers could do that of their own accord now that they were free to combine in trade unions.

Whatever their condition might be, it was clear that the framework knitters could expect no help from Parliament; let us see what efforts were being made to solve their difficulties without legislative interference. The trade union movement, which had been all but annihilated in 1824, appears to have recovered somewhat in the thirties, particularly in Leicester, where in 1839 wages were reported to be considerably higher than in Nottingham.[33] But there was now no attempt to organise the trade as a whole; the new unions were relatively small bodies established on a branch basis. One of the earliest and most successful was the Sock Branch Union which was brought into existence in 1830 when about a thousand Leicestershire sock hands who had already suffered two reductions in wages struck for an advance. They had no funds, but managed to maintain themselves for three weeks by parading with bands and begging at farms; in the end an advance of sixpence a dozen was conceded, and the increase in prosperity may be judged from the fact that in the township of Thurmaston, where nearly all the workers were sock hands, the poor rate was halved. After this the union was maintained by contributions of 6d from men and 3d a week from youths; in 1833 the funds amounted to between £600 and £700, and the men were on good terms with their employers.[34]

In March 1836 the wrought hose workers of Leicester were being urged to follow the example of the sock and glove branches, which had 'done wonders by union'.[35] It is not clear whether any permanent union was organised in this case, but in May the branch were able to announce an advance of 3d a dozen, at the same time expressing their gratitude to the employers for acceding to their request so promptly.[36] They also hoped for the support of the country workers and requested each village to send a deputy to a general meeting of the branch, but there is no record of it taking place.

It is evident that little permanent improvement in wages was to be expected from piecemeal efforts of this kind. No branch had a monopoly of skill, and there was always the competition of the unorganised country workers to reckon with. It was alleged, moreover, that the unions confined their attentions to the large hosiers while any small manufacturer was permitted to invade the statement.[37] Yet the imperfectly organised unions were bound to adopt an opportunist policy, and although they seem to have been encouraged by the larger employers[38] it was impossible for them to bring all into line without more support from the other side.

In 1838 an effort was made to overcome this weakness by forming a joint union of employers and employed. The following extract from a letter of the Operatives' Committee to the Hosiers and Manufacturers of the Town and County of Leicester brings out the aims of the proposal:

> It is not our intention to recommend to our fellow workmen a union upon former principles, which must ever prove abortive while you continue disunited and foster that spirit of competition—that monster which has injured you and ruined us. It may be urged that unions have tried and failed. But we beg to remind you that no union of masters has been tried except in opposition to that of workmen. Let us, we pray you, lay aside all petty jealousies and act upon more enlightened principles, believing that the interests of employer and employed are identical; let both combine their efforts to maintain good prices, instead of acting in opposition to each other. If stockings were one penny per pair cheaper would there be any more consumed? If one penny per pair dearer would consumption be less? Yet what a vast amount of happiness depends upon this paltry sum! If a list of remunerating prices were agreed to and it was determined upon by you and us to maintain them, what is it that could break through such a phalanx?[39]

At a meeting arranged to consider the scheme the chairman

gave an account of the Hinckley Union which, although more general in character, had similar aims. The finances, aided by subscriptions from local tradesmen, were managed by a committee of twenty-one principal inhabitants, and the union had power to regulate prices and take such steps as were thought proper with regard to reductions. During the seven years of its existence, it was said, there had never been a single deviation from the price fixed, and the hosiers were able to manufacture with confidence; instead of lowering prices when trade was bad they gave out less work.[40]

But no success attended the Leicester project; at the next meeting on 21 June only half a dozen manufacturers were present, although 140 circulars had been sent out. It was resolved, therefore, that 'the manufacturers have by their indisposition to attend and confer with the working classes thrown them upon their own resources'.[41] How powerful those resources were may be judged from the tone of the resolution passed a few days later when the Operatives' Committee appointed delegates to wait upon the hosiers: 'That this meeting hopes that the manufacturers will take into their most serious consideration our peaceable conduct during our heavy privations and if it is in their power, without being detrimental to the welfare of the trade, to grant our humble request, we as operatives shall feel ourselves in duty bound to return them our grateful acknowledgments.'[42]

Apparently the Hinckley Union did not survive much longer, for in 1843 fresh plans were being made for a 'Union of All Classes'. A general fund was to be raised by donations from the wealthy, subscriptions from the middle classes, and contributions from the operatives at the rate of a penny a week for adult males and half that amount for youths and women; each village was to have its quota of funds administered by a local committee. The general committee were to publish a list of fair prices, anyone failing to obtain the standard rate being entitled to draw on the funds; but no sick or unemployment payments were contemplated.[43]

On paper the Hinckley plan looks promising enough, but unfortunately there was no opportunity of testing it in practice owing to lack of public support. The only other schemes of any importance were those for providing framework knitters with allotments. Felkin, who was well acquainted with conditions in Saxony, reported that most of the stockingers there were primarily agriculturists who worked at the frame in the evenings; they enjoyed a fairly independent status, buying their yarn and selling the produce to hosiers; many had their own frames, and their homes were on the whole much better furnished than those of English framework knitters.[44] To establish such conditions here, however, would have meant a reversal of the whole trend of development both in manufacture and in agriculture, and no such revolution was contemplated. All that could be hoped for was to provide means whereby the worker could eke out his scanty earnings and fill in the periods of unemployment. Allotment societies existed at several places in the three counties in 1845,[45] but although framework knitters were mostly keen to get holdings they were often too poor to be able to cultivate them properly; rents, too, were high—as much as £6 an acre in Nottingham—and many were forced to give up their allotments on that account.

It is clear that in the present overcrowded state of the trade there could be no great improvement in the condition of the framework knitters, whatever palliatives might be tried. Neither was there any incentive to improvement in methods of manufacture. But the industry had never been lacking in mechanical genius, and however unpromising the prospects of reward might be, the fertile brains of the inventors had not been idle during these years of stagnation. Unobtrusively, but none the less soundly, the foundations were being laid on which a new system of production would eventually arise.

It is true that there were special difficulties in the application of power to knitting machinery, and this partly explains why the hosiery trade lagged so far behind the other textile industries in this respect; but by 1845 at least the preliminary difficulties had been overcome. Obviously the first problem was to devise some method of working the frame by rotary motion, but this was accomplished quite early in the century by Cordell of Hathern, with whom Heathcote, who was at that time a framesmith, entered into partnership.[46] The most interesting invention of this period, however, was that of the French engineer, Brunel, who patented his 'tricoteur' in 1816.[47] This machine, the forerunner of the type on which the bulk of hosiery is now made, introduced a different principle from that established by Lee, its needles being arranged in the form of a circle; it was small enough to be screwed to a table, and was operated by turning a handle. But the tricoteur was regarded merely as a curiosity, apparently no attempt was made to introduce it as a practical proposition, and the model was eventually sent to Paris.

The lack of interest in Brunel's invention is easily understood when we remember the prejudice against 'bag work', as the un-fashioned hosiery was called; for the circular frame necessarily produced its fabric in tubular form, having to be cut out and seamed or, in the case of hose, pressed and steamed into shape. A frame on the tricoteur principle was 'one of the most curious machines' on show at a Nottingham exhibition held in 1840; but it was 'looked at with a distrustful eye by our framework knitters as destined at some future period to supersede existing machines in the manufacture'.[48] Their forebodings were well founded, but as yet there was nothing to fear, for the wide frames could produce all the bag work that was required.

The first attempt at driving a hosiery frame by steam power was made by Warner's of Loughborough, who in 1829 set up a machine 'adapted in the pressing and slur drawing movements to act by carriers without hand direction';[49] but it was probably slow and clumsy in operation, giving little advantage over the wide hand frame, for the experiment was not persevered in. A much more difficult problem was the production of fashioned work by power; indeed, it was long considered insuperable. 'Stockings can-not be made by power,' said a Belper manufacturer in 1844; 'a stocking is not merely a texture, it is a garment; and you may as reasonably expect to weave a coat by steam as to weave a stock-ing.'[50] The difficulty was to reduce automatically the number of stitches in the courses where the hose was narrowed to give it shape, and although it was partly overcome by Luke Barton, an Arnold hosier who patented his apparatus in 1838, it was not until many years later that the final solution appeared in the Cotton's Patent frame.

Great as the technical difficulties were, one cannot but suppose that progress would have been much more rapid had it been worthwhile from the manufacturer's point of view. But so long as there was a plentiful supply of cheap hand labour few were prepared to undertake the expense and risk of introducing labour-saving machinery. It was a long time before a diminution in this supply appeared, and it might have been even longer had not the 'slow operation of improved moral cultivation' been assisted by certain measures of government which are described in the follow-ing chapter.

H

CHAPTER 8

THE BEGINNINGS OF FACTORY PRODUCTION

After 1850 the possibilities of applying steam power to the production of hosiery began to be seriously considered by the more enterprising manufacturers. The Nottingham trade especially was feeling the pressure of German competition even in the home market; there were several large steam factories at Chemnitz whose products were said to be superior to the English,[1] and it was evident that unless British manufacturers bestirred themselves they would be beaten on their own ground as they had already been beaten in America. The lead was given by Pagets of Loughborough, who constructed many circular frames after 1844 and demonstrated that they could be worked very profitably by power.[2] Then in 1847 Matthew Townsend of Leicester invented the tumbler or latch needle. This is self-acting, being made to move up and down or backwards and forwards by the action of cams set in the cylindrical body of the machine. The latch needle obviated the need for loop wheels and pressers and thus simplified the knitting mechanism. Townsend's invention was the forerunner of an entirely new generation of knitting machines, but it was many years before its full potential was realised, the bearded needle being preferred for fine-gauge fabric.[3]

At the same time progress was being made with power-driven full-fashioned frames. The pioneer in this work was Luke Barton of Arnold, near Nottingham, who patented his first machine in 1838. Eventually he joined the Nottingham firm of Hine & Mundella and in 1854 they brought out a machine to produce several fashioned hose at once, the narrowing apparatus being actuated by rotary motion.[4]

But the most notable advances in this type of machine must be credited to William Cotton, whose name has become familiar wherever hosiery is made. Born in 1819 at Seagrave, Leicestershire, Cotton had early opportunities of applying himself to the

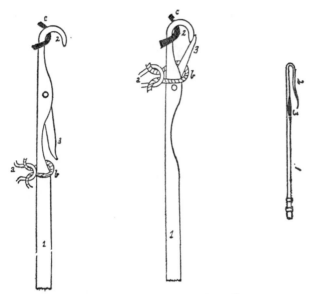

Latch needles and bearded needle

improvement of hosiery machines while employed in the patent shop of Cartwright & Warner of Loughborough where some of the first rotaries were built.[5] He remained with the firm twenty years, and during that time sixty or seventy of these machines were turned out. Cotton then established a factory for the manufacture of warp fabrics, and it was here that he began to work out his ideas. He had no knowledge of the principles of engineering or of drawing, and his method of making sketches and then getting his ideas roughed out involved much useless labour; but after twelve years, in 1864, a patent was issued for the machine which became the basis of the Cotton's Patent type (see p 120). This was a flat frame driven by rotary mechanism and remarkable for its adaptability; the later models were large enough to produce a dozen or more hose at once, and could be used for all kinds of fashioned garments.

Cotton was induced by the success of his invention to begin machine building as a separate business, and thus established one of the first of a class of engineering firms that sprang up as an adjunct of the new hosiery manufacture. He employed only a dozen men and turned out about six machines in the first year, entering into an agreement with Hine & Mundella (later extended

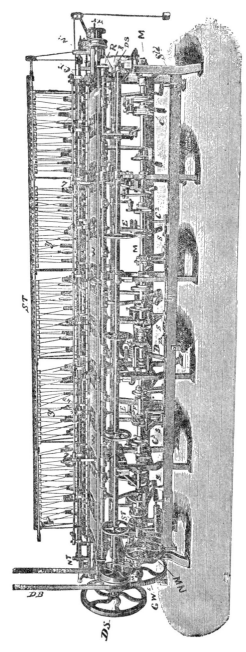

COTTON'S PATENT ROTARY FRAME.

A typical example, late nineteenth century

to I. & R. Morley), for their exclusive use. In 1878, however, the inventor began to build on his own account, and the business steadily increased until it employed some two hundred workers and had an output of a hundred machines a year. Cotton's progress is typical of a process of development common to the textile trades and with many examples in other industries. In the early stages the mechanical inventor, if not already a manufacturer, would either set up as one or try to induce some enterprising firm to adopt his machine on mutually favourable terms. The later stage, where we have firms specialised in producing machines for general sale and of their own accord initiating technical developments, was now beginning in the hosiery trade.

But this is to anticipate the main course of events. From what we know of conditions in the industry we should hardly expect the introduction of power-driven machinery to have produced rapid changes in organisation; and in fact the transition to the factory system was a long drawn out process. Following Pagets of Lough-borough, Hine & Mundella established their Nottingham factory in 1851. Both these firms were important merchant hosiers, the Pagets having also family connections with a Leicester banking house. But other such firms were reluctant to change. It was not until 1866 that I. & R. Morley started factory production, at the same time as the Leicester firm of Corah. Yet it is clear that some progress was achieved in the intervening years, for according to a report by the Nottingham Chamber of Commerce in 1860 the town had some 1,500 flat frames and about the same number of circulars, all driven by steam. Since Hine & Mundella would have nothing like that number, there were evidently other firms employ-ing the new methods and investigation has shown that these were often new enterprises rather than old-established merchant hosiers.[6]

Small-scale factory production was encouraged in Nottingham by the building of tenement factories in which a room with power could be rented. They were provided primarily for the lace industry, which was already a factory trade, but they offered suitable accommodation for small hosiery manufacturers too. Many of these were craftsmen, and with the new frames costing between £100 and £200 their capital resources were strained and failure was common. The bigger firms were not so handi-capped, but they were often reluctant to commit themselves to the new system. Their hundreds of hand frames, let out to rent, yielded a steady return even when not fully employed. In any case the re-equipment of the industry must have taken considerable time. Even Hine & Mundella and similar firms that had set up factories still had many outworkers on hand frames. Allen Solley, of Arnold near Nottingham, one of the best-known firms in the trade, did not start factory production until the 1880s; nor did J. B. Lewis & Sons, another important Nottingham firm. In the towns, however, there was a tendency to concentrate frames in workshops. At Leicester, for instance, one shop had 80 frames in 1863, many had 35 or more and few less than six.[7] The main motive here was to secure better discipline among the workers and greater control over output.

The great obstacle to change in the 1860s was still to be found in the condition of the labour market, where supply remained plentiful and cheap. At first sight it seems remarkable that so many should have been content to stay in an industry where earnings were small, hours long, and work irregular; for the period after 1850 was one of general trade prosperity and rapid industrial expansion with a consequent brisk demand for labour. But as was demonstrated much later[8] such conditions are not incompatible with the persistence in some trades of antiquated methods of production and extremely low earnings; and so it was in the hosiery trade. Generations of grinding poverty had almost killed the spirit of enterprise among the stockingers, and in the hosiery villages, where they lived comparatively isolated from the social and industrial life of the outside world, children followed their father's trade as a matter of course, for the main alternative, that of agriculture, offered even worse prospects. Again, the extremely irregular conditions of work in the hosiery trade had reacted on succeeding generations of stockingers and produced a type of worker who was, almost by nature, irregular in his habits; the trade had also proved particularly attractive to those who found discipline irksome. The stockinger prided himself on his 'independence'. 'Each man has full liberty to earn what he likes and how he likes and when he likes; we have no factory bell, it is our only blessing,' declared a witness before the Factory Commission in 1833. The statement is significant; it was this obstinate clinging to liberty in working conditions that kept the hosiery worker in his squalid domestic workship when the factories had become much more desirable places than they were in 1833.

Another powerful retarding influence was the prevalence of

frame renting. The workers were still agitating for the abolition of compulsory deductions from earnings and in 1854 succeeded in getting a parliamentary committee of inquiry appointed. The evidence was depressingly similar to that adduced ten years before, but on the subject of frame rent the committee expressed themselves in unequivocal terms.

> An indirect profit accruing to the employers of manufacturing labour, beside and beyond the profit arising from the sale of goods, is, so far as Your Committee are aware, recognised in no other manufacture. Your Committee are of opinion that the profit in question is an abuse such as was intended by the Legislature to be guarded against in the Truck Act, 1 and 2, Will. IV. c. 37, which forbids payment of wages otherwise than in the coin of the realm. Your Committee therefore recommend a law analogous to the aforesaid Act prohibiting stoppages from wages in hosiery manufacture.

If such an Act had been passed there is little doubt that the transition to factory production would have been speeded up, for most hosiers contended that the very existence of the domestic system depended on frame renting. But Parliament was not prepared to interfere.

It is difficult to compare the earnings of factory workers with those in the hand branch owing to the very wide differences among the hand frame workers. On the hand machine strength, quickness, and skill counted for more than on the power frame, while it must be remembered that many hand frames were worked by old men who had been driven by failing sight into the coarser and poorer paid lines and by young boys and women who had hardly strength to work a frame. In 1860 earnings in Nottingham varied between 6s and 24s a week on narrow frames, while on wide machines knitting 25in or 30in fabric, 16s to 30s could be made;[9] but only the strongest could work these frames. Moreover, if earnings on hand frames seem in some cases to compare not unfavourably with those of factory workers they were gained at the expense of longer hours. A Nottinghamshire manufacturer stated that a man working regularly from seven in the morning until nine or ten at night could make 25s a week even on coarse work when trade was good, though another on similar work might earn no more than 8s or 10s.[10]

These earnings were of course based on piece rates and the same system applied in the factories. But here hours were necessarily more uniform, giving a narrower range of earnings. In Nottingham men on rotary frames earned from 20s to 30s in a week of 56 hours and as much as 35s on circular frames, while women made between 12s and 20s. Wages in Leicester were not nearly so good; it was said that a man and a girl working two power frames between them would make 12s to 15s and 9s a week respectively. As yet Leicester had less factory employment than Nottingham, but when Corahs opened their St Margaret's works in 1866 they claimed that wages had recently been increased by fully 25 per cent. Thus for those able to find factory work and willing to accept its discipline the new system offered substantial benefits, but their wages were still under pressure from the mass of cheap labour outside the factory system.

The limited scope of factory development may be judged from the fact that out of an estimated total of 120,000 employed directly or indirectly in the hosiery trade only 4,063 came under the Factory Act in 1862.[11] On the whole, the Commission on Children's Employment found the organisation of the trade practically unchanged since the previous inquiry nearly twenty years before. In the hosiery villages and even in the towns the old domestic system with all its attendant evils persisted. Arnold, a place only four miles from Nottingham, was typical. Here was a population of 4,600, and three-quarters of the thousand houses contained frames, of which there were about 1,200 altogether; most houses had less than four frames and none more than ten.[12]

In earlier times the characteristic grievances of the framework knitters—low earnings, long hours, and irregular employment—might be attributed in some measure to bad trade. It is true that trade was not uniformly good in the early sixties. The cotton branch was suffering from a shortage of raw material due to the American Civil War, and also from the competition in the American and Continental markets of cheap goods made in Saxony. The glove trade too, had fallen off with the increasing substitution of kid for silk knitted fabric, and the rent for glove frames was only half what it had been in more prosperous days. Most manufacturers agreed, however, that orders in both cotton and woollen branches were fairly regular. In the natural course of things, it was stated, a cotton hosiery manfacturer could begin in December to prepare his next summer's stock, knowing perfectly well beforehand what he would want. The busiest time in the Leicester woollen trade was in the second half of the year, but after the busy period in

the home market there followed the Australian season of a month
or two, while the Canadian demand came in the spring and
summer.[13]

It is evident, therefore, that bad conditions in the domestic
hosiery trade were not now due to widespread trade depression
and uncertainty, but to evils inseparable from the domestic system
itself. In some lines the hand frame worker was now at the further
disadvantage of having to compete with power-driven machines;
but even on the better-class goods which, it was thought, must
always be made in the old way, earnings were extremely low.
Paradoxical as it seemed, the factory worker supplying the needs
of the poor Hindu got better wages than the skilled framework
knitter who made the trousseau for a princess.[14] The employment
of children, with all its potentialities of abuse, was almost inevitable in such an industry. Winding, for example, was work requiring little skill, it was wanted at irregular intervals, and must be
done as cheaply as possible. In the factories winding machines
had been introduced, but yarn for the hand frame was still prepared by boys who began at about eight years of age, one winder
generally supplying three frames. Seaming was another job in
which children were particularly useful, and it was here that the
worst evils were brought to light. The problem was the more
serious because of the large number employed in this occupation. Although some of the work was done in the factories on
treadle or power sewing machines, a great deal was given out to
home workers both in the towns and villages, and probably there
was more domestic seaming than ever now that this was added to
the supply from the thousands of hand frames still at work.

Some idea of the conditions of children's employment in seaming may be gathered from the evidence of a witness before the
commission:

> Little children here begin work at stitching gloves very young.
> My little sister, now five and a half years old, can stitch a good
> many fingers and is very clever, having been at it for two years.
> She used to stand on a stool so as to be able to see up to the
> candle on the table. I have seen many begin as young as that,
> and they do so still because it makes them cleverer if they begin
> young. Parents are not particular about the age; if they have
> work they must do it. Little children are kept up shamefully
> late, especially on Thursday and Friday nights when it is often
> till eleven or twelve. They have to make two days out of Friday.

Children younger than seven but not younger than six are kept up as late as that. Mothers will pin them on their knee to keep them to their work, and if they are sleepy give them a slap on the head to keep them awake. If the children are pinned up so they cannot fall when they are slapped or fall asleep. . . . The child has so many fingers set for it to stitch before it goes to bed and must do them.[15]

One reason for the long hours in seaming was the extremely low rate at which the work was paid. Stocking legs were less than twopence a dozen, and a child of four managed to do ten legs a day, working from breakfast time until five in the evening.[16] Another reason was the irregularity of the work, due partly to delay in giving it out from the warehouse and partly to the irregular habits of the stockingers themselves.[17] It was a common practice for women seamers to work all night before taking-in day in order to make up for time lost at the beginning of the week. In any case late hours were inevitable since seaming had to be done in the intervals of household work.

Frames were not usually worked by very young children. At one time boys might begin at seven or eight years of age and girls as young as nine years, having the seats and treadles raised for them so that their legs and arms could reach. But now the common age to start was eleven or twelve. On the whole, the number of children put into frames seems to have been decreasing. The growing use of wide frames demanding strength to work them was reducing the field of employment for women and children in the knitting processes. Moreover, stockingers were beginning to realise that the trade was hardly worth learning, and wherever alternative employment offered there was a tendency to turn their children into other occupations. The coal mines absorbed increasing numbers, and those living in or near the town often found work in the factories or bleaching yards. But the movement was gradual; in the early sixties it had hardly begun, and in many places no alternative employment was available.

By contrast with conditions in the domestic hosiery manufacture those in the factories and warehouses were an immense improvement. The hosiery factories were from the beginning subject to the Factory Acts. No child under ten years of age could be employed in them, while the period of employment for women and young persons was fixed between 6am and 6pm in summer and between 7am and 7pm in winter; further, $1\frac{1}{2}$ hours must be allowed for meals, and a half-holiday on Saturday. The maximum legal working day for protected persons was $10\frac{1}{2}$ hours, and the week $56\frac{1}{2}$ hours. Although not regulated by law, conditions in the warehouses were equally good in the main. The workers were generally of a better class than those in the factory branches, though the wages of women workers were about the same, and few children were employed. Most warehouses worked from eight in the morning until six or seven at night, with a half-holiday on Saturday; long hours were said to be exceptional, manufacturers agreeing that they did not pay.[18] The introduction of rail transport also had an important effect on warehouse hours. Formerly goods were sent by carriers, who would wait perhaps until midnight, but now orders sent by rail to London and other distant places must leave not later than eight o'clock.[19]

That one branch of the trade should be under state regulation while the other remained entirely free was a manifest anomaly which left the employer of domestic labour with many advantages over factory production even when the technical difficulties of using power were being overcome. Under these conditions domestic production on a large scale might have persisted indefinitely, cheap labour competing with power as, in India today, the domestic weaver competes with the products of Lancashire. It was evident that conditions in the lesser trades could only be improved by a policy of regulation such as had been so successful in the factory industries, and the sequel to the Commission on Children's Employment was the Workshops Act of 1867.

But it was much more difficult to enforce the Workshops Act than the Factory Act, the existing organisation of inspection being quite inadequate to deal with the thousands of small domestic workshops whose location could only be traced by people familiar with all the back streets and alleys of the town.[20] In the hosiery villages it was even worse; here practically every house was a workshop and it was particularly difficult for inspectors to pay night visits. Hours were still long and irregular, and earnings often extremely low in spite of good trade. The chairman of the Factory Acts Commission of 1876 relates how he visited some cottages of stocking seamers at Ruddington, near Nottingham.

> The cottages were tidy and not very poor looking. In some were women and girls assembled and at work, some being hired assistants. The women said they had to work very long hours to make their wages. They were paid 1s. 9d. or 1s. 10d. a dozen for

stockings; two dozen took about fourteen hours. A girl of eighteen said she worked from 6 a.m. till dark, say 8 p.m. They did not consider this long—'ten hours would not be to call work,' they said.[21]

It might be thought that higher wages and better working conditions in the factories would by this time have attracted all the domestic workers who could be conveniently absorbed. Yet factory owners complained of the difficulty of attracting women and young persons who, it seemed, still tended to cling to the workshops where they had been accustomed to earn their living free from the restrictions of factory employment.[22] There was still the reluctance to break with old habits, so characteristic of workers in this ancient industry, but conditions were slowly changing especially in and near the towns. As children grew up, they were no longer content to add their meagre quota to the family income by tedious labour in the home; in the towns home-work, as distinct from that carried on in the workshop, was mostly done by older women whose domestic responsibilities prevented their going out to work.

The slow growth of factory production is again indicated by comparing the factory inspectors' statistics for 1862 with those for 1874. It is true that the number of hosiery factories doubled in these twelve years, but the total was only 129 in 1874. The number of factory workers increased by some 115 per cent, but the horse power used was rather less than double the amount at the earlier date. Thus the average size of factory had increased hardly at all and the total number of factory workers was still only a small proportion of all those engaged in the industry.

But mere figures do not adequately represent the extent of the change that was taking place. It is the change of outlook, reflected particularly in the attitude of employers and workers towards factory legislation and education that is significant. We find abundant proof of this in the evidence taken by the Commission on the Factory Acts; it was becoming apparent that the main hope of improving conditions in the hosiery trade lay in the absorption of more and more workers into the factories and warehouses which could be efficiently supervised by inspectors. Employers were coming to realise, too, that it actually paid to introduce decent working conditions, and often went beyond mere legal requirements in these matters. Moreover, trade unionism was a growing force among the factory workers and collective bargaining was able to secure higher wages and shorter hours. A representative of the Nottingham hosiery and lace manufacturers reported that nearly all factories in the town had adopted a 54 hour week. 'The fact is that the workpeople have had sufficient power to insist on that limit by the action to a certain extent of trade unions,' he said. 'Not that we have trade unions amongst the females or the children, but the men having insisted on their labour being limited to fifty-four hours, it has necessitated the labour of the females and children ceasing at the same time.'[23]

These were factors making for the improvement and extension of the factory system; but at the same time another force was beginning to operate which struck at the very foundations of the older organisation. The domestic system was largely dependent on child labour; deprived of education and accustomed from their earliest years to the sound of the frame and the atmosphere of the workshop, there is little wonder that stockingers' children were lacking in enterprise and in their turn perpetuated the chronic evils of the trade. In any case the facilities for working-class education before 1870 were poor enough, but framework knitters' children had small chance of benefiting by such as did exist. Many received their only teaching at Sunday-school, Sunday being the only day when they could be spared from work, or else their parents could not afford the small fees demanded by the ordinary schools. Often little girls went to 'seaming schools' to be taught a smattering of reading, giving their work in return; if kept at work very late they might get a halfpenny for it or be rewarded with a 'knob o' suck'. As late as 1875, these places still existed in some districts, and were classed under the Workshops Act, the children being required to attend ordinary schools for a minimum of ten hours a week.[24] Even in some of the ordinary schools, however, it was found necessary to allow girls to bring seaming in the afternoon. When this privilege was introduced at Hinckley the number attending school doubled; but it was a common thing to hear of a boy of five or six: 'he's left, he's winding', or of a girl: 'she's left, she's seaming'.[25]

The Factory and Workshops Acts provided that children under thirteen should attend school part time, but one of the chief difficulties of making the educational clauses of the Factory Acts effective had always been the shortage of schools to which workers' children might be sent. This difficulty was overcome by the Education Act of 1870 which made provision for elementary education in all districts where existing facilities were inadequate. Finally in 1876, school attendance was made compulsory between the ages of five and fourteen, though children who had reached a certain standard of proficiency might obtain partial or total exemption after the age of twelve.

These measures went far towards undermining the domestic system in those trades where, in its debased form, it still existed. There was at first some difficulty in putting the provisions of the Education Act into operation in the hosiery districts; opposition from parents was naturally encountered, but it rapidly lessened. With higher earnings in this period of good trade parents could better afford to send their children to school. Moreover, there were indications that the stockingers were awakening from the appalling apathy that had fallen upon them in the poverty-stricken years of the first half of the century and which was so apparent at the time of the Children's Employment Commission. Now parents were coming less and less to regard their children as potential wage-earners, while employers and trade union officials lent their influence to discourage child labour,[26] many of them being actively interested in the new educational system as members of local school boards. Further, as more schools were built there was less excuse for evasion, while the improving system of inspection ensured greater efficiency and made evasion more difficult.

A comparison of the census figures gives some indication of the decrease in the number of children employed in the trade. In 1851, approximately 13 per cent of hosiery workers were under 15 years of age; by 1871 the proportion had declined to 8 per cent, and in 1881 it was only 5 per cent. The accuracy of the figures for occupational groups may well be doubted, however. The census of 1851 gives a total of 58,923 hosiery workers in England and Wales, whereas the estimate of the Children's Employment Commission is double that number. It is highly probable that many women and children engaged part time or even full time in the domestic hosiery trade would not be returned as occupied persons, so that the proportion of juvenile workers, especially at the earlier dates, may well have been very much larger than the census figures suggest.

Though many years were to elapse before the industrial revolution in the hosiery trade was completed, the pace was rapidly accelerating in 1875; and among the various factors, internal and external, that combined to impel the change not the least impor-

tant was the growing shortage of cheap labour. Once the change
had begun, the impulses continued with cumulative force. The
development of one class of machines and their adaptation to
power necessitated similar developments in other machines and
processes. So with the various classes of workers; when the
obstacles were removed the tendency towards concentration in
factories continued almost inevitably. Where framework knitting
survived it was due not to cheapness but to the supposed
superiority of the product, which thus commanded a higher price.
In a limited section of the market it could still compete with
factory production at the end of the century. I. & R. Morley, who
by this time had seven factories in Nottinghamshire and Leicestershire, still had some 3,000 framework knitters delivering to their
Nottingham warehouse.

There remains to record the legal abolition of frame renting.
Bills were introduced in two sessions following the Report of
the Truck Commission in 1871; but Parliament, it seemed, was
too busy to concern itself with what it regarded as merely a matter
for arrangement between employer and workmen; if the hosiery
workers disliked the system let them combine and abolish it themselves.[27] Samuel Morley, interviewed in 1874, said he was really
tired of the name of frame rent and charges, but consented to
speak for the Bill if time allowed; he understood that the payment
of net wages had been mutually agreed upon some time before.
This was true, but the agreement had never been loyally carried
out and the workers were afraid that they would all be forced
back to the old system at the first trade depression.[28]

The opposition of Parliament had now changed to indifference,
for it was clear by this time that the problem would largely solve
itself. Although frame renting was still general in 1871 where
machines were let out through middlemen, and the old practices
of stinting and spreading work were still resorted to in slack
times, it was seen that factory production was bound to absorb
an increasing proportion of the trade, and that with this development frame renting would tend automatically to disappear. Whatever plausible reasons there might be for charging rents on frames
given out to domestic workers, there was certainly no justification
when machines came to be concentrated in factories, and in the
new steam factories of Nottingham and Leicester rents had already
been abolished. The employer's property was secure; as one of
them remarked, 'we can lock our doors and know that our neigh-

bours are not working our frames'.[29] When at length the legislature found time to deal with it the Bill to abolish deductions from wages passed with little opposition;[30] it was directed against a system that was already doomed, and the erstwhile advocates of non-interference could console themselves with the reflection that at least the measure could do no harm.

CHAPTER 9

CONCILIATION AND ARBITRATION

The increasing prosperity of the hosiery trade in the later fifties
was accompanied by renewed activity on the part of the trade
unions. For thirty years the workers had been forced to acquiesce
in whatever conditions might be offered. Though here and there
a stand might be made and a brief recognition secured for the
principle of collective bargaining in particular branches, there was
no possibility of effective organisation among the body of
stockingers or among the employers either. The overcrowded
state of the trade and its scattered distribution had proved insuperable obstacles. But now conditions were changing; trade was
expanding, there was an increasing demand for labour, especially
for the new factories, while factory development was also bringing
the workers together and providing the nucleus of a new trade
union movement.

In these circumstances the hosiery workers' organisation gained
formidable force, and strikes on the rising market became increasingly frequent. The Nottingham stockingers in the wide frame
branch came out three times in 1860, one dispute lasting eleven
weeks, and manufacturers were unable to meet the heavy demands
of the American trade. Although the strike was in this instance
confined to one branch, other sections, including the power frame
workers, lent support to the struggle for higher wages by contributing to its funds. A general lock-out was threatened as the only
way of breaking the men's resistance, but at this stage the three
largest employers, led by A. J. Mundella, resolved to make conciliatory advances, and invited representatives of the workers and
a number of middlemen to a conference. The employers declared
that the present system of strikes and lock-outs was 'mutually
predatory', and that some means for the peaceable settlement of
disputes ought to be adopted; the men were very suspicious at
first and some of the manufacturers felt that they were being
humiliated, but the outcome of the conference was the establish-

I 133

ment of a Board of Arbitration and Conciliation for the Hosiery Trade.[1]

Before describing the board and its working it will be well to say something about the antecedents of this important step in the development of industrial relations. The idea of a joint body for the regulation of wages was by no means new. As early as 1834 Felkin tried to induce Sir John Hobhouse, MP for Nottingham, to bring in a Bill 'for regulating wages by decisions of a board composed of selected masters and men, and making the scale agreed upon binding on the trade after receiving the signature of a magistrate'.[2] Hobhouse declined to sanction the plan, and in any case there would have been little chance of Parliament lending its authority to such methods; if they were to be introduced it must be by spontaneous action. This was the belief of the Leicester framework knitters who, in 1838, made their proposal for a joint union of masters and men. To its sponsors the mutual benefits of the scheme were so evident that the principle, they thought, had to be stated to gain acceptance, but we know how much success attended their efforts. Felkin, however, continued to urge the necessity for some permanent machinery to deal with wage problems; he was much impressed by the success of the French *Conseils de Prud'hommes,* and in 1834 published an analysis of their laws and constitution. Ten years later, in a paper read before the British Association, he was advocating the establishment of 'trade regulation courts' on the French model, which should be 'local, cheap, frequent, and final'.[3]

Copies of the address were distributed in the principal districts of the hosiery and weaving trades and meetings were arranged in order to get an expression of opinion. One in Nottingham was attended by 1,400 stockingers, who thought the proposed courts 'very desirable, provided that the preponderance of masters were not too great'; it was agreed that decisions ought to be final, for the men could not afford to contest appeals in a court of law. Several other meetings of workers were favourable, though some thought a legal minimum wage desirable and there was a feeling that higher wages would not be possible until wide frames had been abolished. The employers were more sceptical; they did not think the system could be applied in England.[4]

It is indeed doubtful whether councils on the lines contemplated would have been able to do much towards solving the problems of the industry. As the Webbs pointed out, the *Conseils de*

Prud'hommes had always been 'strictly confined to the settlement of disputes arising out of existing contracts, or (as regards minor matters) the application of the law; in no case do they presume to fix the rate of wages for future engagements'.[5] In so far as it ensured uniformity and prevented price-cutting this in itself would have been a useful service; but the real need of the framework knitters at this time was for some means of raising wages without recourse to ruinous strikes.

All these efforts, though fruitless in themselves, at least prepared the ground for the successful experiment of 1860. Hitherto, the main obstacle had been in the attitude of the employers; but now the position was reversed, the trade unions appeared to be gaining the upper hand, and it was in their own interest that the manufacturers took the lead in inviting the men to a conference. A further difficulty had been the lack of any permanent organisation representing the manufacturing interest, but this was supplied in the newly formed Hosiers' Association, while the establishment of the Nottingham Chamber of Commerce in 1860 also helped to bring the employers together. There was, in fact, a close connection between the chamber of commerce and the board, the meetings being held at its offices, and the Hosiers' Association elected the employers' representatives.

Apart from its significance in the progress of industrial relations in the hosiery trade, the Board of Arbitration and Conciliation has a more general interest as the forerunner of many similar bodies set up in other industries during the sixties and seventies of the last century, and it is unfortunate that no records of its meetings have survived. Owing to the attention which it attracted, however, several accounts were given, notably by A. J. Mundella, the chairman, and from these we are able to learn a good deal about the board and its methods.

The declared object of the board was to arbitrate on any questions relating to wages that might be referred to it by the employers or operatives, and by conciliatory means to interpose its influence to put an end to any disputes that might arise.[6] It consisted of ten manufacturers and ten workers, the latter elected by their respective branches; all the deputies served for one year and were eligible for re-election. The president, vice-president, and two secretaries were elected at the annual meeting, the offices being shared equally between masters and men. For the transaction of ordinary business the board was to meet quarterly, but a special meeting could be convened at seven days' notice. All complaints submitted for investigation were to be embodied in written statements sent in at least one week prior to the board meeting; these were referable to a committee of inquiry consisting of four members.

In practice most of the work was done by this committee. They were directed to use their influence in the settlement of disputes, but in no case could they make any award; if they were unable to effect an amicable settlement the business had to be submitted to the board. It was said, however, that three-quarters of the disputes referred to it were settled by the committee and only came before the board in a formal way.[7] When the board was called upon for a decision the members were supposed to vote on the issue and the rules allowed the chairman a casting vote. This placed him in the position of an arbitrator, and Mundella admitted in 1867 that his casting vote had twice caused trouble and consequent secessions from the board, so that for the past four years the practice of voting had been abandoned altogether.[8]

The significance of this change lies in the fact that the board was no longer a means of arbitration according to the strict interpretation of the term; indeed, if 'arbitration' involves decisions by an independent umpire it never had been. But Mundella himself made no distinction between arbitration and conciliation. 'The sense in which we use the word', he said, 'is that of an arrangement for open and friendly bargaining . . . in which masters and men meet together and talk over their common affairs openly and freely.'[9] As it was, however, the board continued to do most useful work.

From March 1862 to January 1865, no formal meetings were held owing to the trade depression caused by the American Civil War, but the committee of inquiry continued to function. Then came a period of intense activity stimulated by the fall in the price of cotton, and all the efforts of the board were required to adjust rates and prevent disputes. The difficulty of the task may be gathered from the fact that the lists covered nearly 5,000 different articles;[10] indeed, it was the great variety of the trade that had always proved the main obstacle to the establishment of definite schedules of prices. But now it was possible not only to introduce printed lists, but for the first time to secure a great measure of uniformity throughout the districts of Nottingham,

Derby, Belper, and Loughborough, which was the area covered by the Nottingham board.

It must be admitted that the prosperous condition of the trade was favourable to success; nevertheless the efficiency of the board's methods was remarkable. For instance, on one occasion in 1867 the workers in an unrepresented branch held meetings to frame a scale of prices without consulting the employers and a dispute was feared; the board intervened, however, and was allowed to draw up a statement which proved mutually satisfactory. About the same time the Loughborough stockingers complained about the variation in prices for heeling; it was found that the rate per dozen varied between $\frac{1}{2}$d and 2d in different places, but the board was able to arrange for a uniform rate throughout its area. Sometimes there was difficulty in enforcing these decisions, especially in the case of small manufacturers, but any refusal to pay the statement price would be referred to a committee, who interviewed the recalcitrants and usually brought them into line. Persistent opposition was said to be very rare; as a last resource, however, the men would be directed not to take out work at less than statement price.[11]

It was comparatively easy to secure the workers' adherence so long as the board was able to induce the employers to concede their requests; but even where this was not possible the decisions appear to have been accepted with equal loyalty. The wrought hose workers only averaged about 12s a week as compared with the power frame operatives' £2, and their request for an advance was felt to be reasonable enough. It was pointed out, however, that the demand for their class of work was declining and would probably fall still more if the price were increased. Foreign competition was also a factor in this branch, and in order that the men might have first-hand information two of them were sent to France and Germany in 1866 to investigate the wage conditions there. 'The men,' said Mundella, 'are convinced by their own senses of the justice of what we say, and by their knowledge of the laws that govern trade; this system has been a complete educational process for our men, they know as well as we do whether we can afford an advance or not.'[12]

Through long experience the framework knitters had grown painfully familiar with the 'laws that govern trade'; but now that confidential relations with the employers had been established they were able, at least, to ascertain the facts which conditioned the operation of these laws. Moreover, some of the employers themselves were beginning to see that the principles of wage determination were by no means immutable. Though confessedly a strict believer in political economy, Mundella was prepared to admit that it was 'carried too far'.

> We find that what is called market price is not always market price, but that in flat seasons the price is governed very much by the unscrupulousness of certain manufacturers. For instance, one manufacturer who is a very honourable man will be content to pay 7s. for a certain article, another will not be content unless he gets it for 6d. less than his neighbour, and takes advantage of the flat season to screw the men down. Now though we do fluctuate under this Board we never fluctuate to the same extent as under the other system.

This was the very point that was made by the Leicester stockingers in 1838; and the mutual advantages of restricting competition which they emphasised were now being obtained. Contracts could be taken with confidence and delivery guaranteed. 'I can lay up stock now,' said Samuel Morley, one of the largest manufacturers in the trade; 'before I could not do that because I was afraid of some unscupulous employer cutting me out with lower prices.'[13] The workers had confidence in the system, too, and the heavy trade union subscriptions formerly required to maintain strike funds were now reduced to a merely nominal amount.[14] It had taken some time to establish this mutual confidence; not more than half the manufacturers adhered to the board at first, and the very men they dreaded were sent as the workers' representatives; yet these were found to be 'most straightforward', and suspicion so far disappeared that in 1867 only two or three employers remained aloof, while fully 20,000 workers were represented.

Besides preventing wage disputes the board was also successful in the suppression of truck where the practice still existed. It could exercise direct authority over those middlemen to whom its members let out machines, and in cases of independent masters found to be trucking prosecutions were undertaken. The board also put a stop to the custom, highly inconvenient to the housewife, of paying wages late on Saturday night or even on Sunday morning, and it drew up a list of frame rents in 1866 which was recognised by most of the masters.

There was thus some reason for the optimistic tone of the

boards' report for this year.[15] Strikes and lock-outs had ceased, inflammatory handbills were no longer seen—never in the history of the trade had there been so much good feeling. During the past two years, when agitation on the question of wages had been prevalent throughout England, the hosiery manufacturers had been able to accept contracts without apprehension and execute them without delay. Six years' experience of the system had thoroughly convinced the board that in a free country where workmen and capitalists have a perfect right to enter into combination, the simplest, most humane, and rational method was arbitration and conciliation.

The success of the Nottingham Hosiery Board led to the formation of similar bodies elsewhere. In 1866 a board was set up at Leicester and one for the Nottingham lace trade was established in the following year. Hawick followed the example of the Midlands in 1867, but in this case a neutral referee was added so that true arbitration was possible. There had been a good deal of trouble in the Hawick trade owing to the workers' strenuous opposition to the introduction of wide frames; it was only within the last ten years that they had been allowed at all, and then it was on condition that the old rates were retained; consequently the Hawick stockingers were better off than the hand frame workers in the Midlands, their weekly earnings averaging about 18s on improved machines and 13s or 14s on narrow frames, while on ribbed work as much as 35s could be made. It was stated that the board had been successful in improving the relations between employers and workers, but the conditions were favourable to the maintenance of relatively high earnings since Hawick enjoyed almost a monopoly in certain lines of the best-quality woollen hosiery trade.[16]

We have seen that one of the essential preliminaries to the development of conciliation machinery was the creation of effective organisation among workers and employers respectively. Such organisation was still necessary to secure the general acceptance of the board's decisions, and perhaps the main reason for the success of the joint bodies was the readiness with which the organised employers lent their aid in bringing the rest of the manufacturers into line. Both before and after this period the whole responsibility for enforcing uniform rates fell on the trade unions, and when they failed the manufacturers might advance this as an excuse for breaking the terms of an agreement. But at this time both employers and employed were working from their respective sides towards the same end. 'The men look pretty sharp after those outside the Board,' said Mundella; 'the employers exercise influence with the manufacturers and the men with men; if the manufacturers do not bring them in the workers bring in their men.'[17]

The existence of the boards, therefore, far from weakening trade unionism, tended to strengthen it; this was reflected in the movement towards closer union among the hosiery workers of the three Midland counties which occurred at this time. There was, of course, nothing new in the idea, but apart from the short-lived Society for Obtaining Parliamentary Relief no progress had been made. Meetings of the three counties were frequently held in times of general difficulty and distress, but united action was always hampered by the varying conditions in the cotton, woollen, and silk branches in which each district was more or less specialised. In 1866, however, a delegate meeting of the whole area met at Nottingham and resolved to form 'a general amalgamated and consolidated union to be called The United Framework Knitters' Society'. Legislative power was to be vested in an annual conference of delegates from the several local unions, the executive committee being composed of the local officials; each branch was to have control of its own funds and pay one penny a month per member towards general expenses. The meeting declared its recognition of the power and assistance of the conciliation board.[18] Although the scheme looked sound enough, little came of it owing, apparently, to the aloofness of the Leicester workers, who had only one delegate among the thirty-five present at the inaugural meeting. Some years later the National Hosiery Federation was formed to co-ordinate the activities of the various unions, but there is still no complete amalgamation of hosiery workers.

CHAPTER 10

PROBLEMS OF THE TRANSITION PERIOD

In spite of remarkable technical progress the last quarter of the nineteenth century was a period of recurrent depression in the hosiery industry. The old evils of the domestic system went with it, but the transition to factory production brought new problems for both employers and workers, demanding an adjustment of outlook and methods that could be attained only gradually as the nature of the changes came to be realised. But apart from these internal difficulties, in themselves serious enough, a new factor now entered the situation. In the eighties the hosiery trade, like many other British industries, felt the pressure of increasing foreign competition, particularly from Germany, whose manufacturers were able to supply the growing demand for cheap goods at prices which British firms could not touch. Added to this, the United States market, hitherto a great outlet for British hosiery, was severely restricted by increased tariffs.

The trade journals of the time may have exaggerated the difficulties, particularly those due to intensified competition, for most of the bigger firms, which had been cautious in their approach to factory production, now continued to expand. I. & R. Morley was the outstanding case with six factories acquired between 1875 and 1890. Other instances of former merchant hosiers that expanded steadily as manufacturers were Corahs, Allen Solley, J. B. Lewis & Sons and William Gibson. These were all firms with adequate capital and good commercial connections. It was the small firms, often started by technical men with little business experience, that found it hard to survive. The majority of enterprises were of this type and their difficulties were a source of instability for the trade as a whole.

Technical progress in all kinds of machinery benefited the consumer by cheapening production; but it was not always an advantage to the manufacturer whose existing plant depreciated with each innovation and who at the same time was severely handicapped if he failed to keep pace with up-to-date competitors. In such circumstances the only policy for an enterprising firm was to write down the value of its plant and, if necessary, scrap the old machines and install the latest type. But instead of cutting their losses in this way many hosiery manufacturers persisted in reckoning obsolete machinery, even if standing, at the valuation of former years when it was being worked to full capacity. Many hand frames that might never work again were still reckoned in at stock-taking, often at a figure out of all proportion to their market value. Consequently, when it became necessary for a manufacturer to realise his assets the plant might turn out to be grossly over-valued; machinery valued at £400 or £500 would be sold at scrap prices, and perhaps twenty hand frames would fetch no more than £5 at auction.[1]

Not only the valuation of plant but the whole business of costing was becoming more and more difficult. With the coming of factory production, status and function began to change. Under the old system the true entrepreneur was the large hosier who collected orders, bought materials, and arranged for the manufacture of goods. Although usually called the 'manufacturer', most of the manufacturing processes were not under his direct supervision. But now he became a manufacturer in the modern sense with a factory for the primary processes and a warehouse for finishing goods, storing and dispatching orders. In addition a new class of small manufacturers now sprang up out of the ranks of the middlemen—the 'putters-out' under the domestic system. There had been an element of the entrepreneur function in their business in so far as they employed direct and had their own workshops and frames; but mostly they acted as agents, more or less independent, of the hosiers. As an agent, the middleman got his yarn from the hosier's warehouse with instructions for its use, a certain allowance was made for waste, he was charged a fixed rent for frames (unless using his own), and he in turn charged the stockinger a frame rent. Other overhead expenses were definitely fixed and were deducted from wages. When work was finished the middleman was paid by the hosier and the difference between the hosier's price to the middleman and the latter's price to the worker was the agent's commission or profit. Thus his position was practically secure; in all his operations the amounts received and the amounts paid were based on rates that became customary or which, when they did change, moved generally against the worker, who was always the weakest party. In such a business there was little room for risk or opportunity for speculation, and the gains were more in the nature of commission than profit.

The growing concentration of production made the middleman superfluous while at the same time it opened up the way for the small independent manufacturer, so that whereas the distinction between the large and the small business had formerly been one of kind it now became one of degree only. Both large and small manufacturers were now true entrepreneurs and risk-bearers. The small man no longer got his raw material with definite instructions as to the goods required. He had to buy his yarn from the spinner or through an agent and to decide for himself what to buy and when to buy. He had to fix his prices to attract buyers, and in so far as he produced in advance of orders, either for stock or samples, he must decide as to the kinds of goods likely to be wanted.

Obviously these operations involved risk at any time, but in this period of trade uncertainty the risk was considerably increased, and often fell upon inexperienced people ill-fitted to bear it. If the manufacturer were making to order he bought his yarn on receipt of the order at the current market price, or committed himself to pay that price when the account was due. But it often happened that the terms of an order were 'for delivery as required', and during the period over which delivery extended there might be a considerable fall in the price of yarn. It became a common practice, when this happened, for wholesalers to refuse to take the rest of the order except at a price lower than that of the original contract, and the manufacturer had to choose between accepting the terms offered and being left with a stock made to certain specifications which might be difficult to sell elsewhere.[2] In making for stock during the slack season there was even more uncertainty, for apart from the cost of carrying stock there was always the danger of depreciation. The uncertainty was in fact the chief burden, for the cost of making a long way ahead of delivery was eased by the system of long credits. The manufacturer often did not pay for his yarn until nine months after delivery, although the spinner had to meet his account within thirty days. Similar terms were, in turn, given to the wholesaler who usually allowed somewhat shorter credit to the shopkeeper.[3] There is no doubt that this system of long credits, while an advantage in some ways, was on the whole injurious to all parties in the trade. The actual cost of extended credit was, of course, spread throughout the industry, for the spinner, on whom the burden would seem to fall, allowed for it in pricing his yarn. But the real evil of the system was that it encouraged buyers, particularly small shopkeepers, to place larger orders than they could safely carry and to undertake commitments the extent of which was not fully realised until the time came to settle the account.

All these difficulties were greatly accentuated by the reckless competition among manufacturers. In the old days the business of finishing and selling to wholesale merchants was mostly in the hands of a few large hosiers; small men could not undertake the costly finishing processes involved in preparing goods for the market and merely worked to the orders of the large firms. But now, with the cheapening of finishing processes and the growth of firms doing such work on commission, many of the handicaps that had hitherto limited the independence of small manufacturers were removed and they were able to put their goods on the wholesale market in the same way as the large firm. Nor was lack of capital an effective barrier to the entry of small firms, for in many ways the growing concentration of operations, which distinguished factory production from the domestic system, favoured the establishment of small businesses. It was now comparatively easy for anyone with a practical knowledge of the trade to set up as a manufacturer. He could rent perhaps a single room in a factory with power included, and with a few power frames and sewing-machines could secure an output that would have required a very large number of hand frames and people working in their own homes. Although power machines were costly, makers were prepared to supply them on the credit system.

It might be thought that the large, old-established firm would still have an advantage in competing for the market, and no doubt it had in the long run, but in the meantime the short-period conditions were working havoc in the industry. Yet it is well, before passing judgement, to notice certain real economies that enable the small man to produce at less cost than his bigger rival. His overhead expenses were small and easy to calculate. He might save something in labour costs by employing members of his own family, and in any case the influence of trade unionism, working to raise wages, was weaker among the employees of small firms. Moreover, personal supervision counts for a good deal in the small firm where the owner is himself an active worker in close contact with everything, and showing a zealous concentration that would hardly be expected in the salaried employee with no personal interest in the business. These were real advantages favouring the small manufacturer and have to be weighed against those of producing on a larger scale.

But the chief reason why small manufacturers were able to put their goods on the market at such low prices was their failure to take full account of all working expenses. It is impossible properly to understand the difficulties of this transition period unless we appreciate the effects of the changed organisation on the problem of costing. Indeed, the problem hardly existed under the domestic system where practically all the expenses of production were direct charges on the product, being deducted from the worker's earnings. Again, machines depreciated very slowly and even when their selling value fell through bad trade those out at rent might still yield an income. But now, besides the heavy depreciation of plant due to constant innovations, there was the problem of assigning to each item of output its proper share of overhead charges. If mistakes were made goods might be produced at a loss, and it was a common thing for manufacturers to lose on a part of their output without knowing it; for where prices were cut very fine quite a small error made all the difference between a profit and a loss. In their eagerness to attract custom, firms would accept orders at prices that merely covered the prime costs of manufacture and left nothing for fixed charges, hoping to get more profitable orders later on.

Ignorance of costing methods and reckless price-cutting were not confined to small firms, however, though they were usually the worst, being run by men whose business ability was seldom equal to their practical knowledge of the manufacture. But all firms, large and small, were affected by the spirit of cut-throat competition that was characteristic of this period of transition and rapid expansion. In these circumstances the manufacturer was always at the mercy of the wholesale dealer who took advantage of the situation to play off one against another. Formerly the tendency was for the merchant to seek the manufacturer and give his orders, but now the manufacturer had to produce samples based on his own estimate of the market and submit them to buyers who placed orders after comparing the goods for quality and price with those of other makers. There were constant complaints about the samples of one firm being submitted to another with the request for a lower quotation, upon which the second firm, seeing a chance of getting some of its idle machinery to work or of working up some yarn that was in danger of depreciating, might quote a price that left only the barest margin of profit and which could not possibly pay in the long run. It was this reckless competition, too, that made possible the frequent cancelling of orders to which reference has been made. Wholesalers could do this almost with impunity, for if the manufacturer declined to accept a reduced price for the remainder of an order when the price of yarn fell the merchant could always find someone else who was buying yarn at the new price and so could produce more cheaply. It is true that there was the possibility of resort to law for breach of contract, but the manufacturer well knew that such a course meant permanently losing a customer and perhaps being victimised by other dealers.

In this state of affairs there was a complete lack of confidence among all engaged in the industry. Each manufacturer carried on his business in jealous fear of his neighbour while trying to preserve as much secrecy as possible in his own operations. For the middleman was ever in search of information that would enable him to make his own terms with the manufacturer, and was often known to carry information from one firm to another. Although each year showed an increase in the output of the industry the demand was always for cheaper and cheaper goods, and profits were so low that many large firms could pay only a nominal dividend and in some years none at all. Among the weaker businesses, and even among those that had been considered as the pillars of the industry, failures were frequent. In 1891 a contemporary observer calculated that in twenty-eight years out of 105 firms that began business in the hosiery trade 27 failed, 27 closed down through making no profit, 13 had transferred their businesses, 17 were still in business, and of the remaining 21 there was no information.[4] This was bound to be the result in the long run, but as some producers were eliminated there were always others coming along who thought they could do better, so that the aggregate number of firms tended not merely to remain constant, but actually to increase.[5]

It is evidently impossible to say how far the depression in the hosiery trade after 1875 was due to the conditions we have been describing, but it is obvious that an industry in this state was ill-fitted to encounter the troubles that beset British trade generally in the eighties. In the earlier years of the transition period the full effects of the profound changes that were taking place had not been felt. With improved methods of production the efficiency of labour in terms of output was increasing faster than its cost, and even though prices might fall with increasing production the demand at home and abroad was sufficient to absorb larger and larger quantities of goods at prices that allowed a satisfactory margin of profit for the manufacturer. But the general trade depression that followed these few years of exceptional prosperity came just at the time when the hosiery trade was beginning to experience these internal difficulties, and when, with the spread of trade unionism among its workers, the demands for higher wages were becoming more and more insistent. At this critical stage in the development of the industry there came the decline in the purchasing power of the home market owing to the depression in the staple industries, while the hosiery trade felt as severely as any that increase in foreign competition which was one of the main causes of the general depression.

In hosiery, as in the other textile trades, England had been a pioneer; the knitting frame was an English invention and it was in this country that all the chief improvements in knitting machinery during two hundred and fifty years' development had been made. There was a period in the eighteenth century when foreign competition threatened, especially from France; but protective legislation and, later, political disturbances on the Continent put an end to this menace and left the British manufacturer supreme. The prohibition of the export of frames was still in force in 1841 when a select committee was appointed to inquire into the state of the law with regard to the export of machinery.[6] Prohibition only applied to certain classes of machines specified in the various Acts, and even among these there were several kinds for which export licences could be obtained without much difficulty; but licences were never granted for the export of hosiery frames which, like looms and spinning machinery, had seemed to call for special protection. It is difficult to say how far prohibition was effective, however, for as the evidence before the committee showed, it was impossible to check all machinery destined for export, and smuggling was rife.

The hosiery and bobbin net manufacturers were afraid that the free export of frames would lead to an expansion of the trades in

France and Saxony, though they admitted that there had already been considerable development in both these countries without the aid of English machinery.[7] In the forties, however, the hosiery trade on the Continent was in an even more backward state than in this country. Some progress had been made in France, the circular frame being a French invention, while the rotary frame was introduced in 1844 and adapted for automatic fashioning a few years later. But it was after 1855 that the French hosiery trade began to expand so rapidly; by 1860 the value of the output was 70 million francs (£2,800,000), and in 1860, 90 million francs (£3,600,000), of which 55 per cent was cotton, 35 per cent wool, 9 per cent silk, and 1 per cent linen.[8] In Saxony the frames were of a primitive type made partly of wood, and in 1840 earnings were even lower than in England, though the workers had the advantage of being able to combine agriculture with framework knitting. The number of wood hand frames in the Chemnitz district was given as 26,378 in 1863, but about this time English iron frames were introduced; the first circular frame went to Chemnitz in 1851, and in 1863 there were 303 French round frames, 1,774 English round heads worked by hand, and 2,484 power-driven, though only half of these were at work.[9]

The British hosiery manufacturers who led the way in the development of power-driven machinery had little to fear from the competition of foreigners so long as they continued to produce mainly on hand frames. Even with cheap labour hand frames could not compete with power except perhaps in the best-quality goods. But the revolution in the British hosiery trade quickly spread to the Continent and in Saxony its progress was particularly rapid; it was, in fact, typical of German industrial development after 1870. By 1882, of the 45,000 employed in the Saxon hosiery trade, 11,500 were factory workers; in 1892 the total number employed was 50,000, the machines in factories had increased by 12,000 and 3,000 hand machines had been added. It will be seen that hand workers still predominated, many carrying on the trade as a part-time occupation in their homes, but the output of the factories was, of course, much greater than that of the domestic industry. The total daily output was estimated in 1894 at 50,000 dozen stockings and socks, 15,000 gloves, and 3,000 dozen vests and other articles, while the value of the annual production was about £5,000,000.[10]

The Germans concentrated on cheap cotton goods mainly for

the export trade, and with their low labour costs they were able not only to drive us from foreign markets, but also invade the home market for this class of goods. 'We cannot expect the hosiery trade to be ever so prosperous as it was fifteen years ago,' says a writer in 1888, commenting on the numerous failures in the past year among prominent firms. Machinery exported from England was making competition still more severe, it was said.[11] Moreover, there were constant complaints that English manufacturers, instead of developing the better-quality trade in which they were still pre-eminent, seemed compelled to respond to the prevailing cry for cheapness and to use each new improvement as a means for turning out still bigger quantities of low-grade goods in efforts to drive the Germans from the home market and win back the American trade which had so largely fallen into their hands. The United States had been one of the chief markets for English hosiery, but in the four years previous to 1896 our exports there were only one-tenth of those from Saxony.[12]

The following figures enable us to trace the development of overseas trade over the period 1861-1910:

BRITISH FOREIGN TRADE IN WOOLLEN AND COTTON HOSIERY (EXCLUDING GLOVES)

Years (Average)	Wool	Exports Cotton	Total	Net Imports (Cotton only)b
	£1000	£1000	£1000	£1000
1861-5	348	443a	791	66c
1866-70	286	756	1,042	107c
1871-5	288	1,026	1,314	116
1876-80	294	866	1,160	202
1881-5	420	1,102	1,522	240
1886-90	794	768	1,562	365
1891-5	759	450	1,209	357
1896-1900	856	374	1,230	374
1900-5	1,007	461	1,468	741
1906-10	1,415	493	1,908	1,311

a Four years, 1862-5; exports of cotton hosiery separately entered only since 1862.

b Imports of woollen hosiery only recorded since 1904. Average 1906-10, £331,000.

c Gross imports, net imports were probably £10,000 less.

It will be seen that while exports of woollen hosiery show on the whole a steady increase, those of cotton hosiery reflect violent fluctuations with a marked decline after the period 1881-5. On the other hand, the imports of this class of goods increased 50 per cent between 1886 and 1890 as compared with the average for the previous five years. There were further remarkable increases between 1901 and 1905 and between 1906 and 1910, and although exports recovered somewhat during the same period they never reached half the high average of 1881-5. These figures show the extent to which the trade in cotton hosiery was passing out of our hands, but they indicate that we were still holding our own in the woollen branch where the superior quality of our products enabled us successfully to meet foreign competition and, in spite of tariff barriers, to find entry into foreign markets.

Between 1891 and 1895, however, there was a decline both in woollen and cotton hosiery exports which was mainly attributable to the United States 'McKinley' Tariff of 1891. The new tariff with its increased duties on knitted goods had very serious effects on the Nottingham trade in particular, which was largely engaged in supplying the American market, some small firms producing for it almost exclusively. Indeed, the decline in exports and the flooding of the home market with German goods at prices which English manufacturers could not touch combined almost to extinguish the trade in cotton hose and half-hose which had been the speciality of Nottingham and Hinckley. But at the same time the home consumer was beginning to prefer woollen hosiery, and as the cotton trade declined it was replaced by the increased production of black cashmere plain and ribbed goods.[13] After about 1890 these lines became so important in the Nottingham trade that its production of woollen goods came closely to rival that of Leicester. A big trade also developed in fancy embroidered goods, and in some parts of the county cheveners were unable to keep pace with the manufacturers' demand.[14]

By such adjustments the British hosiery trade met the changing conditions of production and of demand.[15] But as with so many of our manufacturing industries foreign competition was henceforward always a force to be reckoned with. Manufacturers, as usual, laid great emphasis on the advantage of cheap labour enjoyed by their foreign rivals,[16] but it would be a mistake to attribute the latter's success entirely to this. Low wages undoubtedly gave them an initial advantage; but, as the factory industry developed, improvements in technique became increasingly important. Continental industrialists quickly realised the importance of technical education and, aided by state and municipal authorities, well-equipped schools were established at all the chief centres, as, for example, at Chemnitz and Roubaix. England lagged far behind in this respect, her manufacturers being slow to realise that the old rule-of-thumb methods that had served well enough in the past were quite inadequate for the age of science and system that was beginning in industry.

There were exceptions, however. As early as 1867 we find A. J. Mundella, the Nottingham hosiery manufacturer, moving a resolution at a meeting of the Associated Chambers of Commerce that the government be urged as to the necessity of technical schools such as had been established in Germany and elsewhere on the Continent, to which 'the rapid progress and high excellence of Continental manufactures are mainly attributable'. In the same year the Nottingham Chamber of Commerce produced a report on the subject.[17] They acknowledged the advantages of the schools of art, but complained that high fees deterred the poorer classes from attending. Yet the need for instructing artisans in design and especially in machine-drawing was imperative. Without such knowledge the inventive powers of the workman were often misdirected and many valuable inventions were never perfected; when improvements were made they were generally the result not of scientific induction but of numerous trials and failures. No less urgent was the need of instruction in chemistry for the dyeing and finishing trades. In Germany, it was said, technical education could be obtained 'on the spot at a cost of as many shillings as it requires pounds in England'. For the artisans of Nottingham there was no instruction that could compare with that available for the same class in Chemnitz, at small fees which were remitted in deserving cases. Moreover, in many parts of the Continent primary education was superior to that provided in this country where the workers were generally 'utterly ignorant of the properties of the materials they used'. Twenty years later similar complaints were still being made; although technical schools were being established in England they were far behind those in other countries; there was a lack of support for this kind of education in England. The now familiar complaint of lack of selling enterprise on the part of British merchants was also coming to be heard.[18]

CHAPTER 11

LABOUR
UNDER THE FACTORY SYSTEM

Accounts of the Industrial Revolution usually represent the advent of the factory system as something of a disaster for the mass of the workers. It would seem, however, that this view is only justified when comparison is made between the domestic system at its best and the factory system at its worst. In the framework-knitting industry the domestic system is revealed at its worst, with all its characteristic evils of low wages, long hours in unhealthy surroundings, the abuse of child labour, and the petty tyranny of the truck master. It was only under the factory system, reformed as it had been by the efforts of two generations, that such evils could be eliminated. The transition to factory production was, therefore, on the whole of immense benefit to the hosiery worker. But the period had its problems for workers as well as for manufacturers, especially as changes in methods of production were impinged upon by trade depression and fierce competition, and so far as the hosiery trade was concerned these special problems accentuated the general labour unrest that marked the closing decades of the nineteenth century.

There was first the problem of the hand-frame worker who still existed in large numbers long after factory production had become the general rule. It is impossible to give the exact numbers, but there were said to be quite five thousand framework knitters in the Midland counties in 1892, with a further five or six hundred in Hawick and the surrounding district.[1] No new frames were now being built in the Midlands, but old skeletons were constantly recruited, over thirty men being kept fully employed on this work in the Nottingham district.

Despite the great decline in the hand branch its workers were far from regarding its extinction as inevitable. In fact they were making strenuous efforts to preserve and extend it, claiming that there must always be a market for their goods on account of their superiority to the factory product. If the public knew the superior wearing qualities and greater elasticity of hand-made fabric, those who could afford would always buy it in preference to power-made goods. But unscrupulous, or perhaps ignorant, dealers would often sell factory goods as hand-made, charging a high price and at the same time bringing hand work into disrepute. It was therefore necessary that buyers should be able to distinguish between the two classes of goods and be able to prove that the hand-made article was really worth a higher price, which, however, could only be tested in wear, it being difficult to tell one from the other by mere examination. In order to further their case the hand workers had formed the Framework Knitters' Federation which extended over the three Midland counties and included Roxburgh and Dumfries in Scotland.

We find the federation particularly active with inquiries in connection with the Merchandise Marks Acts. Already these Acts, by requiring goods to be stamped as products of the country where they were made, had done much to prevent foreign articles being sold as British; and now hand workers in several trades, notably hosiery and Sheffield cutlery, were demanding that the same method should be used to protect them against unfair competition from the factory product.[2] But however desirable it might be that hand-made goods should be stamped as such there were serious difficulties in this. While some goods were entirely made on the hand frame, many workers made only parts of garments, the rest being made by power; for instance, three or four machines might be used in making a stocking, the heel and foot, where there was most wear, and fancy parts like lace ankles, being hand made, while the leg was knitted on the power frame. Moreover, frame-work knitters had difficulty in proving that their work was always superior to the factory product; it was contended that if the same high-quality yarn were used for the latter it would wear quite as well. Many manufacturers were opposed to the policy of marking goods, with all its attendant difficulties, in the interests of what appeared to be a dying industry. As for safeguarding the public against fraud, it was suggested that the existing law under which the Board of Trade could take proceedings against dealers selling power-made goods for hand-made was sufficient.[3]

It is evident that the hand-frame workers were fighting a losing battle; even though their trade might survive for some time it was plain that they could only hope to find work in a very restricted field. Indeed, they themselves recognised this; they were not opposed to the new machinery, they said, only they wanted the public to be able to buy hand-made hosiery if they preferred it. At Hawick the framework knitters were reported to have a constant supply of work, the trade having been fostered by the manufacturers who stamped the goods as hand-made.[4] But the Scottish trade was of a different type from that carried on in the Midlands; there was no striving for mere cheapness, and in the production of quality goods the hand frame could still hold its own on account of the high prices obtainable. Even here, however, a change was taking place, and the old frame worked by hands and feet was being superseded by the flat knitter of the Lamb type which had been developed chiefly in America. This machine was operated by a handle with a sideways movement, but it required less skill and found work for women rather than men. In the Midlands there was also a certain amount of high-grade work in which hand frames were used, but an important source of supply were the government orders for military socks and pants made from cheap yarn, but of such specification that the garments could only be knitted on the hand frame.[5]

Some of the worst abuses in the trade were in connection with these government contracts. There were constant complaints of orders being taken by people who had not enough machines to do the work, but hired machines or let out part of the order at a profit to subcontractors who, in turn, expected a profit, the worker being the victim at the end of this series of transactions. In accordance with the Fair Wages Resolution of the House of Commons (1891), the government now stipulated that the standard wage of the district should be paid on all their contracts; but it was said that men often got 3s or 3s 6d a dozen less than the statement price, while subcontractors would make as much as 8s to 10s a dozen of pants.[6] Nor had the worker much chance of improving his position. Trade unionism was necessarily weak among scattered workers, and even where attempts had been made to organise them it was almost impossible to prevent people working under price at home. Again, the middlemen, unlike the majority of larger manufacturers, were often definitely hostile to trade unions and victimised any of their workers who became members. The rates for hand work in the Nottingham district were nominally still based on the list drawn up by the Board of Arbitration as long ago as 1866, but the board had ceased to function and the workers had no alternative but to take what the employer chose to offer. They were not only competing among themselves, but competing with the factories, and in this they well knew that their only chance of securing work (apart from that which could not as yet be done by power machines) was by their cheap labour.

No doubt some improvement could have been effected by bringing the hand frames into the factories. Except in the outlying districts, this would not have been difficult now that they were so few; in fact some firms had already brought in their frames or had housed them in workshops adjoining the factory.[7] But whatever might be done, the hand worker could never escape the fact that the demand for his labour was always a question of comparative costs; he could only hope to get work in competition with the factories by improving the quality of his product and by keeping down its labour cost. Obviously the possibilities in either direction were extremely limited, but with power-driven machinery they were almost infinite; in these circumstances the complete extinction of the hand-frame stockinger seemed merely a matter of time.

The decline of the hand branch was the natural result of the transition to factory production, but it was not accompanied by anything like a proportionate increase in the number of factory workers. Thus the total number employed in the trade decreased markedly with the extension of the factory system. It is impossible to measure the extent of this decline with any precision owing to the unreliable character of the available statistics. Felkin's estimate of 150,000 workers in 1867 may have been exaggerated, but the figure of 120,000 given in the Report of the Children's Employment Commission far exceeds that of the census return for 1861, which is 45,869. It seems likely that both these estimates included many children and part-time workers who would not be classed as 'occupied' in the census, the returns of which would doubtless be far from complete in any case. The later census returns are probably more reliable, but that for 1881 gives only 40,372 hosiery workers for England and Wales. Here again, however, there may be important omissions especially of outworkers, who are said to have numbered at least 25,000 as late as 1907.[8] But whatever qualifications may be necessary on these grounds, the fact of the decline is sufficiently evident, and this, taken with the increasing output of the industry, affords some indication of the greater efficiency of factory production.

The decline in employment affected both men and women workers, but not in the same degree. It is difficult to say what were the proportions between the sexes in the old domestic trade, for Felkin's estimate in 1866 of 100,000 menders, seamers, winders, cutters, finishers, and makers-up, most of whom were women and children, is evidently only approximate and would include many part-time workers; nor do we know how many of the 50,000 frameworkers were women. Taking the trade as a whole, however, we can say that roughly it employed twice as many women as men. As will be seen, the ultimate effect of the development of factory production was greatly to increase the proportion of female labour employed. This was not apparent at first, for although women were employed to some extent on power-driven circular frames the demand in the early factories was mainly for men. Rotary frames, especially, required considerable skill in operation, and men, moreover, were able to get the most out of these expensive machines by working overtime and night shifts when required. It was some time, therefore, before there was any serious attempt to introduce female labour on power frames. But as machines became more automatic in operation and called for less skill on the part of the worker, the process of substitution began in the circular branch and even, though with less success, on rotary frames like the Cotton's Patent.[9] But the machine that did more than any to increase the number of women knitters was the automatic seamless hose and half-hose frame. Not only did this machine provide a new field for female labour, it also severely affected the demand for full-fashioned goods made on rotary frames. The prevailing desire throughout the trade was for cheaper and cheaper goods, and the seamless automatic frame cheapened production in two ways: it made possible a far higher rate of output by turning out the hose practically complete in one operation, and it required only semi-skilled labour to work it.

In the late eighties and the nineties we find the unions constantly complaining of cheaper women's labour displacing that of men, many hundreds of whom, it was said, had been driven to seek employment in other trades.[10] But the question as to whether particular work should be done by men or by women was not necessarily determined on the purely economic basis of labour cost, for custom, strengthened by trade union influence, played a big part. Where women had always been employed on frames in large numbers it was comparatively easy to increase the numbers; on the other hand, certain branches had come to be regarded as men's work, and here any attempt to introduce women provoked strong resistance. Distinctions varied in different districts; for instance, in no other district was the circular branch considered as men's work to such an extent as in Nottingham.[11] Outside the towns women were working power machines at set wages of 13s a week in 1890,[12] and at Hawick women were employed at set wages on what the Nottingham trade unionists called men's machines. Conditions varied, too, with different firms, and where only non-union labour was employed the proportion of women would be much higher than for the trade as a whole.[13]

The figures of hosiery workers employed in factories do not, of course, indicate the extent to which women were encroaching on what had been the province of men, but they do show that hosiery was becoming more and more a women's trade. In 1890 there were 9,208 men employed in hosiery factories,[14] the bulk of them, presumably, on frames; so that together with the 5,000 hand framework knitters already mentioned there would be about 14,000 men in the occupation, probably a third of the total 30 years before. The census of production taken in 1907 gives only 9,609 male hosiery workers, and even supposing the number of hand framework knitters to have been underestimated there could not have been more than about 10,000 in all branches. On the other hand, the number of women employed in factories shows a striking increase. In 1876 they only slightly outnumbered the men at 5,098;[15] some of these were working frames, but the majority would be on winding and sewing machines and mending fabric. By 1890 the number of women in factories had trebled to 15,630, and in the next 17 years it again increased to over 30,000. But whereas in 1907 practically all the male hosiery workers were in factories there were perhaps 25,000 women outworkers besides factory workers.

The increase of women factory workers is partly accounted for by the substitution of women for men on frames, but what it mainly indicates is the gradual absorption of the seaming and making-up processes formerly done by outworkers. Winders, of course, were brought in early, for theirs was a process which must be carried on side by side with knitting, and the machines being comparatively simple in character, power was easily applied. It was the development of the power-driven sewing machine that drew the other classes into the factories, but progress in this direction was rather tardy. Among the early sewing machines there was only one type which rivalled hand work in the quality of its stitching; this was the linking or turning-off machine, said to have been invented by Campion of Nottingham about 1858, which joined the selvedged fashioned fabric loop by loop with a chain-stitch. But for cut work with no selvedge the linker could not be used, and in any case it was too slow for cheap goods. The introduction of a machine which neatly trimmed the edge of the fabric as it seamed gave a great fillip to the cut-out trade, but it was not until 1887 that the 'over-lock', a machine which not only trimmed but covered the raw edge, finally solved the problem of seaming cut-out garments. Cut work now began closely to rival the fashioned article for quality, and was so much cheaper in production as to have serious effects on the fashioned trade. The concentration of women stitchers in the factories now continued more rapidly and had the effect of bringing in other classes, such as menders and cutters, whose work, though done by hand, was so closely linked with the other processes of manufacture that it could most conveniently be carried on in the same place.

As the character of the trade changed, the determination of wage rates in the various branches became increasingly difficult. The task of drawing up lists of prices had always been extremely complicated in an industry with such an immense variety of products and so many different classes of machines, but now the constant technical improvements necessitated frequent revision of such lists as could be agreed upon. Disputes might have been avoided if the machinery for conciliation set up in the sixties had still been in operation, but it is hardly surprising that the system which had functioned so well for twenty years failed to stand the strain of this period of rapid change coinciding with persistent trade depression. Each side blamed the other for the breakdown. The employers alleged that the workers' representatives on the Nottingham board were divided among themselves. There were disputes as to the representation of the three or four classes of workmen, while the power-frame operatives, who got excellent wages for a time on the new machines, had little in common with the old type of framework knitter, struggling to compete. Meetings of the Leicester board were dropped in 1884, about the same time as the Nottingham body ceased to function, the last dispute, concerning work being sent into the country where reduced prices had been agreed upon, having ended in a strike.[16]

But if there was little solidarity among the workers there was still less on the employers' side. When the boards were first instituted the industry was dominated by a comparatively small number of large, old-established firms whose power was sufficient to impose certain uniform standards throughout the trade. But with the development of the factory system there grew up a host of small manufacturers competing among themselves and with the larger firms for orders which, in a period of general trade depression and increasing foreign competition, could only be secured at the very lowest prices. The breakdown of the arbitration system was, in fact, typical of the state of the industry in the eighties and nineties, for no institution that existed to make regulations in the common interest could flourish in an atmosphere of mutual suspicion, where none could be sure that his neighbour would adhere to the terms of an agreement.

The irregularity of prices was the workers' main grievance; nine-tenths of the disputes, it was said, were due to this cause. It was recognised that the high earnings of the prosperous years could not be maintained through the depression, and reduced rates had been generally agreed to; in the Nottingham rotary branch, for instance, the 1889 list was 25 per cent below that existing in 1875.[17] But many received far less than the standard rates, and owing to the difficulty of maintaining uniform statements all were in danger of being forced down to the level of the worst paid in the trade. As might be expected, wages were highest in Nottingham and Leicester where the trade unions were fairly effective; but even here there was a good deal of irregularity, especially among the small manufacturers. There had appeared a new kind of middleman who would rent a room with power, buy a few machines or get them on credit, and fetch work from the larger manufacturers, relying on low labour costs to afford a margin of profit. Such men were 'a curse to the trade', and although at Nottingham most of their workers had been brought into the union by 1892, there was still great difficulty in enforcing standard rates: 'every time we attempt it,' said one of the trade union leaders, 'we have got to bring a shop out.'[18]

It was even more difficult for the unions to secure standard rates for women, the bulk of whom were not members of any organisation. A special problem here was the competition of people working in their homes, a good deal of work such as button sewing and stitching shirt fronts being still done by domestic hands workers who, it was said, were 'cruelly sweated'.[19] Where hand labour was competing with machinery this was probably true,[20] but there was still much fancy work that had to be done by hand. It must be remembered, too, that many of these domestic workers were people not entirely dependent on this source of income. Many were married women trying to earn a little to eke out the family resources, and although to the factory worker their wages may have seemed sweated, yet to them whatever they earned was so much 'found money', and they were not likely to complain too much about the rate of payment, especially where they only got the work because they could do it cheaply. Thus it is probable that the factory workers who saw their standards threatened by cheap domestic labour were more concerned about the low prices paid than were the sweated workers themselves.

But the most serious menace to the town worker's standards came from the country districts. All through the history of the hosiery trade we can trace the play of centralising and decentralising forces. In the early years of the factory industry the former were predominant, but in the last two decades of the century the influences were definitely in the opposite direction. One factor was the introduction of automatic machines for which operatives could be quickly trained. Another was the growing practice of selling by sample, which meant that a factory in the trading centre no longer had its former advantages,[21] while those firms which had begun to deal direct with retailers and secured orders through travelling salesmen could operate their business from almost any centre.[22] Most manufacturers, however, still found it convenient to have a warehouse at Leicester or Nottingham. It was in the factory branch that the process of decentralisation was so marked, and the main factor was the attraction of cheap labour in the country districts. We get constant references, in the trade journals and trade union reports, to the removal of machinery into the smaller towns and the villages, and to the rise of new firms in these places, often working for the town manufacturers. In 1889 it could be said that most of the villages and townships for a radius of twenty miles round Nottingham had hosiery factories, while Nottingham itself was fast becoming merely a sales centre.[23] By 1908 the migration had reached such proportions that there was not 20 per cent of the manufacture carried on in Leicester or Nottingham.[24]

Country labour was somewhat less efficient, but with rates

30 to 50 per cent below trade union prices a saving of quite 25 per cent in manufacturing costs was possible.[25] Competition forced the unions to make concessions from time to time, but the migration continued. Employers would select a poverty-stricken district, where almost any wages would be accepted, in which to establish a factory; if the unions submitted to reductions to enable the town manufacturers to hold their own, and to prevent more machinery being moved, the country employers would retaliate with still lower wages. So the struggle went on, country and town being played off one against the other, and the unions trying to prevent it by extending their organisation through the country districts. This was not at all easy; the workers in some places showed most discouraging apathy, declaring themselves satisfied with their present position, while in others the threat of a lockout was a sufficient deterrent.

The difficulty of enforcing standard rates, although due in part to the continuous changes in technique, shows, nevertheless, to what small extent real collective bargaining was possible. Under the regime of the conciliation boards collective bargaining appears to have been really effective, at all events so far as the actual frameworkers were concerned; but now, in the absence of any joint organisation, each side was left to its own devices. On the workers' side trade unionism was being reconstructed in accordance with changing conditions. Some of the older societies, representing particular classes of workers established on a district basis, still survived at the end of the century; but half the unions in existence in 1899 had been formed since 1884.[26] These newer unions included all classes of workers, which was the more effective method of organisation now that rigid distinctions between skilled and semi-skilled labour could no longer be maintained. At the same time we get a movement towards more unified control, resulting in the formation of the Leicester and Leicestershire Amalgamated Hosiery Union, registered in 1885, and the establishment four years later of the Midland Counties Hosiery Federation, soon afterwards superseded by the National Hosiery Federation,[27] in which practically all the unions were associated for the purpose of trade protection. But in spite of this progress, membership was still small and fluctuating,[28] and the constant insistence, in the union reports, on the necessity for expansion shows that the leaders were conscious of the weakness of their position. On the employers' side no formal organisation remained after the break-up of the conciliation boards, and it was some years before the Leicester Hosiery Manufacturers' Association and, later, the Midland Counties Hosiery Manufacturers' Association were formed. It was stated, however, that in Leicester 'there was no difficulty in getting representatives of both sides together to discuss disputes'; prices had been rearranged several times without strikes and relations were 'fairly friendly'.[29] In Nottingham, on the other hand, price adjustments seem to have been more piecemeal in character. For instance, an agreement was reached in 1886 that there should be no further reductions unless by mutual consent; yet two years later we get reports of reductions by individual firms amounting in some cases to as much as 25 per cent.[30]

Although the organisation of collective bargaining might not be very efficient, the principle, at all events, was recognised in the two leading centres. Outside, the unions were still fighting for recognition. Some employers resented the interference of trade union officials in what they considered to be essentially their own business; as one of them put it: 'Our people do not need to employ anyone to look after their interest, we look after it.' Others were afraid of losing their competitive advantage, though there was apparently no question of forcing up rates to the level of the towns, the primary aim being to secure recognition for the principle of collective bargaining.[32]

So far we have been discussing the irregularity of rates of payment. But more significant are actual weekly earnings, of which piece rates, under the system almost universal in the hosiery trade, form the basis. The ultimate aim of the unions was to secure such adjustments of rates that earnings throughout the same grade of labour might be levelled up. The continuous improvements in machinery, however, made the attainment of this ideal particularly difficult. Clearly, workers on obsolete machines needed a higher rate than those who had the advantage of the latest types, but although their rates might be higher they were not usually proportionate to the difference in productivity. For instance, it was reported that women on the latest type of knitting machine at Leicester were paid 3d a dozen while those working the older pattern got 1s 3d, yet earned 7s a week less.[33] It was, of course, all to the good that earnings should be levelled up rather than levelled down, and the higher the rates that had to be paid on obsolete machines the greater the incentive to substitute new ones. But the principle of substitution is often tardy and uncertain in its action;

the obsolete machine of today might be the latest type of yesterday and by no means worn out, and the manufacturer who could not afford to scrap his plant and yet must compete with more up-to-date firms was tempted to cut his costs at the worker's expense.

Unfortunately we have no complete statistics to indicate the extent of variations in earnings on similar kinds of work, but the instances quoted suggest that they were fairly wide. With regard to average earnings in the various branches we have much fuller information.[34] The returns show that among men frameworkers earnings were approximately equal on rotary and circular frames at about 33s, but considerably higher in the Cotton's Patent branch where the average was 38s 3d a week. This is accounted for partly by the greater skill required and by the rapid improvements that were being made in the latter type of machine; there was also far less competition from low-paid female labour.[35] In nearly all cases women's earnings were less than half those of men, but useful comparison is seldom possible because, except in circular and automatic seamless work, the sexes formed non-competing groups with different sets of wage determinants. Even where women were engaged on the same work as men the conditions were not precisely similar, for the women worked fewer heads or had men to supervise. Thus the competitive power of women was limited by inferior capacity, and although this might be compensated, to some extent, by their willingness to work at lower rates, trade union restrictions were also a factor; for the policy of the unions, while tolerating lower rates for women, tended to prevent their encroaching on the field of men's employment. But in all discussion of wages the powerful influence of custom has to be borne in mind. There are conventional standards which largely determine the relation between the wages of men and women, and the fact that in the present case the earnings of women frameworkers approximate very closely to those of women sewing-machinists, winders and menders suggests that their rates were adjusted in accordance with a notion of what they 'ought to earn' rather than according to the actual productivity of their labour.

In attempting to estimate the position of the hosiery worker at any time considerable allowance must be made for irregularity of employment. The trade had always been subject to seasonal fluctuations, enhanced by the vagaries of the weather, while some branches were constantly having to adjust themselves to changes of fashion and improvements in machinery. Some irregularity in hours and in employment was therefore inevitable. In the busy season, when orders were in urgent demand, the necessary elasticity was obtained by working overtime; while between seasons, unless manufacturers took the risk of making for stock, workers had to go on short time. About three months short time in the year had come to be regarded as normal in the nineties; but in bad years employment was far worse. In March 1895, for instance, one of the Nottingham unions reported that from the beginning of the year an average of one-third of its members had been totally unemployed, another third had not received a weekly average of more than 7s, and of the remainder not more than one-tenth had full employment. At the same time Leicester had 10 per cent unemployed, and not more than 10 per cent on full-time.[36]

Thus, although it was generally agreed that full-time wages were 'very fair' for men and compared favourably with those of skilled workers in other trades,[37] fluctuations in employment, though less severe in effect than in the old days because the workers were better able to meet them, continued to be characteristic of the trade. To a large extent the causes of these fluctuations were beyond the control of those engaged in the industry, but there is little doubt that in some ways a common policy would have been effective. The regulation of overtime is an obvious case. Such rigidity as was implied in the Eight-Hour Day proposal of the Trades Union Congress, supported by the hosiery unions, might have been impracticable. But it was clear that readiness to work overtime tended to enhance fluctuations. It encouraged buyers to leave the placing of orders as late as possible, and manufacturers to accept orders which they could only execute according to promise by working above the normal hours. This highly concentrated activity inevitably increased the succeeding depression. But, with manufacturers in keenest competition, and the workers too imperfectly organised to impose uniform conditions of labour or demand higher rates for overtime, remedy was impossible.

Another factor which must be set against the advantage of relatively high earnings was the increasing prevalence of night work. Employers contended that night shifts were necessary in order to get the utmost out of machines before they became obsolete. Further, the shift system effected considerable savings in rent and other fixed charges, so cheapening production, while it enabled orders to be executed more rapidly. Such savings, resulting in cheaper goods and bigger sales, might ultimately benefit the worker; and shift working was clearly not liable to increase unemployment as overtime did. Nevertheless, the unions had good grounds for opposing a system which robs the worker of his natural rest hours, interferes with his social life, and disorganises his domestic arrangements. For these disadvantages the two pence a dozen extra paid in the towns was regarded as inadequate compensation; but the fear of unemployment compelled submission, for there were competitors in the rural districts glad to get work at almost any price and willing to do night work without extra pay.[38]

Thus the problems of this transition period were numerous and difficult; but there is nothing of the sheer hopelessness that accompanied the stagnation of the forties. It is only by comparison with the conditions of that time that the extent of improvement can be realised. As we have shown, the initial impulse towards change came, in this industry, not so much from technical developments as from legislation. Now there was the problem of controlling the forces that had been set in motion. It must be admitted that on the whole the workers showed better capacity than the employers. Frustrated as they were by apathy, if not by active opposition, and perhaps handicapped by the somewhat restricted outlook of their leaders, the trade unions at least had a policy. On the other hand, the manufacturers seem to have been almost incapable of realising that many of their individual problems were common to the whole industry, and that concerted action was necessary in dealing with them. Keen competition is to be welcomed in so far as it ensures that efficiency gets its reward; but, as we have seen, it was not necessarily the firms of highest technical efficiency that survived. In so far as trade unionism was able to insist on uniform conditions of labour, however, it did tend to secure that the ultimate test for survival should be technical efficiency and business ability. This is an important social by-product of trade union policy.

L

Part Two:
The Modern Industry

CHAPTER 12

HOSIERY AS A GROWTH INDUSTRY

The slow transition from the domestic to the factory system of production in the hosiery trade was virtually completed by 1914. In its earlier stages it was accompanied by a steady decline in employment; but by the turn of the century this trend had been reversed. The first census of production taken in 1907 showed a total employment of 57,016, including 5,803 outworkers, and output was valued at £8,726,000. However, only five years later, when a second census was taken, output had increased to £12,048,000 while employment had reached 70,086.

The 1914-18 war checked expansion but it brought prosperity to many hosiery manufacturers working on government contracts. In 1919 and 1920 much capital was invested in re-equipment and factory extensions; the trade shared fully in the post-war inflationary boom in which selling prices rose faster than costs of production. By 1921, however, the boom had collapsed; the worst-hit industries were those producing capital goods or heavily dependent on export. Hosiery suffered a sharp set-back and there was much unemployment and short-time working, but recovery was fairly rapid and when the first post-war census of production was taken in 1924 total employment, at 97,468, was over 50 per cent higher than in 1912.

The tables on page 170 show the growth of output by value and quantity between 1924 and 1937. Comparison of pre-war and post-war values is of course vitiated by price changes, but the quantity figures for stockings and socks give a fair indication of the industry's expansion generally since these articles were the biggest item in the total output. The general course of prices in the inter-war period was downwards, with a sharp fall in the early 1930s, and this is reflected in the value figures shown in the first table. But if the value figures underestimate the industry's growth the quantity figures exaggerate it somewhat. For, as will be described later, changes in the nature of output and in manufacturing methods tended to cheapen the product. Further evidence of growth between the wars is provided by the returns of insured workers. These give a total of 93,410 in 1924, which increased fairly steadily to 120,800 in 1939. Throughout the period the proportion of female workers remained almost constant at just under 80 per cent.

TABLE 1

OUTPUT OF PRINCIPAL PRODUCTS IN VALUES 1924–37

(Census of Production and Import Duties Act Inquiry)

Product	1924 £'000	1930 £'000	1933 £'000	1935 £'000	1937 £'000
Stockings and socks	19,867	17,032	16,142	16,066	18,370
Underwear	10,824	11,084	10,881	10,743	11,682
Outerwear	11,046	9,754	9,436	9,721	10,027
Other principal products	1,749	1,799	2,757	5,907	5,984
Total	43,486	39,669	39,216	42,437	46,073

TABLE 2

OUTPUT OF PRINCIPAL PRODUCTS IN QUANTITIES
1924–37
(Census of Production and Import Duties Act Inquiry)

Product	1924	1930	1933	1935	1937
Stockings and socks (thousand doz prs)	25,400	24,029	29,358	31,176	35,981
Underwear (thousand doz)	6,514	8,509	11,398	11,627	12,789
Outerwear (thousand doz)	4,067	4,392	5,247	5,064	4,901

The growth of the hosiery industry between the wars is the more remarkable when contrasted with the decline in most of the other British textile trades. Unlike the cotton and woollen industries it was not greatly dependent on exports and it benefited from an expanding home market. Apart from the growth of population and the rising standard of consumption, the trade in hosiery and knitwear was favoured by fashion changes. Shorter skirts enhanced the importance of stockings. Many were still made of silk, but the rapid improvement of artificial silk, or rayon as it came to be called, introduced a cheaper article not markedly inferior in appearance. Finer-gauge stockings were demanded and these were less durable, necessitating frequent replacement. Coloured stockings became fashionable and the wearer needed a varied stock. With men, too, the general substitution of shoes for boots emphasised the importance of socks and here again the increasing variety of shades and fancy effects stimulated demand. The growing sales of underwear for both sexes were partly a reflection of the rising standard of living; there was less patching and darning and more replacement. The demand for variety was also a factor in underwear as with outer-garments. Knitted garments for outerwear were of less importance, but the vogue was beginning. In the inter-war years it was largely a women's trade, but men contributed to the demand in the form of items like sports shirts, pullovers and cardigans.

In some ways the new styles made for cheapness and this, as we have already suggested, helps to explain the increase in volume of output relatively to value. The change was particularly marked in underwear, as the old-style full-fashioned combinations, pants and vests were replaced by lighter and simpler garments. Women's vests, for instance, would be made from a length of tubular fabric which needed little but the addition of shoulder straps to complete the garment. Similarly in men's pants and vests the elimination of facings and buttons made for simplicity and cheapness.

Another factor in the cheapening of some garments was the displacement of wool by cotton and rayon. The popularity of cotton underwear, for instance, was encouraged by the introduction of new types of fabric. The demand for light-weight garments was met by open-mesh or cellular fabrics with good wearing qualities and also by the patented interlock fabric, close-knitted and remarkably fine and soft in texture. Interlock was at first rather expensive and the few firms making it earned big profits; but prices fell substantially when the patent expired. Rayon competed with wool and to some extent with cotton, but its main effect was in the stocking branch. Although the best kinds of full-fashioned stockings were made of silk, the mass demand was met by rayon knitted on seamless hose machines. These articles were often finished with a mock seam in imitation of the full fashioned style. In time, however, rayon was greatly improved; finer yarns were introduced and matt finish gave it a closer resemblance to silk.

The adoption of rayon marked the beginning of a process which, through the proliferation of man-made fibres, was to transform the hosiery industry in later years. In the high-quality trade, however, wool was still favoured. Despite the drastic decline in woollen stockings the combined output of woollen stockings and socks fell by only 20 per cent between 1924 and 1935. This reflected the continuing high demand for wool in men's socks and also in children's wear. In the growing outerwear trade, too, wool was the predominant material.

Although the industry's growth owed so much to external factors—fashion changes and the new artificial silk—it also reflected the enterprise of manufacturers in taking advantage of favourable conditions and encouraging their development. In this they were aided by the machine-builders whose innovations added to the variety of output and the increase of productivity. The main types of modern knitting machines had already been introduced during the transition to factory production.[1] A basic distinction, as we have seen, was that between the flat frame making full-fashioned work and the circular machines, while a further division was determined by the kind of needle used (see p 119). Fashioned work was invariably knitted by bearded or spring needles, as on the old hand frame; most circular machines were fitted with latch needles, though some had the spring type, which is more suitable for fine-gauge fabric. The later innovations involved no change of principle, but remarkable advances were made in the speed and adaptability of existing types of machine (see pp 197-8).

The flat frame, as developed from the Cotton's Patent type, was given a new lease of life by the remarkable expansion of the stocking trade. Here improvement proceeded in three directions. Finer and finer gauges were introduced; frames were extended so that as many as 28 stocking legs could be made at once; speed and reliability were increased by refining the mechanism. Much of the credit for this went to German and American hosiery machine builders and British stocking manufacturers became increasingly dependent on imported plant. Apart from the stocking trade the flat frame was still widely used for other kinds of garment. As the

Circular frame with bearded needles. There were many types but in all cases the essential knitting motions—looping, pressing, landing and knocking off—were made by wheels acting on the needles as they revolved. The example shown is a two-head English machine

demand for full-fashioned underwear declined knitted outerwear increased in popularity and the better-quality articles were made in the traditional way with the various parts shaped in the knitting and then linked together through the selvedge. This branch offered great scope for mechanical ingenuity in the making of patterns, the V bed machine with its two sets of needles being particularly remarkable for its versatility.

Despite the improvements making for greater productivity, knitting on the Cotton's Patent type of machine was still relatively slow. The essential motions were those of the original stocking frame, worked by hands and feet, and the mechanism for linking them with a rotary drive was inevitably somewhat cumbersome. The power loom suffers from a similiar handicap. In the circular frame, however, the essential motions are rotary; the needles, arranged in a circle, are actuated by cams contained in a surrounding cylinder, or by loop wheels in the case of bearded needles. This makes for a simpler mechanism ideally suited to the application of power. Progressive refinement of the mechanism, improved thread control and the introduction of devices for stopping the machine automatically if a thread broke, enabled machines to be driven at higher speeds. Fabric production was also speeded up by increasing the number of points round the cylinder at which yarn was taken up by the needles. Quality was a limiting factor in the use of multi-feed machines, but with improved thread control a twelve-feed machine could make fabric with a perfectly regular texture (see p 51).

Efforts were also directed, in the 1920s, towards increasing the versatility of the circular machine. Much of the output consisted of plain fabric to be cut and made up into garments. Cutting-out was speeded up by the use of electric cutters capable of taking several layers of fabric, and an important advance in making-up was effected by the flatlock seaming machine which made a finer join without the ridge produced by the overlock type of seam. This innovation did much to enhance the status of cut and sewn goods, especially when made from high-quality fabric like interlock. But circular machines proved adaptable to many other requirements. With multi-feed coloured yarns could be introduced to give striped effects. Patterns could be made by varying the action of the needles or the tension on the yarns. Fabrics could be knitted with alternating lengths of plain and rib stitch. Plated fabrics with one kind of yarn showing on the 'right' side and another kind on the 'wrong' side, also offered scope for development. They could, for instance, be brushed to give a fleece-lined appearance and by the use of rayon for the surface yarns an imitation of plush or velvet was possible. In some forms knitted fabric was already competing with woven materials, though as yet it was not sufficiently stable for certain uses. For underwear and some kinds of outerwear its characteristic elasticity was ideal; but this same quality was a disadvantage in articles like men's suitings and shirtings.

Besides producing fabric for making-up, circular machines, in some branches of the industry, greatly simplified the making-up process and indeed virtually eliminated it. Fabric knitted in tubular form could provide the basis for such garments as vests and singlets, the elasticity of the fabric being relied upon for shaping the garment to the body. Quality was sacrificed to some extent but manufacture was cheapened. This line of development was important also in the stocking and sock trade, but here the requirements were more exacting, especially with stockings. These consist of a welt, leg, heel and foot and the aim was to produce all these parts by a continuous process on the same machine. The demand for such machines which, being automatic in action, could be tended by semi-skilled and often female operatives, was greatest in America. It was here that progress was most marked, due not merely to inventiveness but to the opportunities for mass production in supplying the home market. With this advantage American machine-builders were able to penetrate markets abroad and British seamless hose manufacture became largely dependent on American machines.

However, with all the mechanical ingenuity embodied in the seamless hose machine, its product could not compete in quality with the full-fashioned article. It was given shape by pressing or 'boarding', but its inferiority came out in the wash. Its great merit was cheapness and for many consumers this was the main consideration. Later on, as we shall see, the disadvantages of seamless hose were largely overcome, and the stocking trade was transformed.

The increasing production of cheap, low-quality hosiery had been a frequent cause of complaint in the old days and it appeared again in the 1920s. It was directed particularly against imports from Japan where modern machinery and low wages gave a decisive advantage in international trade. Except for the silk duties, introduced in 1925, the British textiles market was freely open to foreign competition. However, under the Safeguarding of Industries Act, 1925, an industry in which employment was seriously threatened by increasing imports could submit a case for a protective tariff. In 1926 the national joint industrial council for the hosiery industry made application for a safeguarding duty on cotton and woollen goods and a Board of Trade committee investigated the position. It found that, for the industry as a whole, employment was not at the time seriously threatened, although the volume of cotton hose and underwear imports was disquieting. However, the applicants failed to prove their case for a duty on such articles; cotton hosiery accounted for less than one-quarter of total output, measured in quantity, and the share of the home market held by British goods of this class was about 65 per cent. Thus if foreign cotton hosiery were excluded altogether there would not be any great increase in employment for the industry as a whole.[2] Imports of cotton goods from Japan, Germany and Czechoslovakia continued to increase until 1931. These goods competed with British products on price. But in the rapidly growing silk and rayon hose market quality was an important factor. This was particularly true of imports from Germany, where manufacturers who had built up a flourishing trade in cotton stockings before the war now repeated their success in other lines. In collaboration with the machine-builders they produced very fine gauge stockings in silk and rayon and it was some time before British manufacturers, equipped with German machines, were able to match them in quality.

The worldwide trade depression, beginning in 1930, caused more foreign goods to be directed to the still-open British market. However, following the monetary crisis in the autumn of 1931, abnormal importation duties of 50 per cent ad valorem were imposed on most manufactured imports, including hosiery. An Import Duties Advisory Committee was then set up to consider the claims of individual industries for a more permanent measure of protection and the recommended rate for most knitted goods was 20 per cent. Although this was less than manufacturers had hoped for, it proved to be a sufficient deterrent for cotton hose and underwear and imports in both categories declined drastically. On the other hand, imports of silk and artificial silk hose recovered markedly in the later 1930s. In the case of rayon hose the increase was partly a reflection of the general tendency for rayon to oust cotton in the cheap stocking trade. A common retail price for rayon stockings was 1s 11d a pair, but the lower qualities of silk hose could be bought for 2s 11d. Germany and Czechoslovakia were our main competitors in this trade, supplying about three-fifths of the imports, while better quality goods retailing at 3s 11d upwards came from the USA, Canada and France.

The revival of foreign competition produced an application in 1938 for an increased tariff. But taking the industry as a whole, imports could hardly be regarded as a serious threat. By 1934 the home market was recovering from the general depression and in all the main branches of the trade the share held by British manufacturers was greater than in 1924. It was highest in underwear, at 96 per cent in 1937, the corresponding figures for outerwear and hose being 93.9 and 88.8 per cent respectively.[3]

In contrast with the home market where British manufacturers, aided by protection, secured a higher proportion of a growing trade, hosiery exports in the 1930s were relatively small. They had accounted for about 15 per cent of total production in 1924; but the general depression in world trade during the 1930s brought a drastic reduction and throughout the decade the proportion never exceeded 7 per cent. Like Britain, other countries protected their home markets, often by increasing existing tariffs. By far the most important category of exports in 1924 was woollen hose, which includes men's socks, and here the decline was particularly marked. The only bright spot in the export trade was woollen outerwear, much of which was made in Scotland and enjoyed high prestige in overseas markets. Ten per cent of production was exported in 1937, and taking into account the fall in wool prices, the volume compared fairly well with that for the 1920s.

As with so many consumer goods industries, the growth of the hosiery trade was sharply checked by the second world war. There was again a big demand for clothing from the services, but from 1941 civilian demand was curtailed by rationing. Mobilisation of women as well as men reduced the labour available for less essential production, which in turn created surplus capacity in factory space and industries so affected were required to concentrate in fewer units. The space surrendered was converted to war uses and much machinery was laid up. It is unnecessary to describe the scheme in detail; but its effects on the hosiery industry with its many small and medium-sized firms was particularly severe. About half the factory space occupied in 1939 was requisitioned and in 1944 the labour force had been reduced to about 53,000.[4]

Recovery after the war was hindered by a number of obstacles. Although factory space was released fairly quickly, new building was subject to licensing. New machinery was hard to obtain, especially the foreign machinery on which some sections of the industry had come to depend, and yarn supplies were controlled. Nevertheless, by 1948 the 1937 level of production had been nearly restored and in 1950 it was exceeded. Then a set-back occurred; the Korean War brought a sharp rise in the prices of raw materials, especially wool, and the subsequent fall contributed to a world-wide recession in textiles. In hosiery, however, this was short-lived. British production recovered rapidly in 1953 and the industry entered a period of further growth. This is not fully reflected in the sales figures for the later 1950s, for 1958 was marked by another fall in yarn prices; the industry's net output

VALUES OF GROSS & NET OUTPUT 1951–69
(Census of Production & Board of Trade 'Business Monitor')

Gross Output	1951 £m		1954 £m		1958 £m		1963 £m		1969 £m	
Fabric	23.3		25.0		20.8		48.5		128.0	
Stockings and										
Socks	75.3		77.9		66.1		69.5		96.9	
Men's		23.3		18.4		14.5		14.0		15.1
Women's		43.3		51.3		45.6		50.0		73.7
Children's		8.6		8.2		6.0		5.5		8.1
Underwear and										
Shirts	31.0		31.6		34.1		43.0		46.9	
Men's		14.4		12.3		11.8		16.9		19.8
Women's		13.7		13.9		15.7		17.6		16.2
Children's		4.9		5.4		6.6		8.5		10.9
Outerwear	46.0		52.9		69.3		104.8		142.1	
Men's		9.9		10.5		15.4		24.4		39.7
Women's		26.9		31.7		43.2		66.0		82.8
Children's		9.2		10.7		10.7		14.4		19.6
Other Products	7.9		7.2		4.4		7.4		10.1	
	183.5		194.6		194.7		273.2		424.0	
Net Output	66.3		79.9		83.8		117.5		N.A.	

was higher in that year than in 1954 and about 26 per cent above that for 1951.

The industry's continued growth from 1951 is illustrated in the tables on pp 178 and 179. It was due partly to influences originating between the wars. Fashion favoured hosiery more than ever. Skirts were shorter still and stockings or tights still more in evidence. There was a general trend towards informality in dress for both sexes which was expressed in a growing preference for knitted garments. But even for formal wear knitted fabrics competed with woven cloth to an increasing extent. They were also coming to be preferred for soft furnishings and for many industrial uses. Some authorities estimated that by the mid-1970s two-thirds of all textiles would be of knitted construction.[5]

If this forecast is realised, it will be largely due to the remarkable technological progress achieved since the last war. This developed along two lines. Firstly, the range of man-made fibres was greatly extended. The best known is nylon, introduced in America just before the war and now the supreme material for

QUANTITIES OF PRINCIPAL PRODUCTS 1951–69

(Census of Production & Board of Trade 'Business Monitor')

Product	1951	1954	1958	1963	1969
Fabric (thousand lb)	41.5	42.0	27.9	56.7	141.3
Stockings and Socks (thousand doz prs)	40.7	40.9	33.5	41.1	50.5
Men's	10.3	10.0	7.3	7.3	7.7
Women's	21.6	22.0	20.5	29.1	36.3x
Children's	8.8	8.9	5.7	4.7	6.5
Underwear and Shirts (thousand doz)	11.5	13.5	14.6	17.3	17.3
Men's	3.8	4.0	4.3	5.4	5.6
Women's	5.1	6.0	6.3	6.9	7.1
Children's	2.6	3.5	4.0	5.0	4.6
Outerwear (thousand doz)	4.8	5.9	7.7	7.2	9.1
Men's	1.0	1.0	1.4	1.4	2.0
Women's	2.3	2.9	3.4	3.8	5.0
Children's	1.5	2.0	2.9	2.0	2.1

x of which 20.5 tights and panti-hose

stockings. It has all the appearance of silk but is stronger and very much cheaper. Further, it has a peculiar thermo-plastic quality whereby a permanent shape can be given to the garment in the finishing process. This transformed the stocking trade. In the five years 1958–63 output increased from 10,623 to 29,130 thousand dozen pairs and the proportion of seamless hose grew from 44 to 76 per cent of the total.[6] During the same period the average selling value of stockings fell by nearly 25 per cent and in 1970 the most popular brands of hose sold at about 3s 6d a pair. With its easy-care properties nylon was also increasingly used for lingerie and men's shirts. Acrylics, too, are highly suited to knitwear, especially outer-garments; they blend well with wool or cotton and have a high bulk-to-weight ratio. Some man-made fibres have remarkable stretch qualities, particularly important for tights, while others make it possible to produce more stable knitted fabrics that can compete with woven cloths for men's suits. A further factor was the progress in dyeing and finishing, which not merely overcame the problems presented by the new materials but extended their uses.

The second line of development was in the continued improvement of knitting machines. Some of the standard types had been in existence for many years but machine-builders in Britain, America, Germany, Italy and elsewhere introduced notable modifications and refinements. Productivity was greatly increased by the further development of multi-feed machines, the earlier difficulties being overcome partly by improved finishing processes (see p 52). For instance, seamless-hose machines with as many as twelve feeds, introduced in the 1960s, could make 65 dozen stockings every 24 hours, or 53 dozen panty hose. They are fully automatic, turning out stockings—welt, leg, heel, foot and toe—in a continuous operation. Shape is given to the stocking by controlling the loop formation, and, as already described, it is made permanent by heat treatment. Seamless stockings, once regarded as an inferior article, now almost ousted the full-fashioned style. In the larger fabric-knitting machines many more feeders were introduced—80 or even 100 in some types. Such machines often use coloured yarns and patterning may be controlled by electronic devices.

Fabric-making on circular machines is often described as weft knitting, in contrast with the alternate method of warp knitting. The progress of warp knitting since the 1939–45 war is one of the most notable developments in modern textile manufacture. Warp knitting has a long history, the first machine being an adaptation of the hand frame generally attributed to Crane of Edmonton near London in about 1775.[7] Its basic principle is the use of warp threads, one to each needle, in contrast with ordinary knitting which, in its simplest form, makes fabric from a single thread. For many years warp frames were used mainly for lace making, the warp giving the necessary stability to the fabric. In the nineteenth century, however, lace manufacture developed as a separate industry with machines based on a different principle and warp knitting remained as a minor branch of the hosiery trade. Its modern revival was stimulated by two complementary factors: the superiority of the warp-knitting principle over that of the loom in high-speed fabric production and the strength and consistency of man-made fibres (see p 215).

One of the first to appreciate the possibilities of warp knitting in competition with weaving was Sir James Morton of Morton Sundour Fabrics Ltd. He, with his colleague Frank Oldroyd, intoduced in 1931 the fly-needle frame, so-called after the improved needle which it employed. The FNF machine attained the remarkable speed of 1,000 stitches a minute and a later version incorporated weft as well as warp threads.[8] In the meantime German machine builders were applying themselves to the improvement of the warp-knitting frame and after the war two firms in particular concentrated their efforts on this principle, but using only warp threads. Unfortunately the British lead was lost and German machines became predominant in British warp-knitting plants. In the 1960s warp knitting was the fastest growing section of the British hosiery industry. Between 1958 and 1963 the annual output of warp-knitted fabric, mostly of man-made fibres, doubled to nearly 25 million lb; by 1969 this had risen to 70 million lb and the Textile Council forecast continuing rapid growth in the 1970s.[9]

This remarkable expansion of warp knitting was mainly at the expense of the weaving trades, especially cotton. In 1969 it was estimated that 50 per cent of men's shirts were made from warp-knitted fabric, while the proportion in women's lingerie and night-wear was 80 per cent.[10] Increasing quantities of sheetings were warp-knitted and laminated cloths for suitings were being developed; there was also an interesting revival of warp-knitted lace; this was made on Rachel machines which, though less versatile than the traditional Leavers type, are much faster and

M

require less skill in operation. Lace-making is, however, only one of the uses for Rachel machines. Indeed, there is reason to believe that this type, which uses latch needles, offers the best prospect of competing with the heavier kinds of woven cloth. The success of warp knitting in competition with weaving depends ultimately on relative costs. In 1970, warp-knitted cloths such as shirtings were said to be up to 25 per cent cheaper than similar quality woven fabrics. The position in regard to heavier cloths was less clear, and in estimating prospects allowance must be made for possible improvements in the rival weaving process such as substituting the traditional shuttle by other means of carrying the weft threads across the warp.

In the light of the conditions we have described the continued growth of the hosiery and knitwear industry seems assured. But what of the British industry in particular? The 1960s saw a remarkable expansion of international trade in knitted goods. This was reflected in the growth of British exports, the value of which more than doubled between 1963 and 1968. For the latter year exports of men's and boy's knitwear were estimated at £13 million, 26 per cent of total production, the corresponding figures for women's and girl's being £112 million or 17 per cent. The USA was much the biggest market, taking 31 per cent of our exports, and our greatest strength was in high-quality, full-fashioned woollens. But other countries were expanding their exports and increasing quantities entered the British market. By far the most important supplier was Hong Kong, followed by Italy, Japan, Portugal and Eire.[11]

Britain's trade balance in knitwear was still favourable to the extent of £9 million in 1968 and the industry's Economic Development Committee estimated that this might increase slightly to £10 million by 1978. The forecast was, however, subject to much uncertainty; on the most pessimistic assumptions an adverse balance of £8 million was predicted, while the most optimistic estimate gave a positive figure of £24 million. One factor affecting the position was tariff policy in Britain and abroad. In 1970 the British tariff on knitwear imports averaged about 15 per cent, but Portugal as a member of European Free Trade Association enjoyed duty-free entry and Hong Kong had a Commonwealth preferential rate. On the other hand British exports often faced high tariffs, particularly in the important American market. If Britain joined the European Economic

Community imports would certainly increase, especially from Italy, but British exports in certain lines would benefit. It was generally agreed that the best prospects for our exports were offered by the trade in high-quality, full-fashioned woollens. In other lines our relatively high wages, together with a loss of leadership in technical innovation, weakened our position in world markets and to some extent in the home market too.

CHAPTER 13

DEVELOPMENTS IN ORGANISATION

The growth of the British hosiery industry between the wars was not accompanied by any great changes in its structure or geographical distribution. Its location in the East Midland counties of Leicester, Nottingham and Derby, originally an historical accident, had, in the course of time been consolidated by the growth of ancillary trades, commercial facilities and the availability of suitable labour. When new firms appeared they were nearly always started by people with experience in the trade who naturally preferred the familiar environment. The main development outside the traditional centres was in Lancashire, where employment increased from about 3,500 in 1924 to 9,500 in 1935; female labour was plentiful, wages were lower than in the East Midlands and deserted cotton mills often provided accommodation. In the 1930s, too, hosiery, like other of the lighter manufactures, felt the pull of the Greater London area and the Home Counties. Proximity to the London market was an obvious attraction for makers of fancy outerwear, but new factories specialising in stocking manufacture were also established. Minor instances of dispersal were seen in a few seaside towns and at one or two places in Northern Ireland. These developments, however, did little to change the pattern of location. In 1935, 56 per cent of hosiery firms, and 64 per cent of workers were in the East Midlands, and they accounted for 71 per cent of the industry's output. The other traditional centre in south-west Scotland remained small with about one-tenth of the total employment.[1]

The resumption of the industry's growth after the 1939–45 war again brought little change in location. The relative importance of the East Midlands declined somewhat; total employment in Great Britain was 133,700 in 1969, of which the East Midlands accounted for 58.7 per cent.[2] But this decline was almost entirely a reflection of expansion in Scotland whose share had risen to 16 per cent with the increasing demand for the section's traditional products. Elsewhere the position was much the same as before the war, though there was some expansion in Northern Ireland.

Changes in structure are rather more difficult to trace because of variations in the census of production reports. The first of these, which relates to 1907, did not give even the number of returns. The report for 1924 gives the figure of 1,097 returns, but adds that there were many very small firms that failed to make returns. The 1930 report was much more informative in that it showed the size distribution of firms in terms of employment. In 1935, however, returns were based, not on firms, but on 'establishments' or plants, of which some firms might have several units. It was only in 1968, when the report on the 1963 census was published, that official statistics became available for both firms ('enterprises') and establishments. The distinction is, of course, significant only when multi-plant firms become common, and this was certainly not true of the hosiery industry in the 1930s or even in the first decade after the 1939–45 war. Throughout this period, apart from the contraction and forced concentration during the war, the industry's structure showed remarkably little change, as the following tables show:

SIZE DISTRIBUTION OF FIRMS 1930

Average number employed	Number of firms	Number Employed	Net Output £'000
11–24	180	3,186	406
25–49	196	7,006	940
50–99	189	13,428	1,854
100–199	126	17,877	2,585
200–299	40	9,461	1,425
300–399	21	7,291	1,183
400–499	10	4,566	805
500–749	21	12,412	1,820
750–999	9	8,303	1,481
1,000 & over	12	21,880	3,855
Totals	804	105,410	16,354

SIZE DISTRIBUTION OF ESTABLISHMENTS 1954

Average number employed	Number of Establishments	Number Employed (Total of operatives and others)	Net Output £'000
11–24	220	3,714	2,065
25–49	319	11,290	6,205
50–99	243	17,061	10,513
100–199	170	23,814	14,267
200–299	57	14,464	9,132
300–399	37	11,526	7,692
400–499	15	6,593	4,121
500–749	25	15,685	11,686
750–999	6	5,243	5,296
1,000–2,999	5	10,760	7,272
Total	1,097	120,140	78,249

The most obvious feature illustrated by these tables is the preponderance of small units. The change from firm to establishment as the basis of returns may have exaggerated it somewhat, and the apparent decline in the largest class after 1930 is explained in this way; but as Pool and Llewellyn showed in their study published in 1955,[3] the great majority of establishments were independent firms. On this assumption, we can say that small firms employing between 11 and 50 workers were half the total in 1954—a higher proportion than in 1930. Firms with between 11 and 99 workers formed nearly three-quarters of the total, and if the 322 firms with fewer than 11 persons is added we find that in 1954 nearly four-fifths of hosiery firms had less than 100 workers.

Some of the small firms were, of course, young businesses destined to grow. The industry had always been one in which entry was easy and the change to factory production made little difference; it was still possible to set up with a plant consisting of a few circular frames and a bench of sewing machines, or, perhaps knitting machines only. A boom in trade naturally encouraged new ventures, but even in bad years, when mortality among firms increased, new businesses continued to be born. For instance, in the two years of bad trade 1932–3, 41 enterprises were reported as having closed down, but 46 new enterprises were started.[4] For about five years after the second world war the hosiery industry, like so many others, enjoyed the benefits of a sellers' market, and there was a notable increase in the number of new firms.

Pool and Llewellyn identified 79 such firms in the East Midlands and all were still in business at the end of 1953, although 31 firms, all established before 1945, had gone out of business. More than half the new firms had started with less than £2,500 of capital, usually provided by the proprietors themselves, which credit was obtained from banks, yarn agents and in some cases from wholesale merchants. Most of the firms economised on initial investment by installing second-hand machines. This had always been a common practice and a subject of complaint by established firms; they alleged that it encouraged the entry of people with inadequate resources who then resorted to weak selling in order to survive. Finding premises for a new business was often a problem in the early post-war years, but it could be less serious for the small firm than for the larger business wanting to expand. For small-scale production a single room in a tenement factory might suffice, old workshops and warehouses, even houses and disused chapels could be adapted. But a larger firm usually required purpose-built accommodation and under the government's distribution of industry policy it might be denied a licence to expand in the neighbourhood of its existing premises. In some cases this deterred expansion, in others it compelled firms to set up subsidiary units outside the congested areas.

By 1953 nearly all the young firms in Pool and Llewellyn's sample had expanded; the mean rate of growth in numbers employed was 36.1 per cent per annum. Four were employing more than 100 workers each, two of them having started as one-man businesses in 1946 and 1947. Most of the firms, when interviewed, expressed a desire for further expansion, but some had only modest aspirations. Many mentioned shortage of capital and the difficulty of finding suitable premises as obstacles to expansion; but in the meantime they were evidently doing quite well on their existing scale, in competition with older and larger firms.

With its multiplicity of firms and its ease of entry the hosiery industry has always been highly competitive, and it might be supposed that a typical or optimum size of firm would emerge. Firms starting with a level far below the optimum would have to grow quickly to survive, while over-large firms would become less profitable. There are, however, many difficulties in applying the concept to an industry with such a varied range of output as the hosiery trade, and in which success depends on commercial relations as well as on economies in manufacture. One section in which small firms appeared to be quite successful was that of outerwear. In 1953 there were in the East Midlands 179 firms making outerwear only and 30 per cent had fewer than 50 workers each. Only 28 firms were identified as confined to making fabric for the trade, but of these 15 were in the 'under 50 employees' group.[5]

Very few of the larger firms specialise in one branch of the trade; most firms grow by extending their range of output. One exception is stocking manufacture, in which several large plants were set up between the wars, equipped with expensive full-fashioned frames. The increasing substitution of seamless for fashioned hose in the 1950s and 1960s placed such firms at a dis-advantage however and much re-equipment had to be under-taken. Some of them decided to spread their risks by diversifying like other large firms and many of quite moderate size. The extent of diversification is only partially revealed in the 1963 census of production report. This recorded altogether 924 firms employing 25 or more persons, 500 of which were shown as specialising in one or other of four broad sections of the trade. This left a total of 424 non-specialised firms. But the actual number would be considerably higher since the census treats firms as specialised on the basis of their principal, not their sole, product. A sample of 71 firms with 200 or more employees, taken from a trade direc-tory[6] for 1967, showed only 10 that could be described as specialised to one line.

There are several reasons for diversification as a hosiery firm grows in size. Much of the trade is seasonal, but fluctuations in the different sections do not always coincide; the peak demand for some products appears in spring, for others in the autumn. Diversification thus ensures a steadier flow of orders and of cash for the firm as a whole and it helps to stabilise employment. A firm offering a range of goods may also achieve economies in selling. On the other hand there are limits to the possible economies of scale in manufacture. In an industry producing mainly articles of clothing extreme standardisation is not feasible. The production processes, too, are essentially the same whether the plant be large or small. The number of stages of production is greater in the case of cut-out garments; they consist of yarn winding, knitting, fabric cutting, sewing on a variety of machines, ironing and folding. But even here a satisfactory balance of machines and operatives can be achieved at a fairly low level beyond which the difficulties of supervision tend to increase without any compensating gains. Mass production is undertaken by a few firms catering for particular markets but the advantages they enjoy derive as much from commercial, as from manufacturing conditions, as when, for instance, they work to bulk orders placed by chain stores.

In some instances the growth of firms takes the form of vertical integration. In a sense vertical organisation has always existed to some extent in hosiery manufacture. Though nearly all manufacturers bought their yarn from specialised spinners, often through yarn agents, most of the processes for converting it into garments ready for sale were carried out in the same factory. Some fabric was sold as such, but until the 1960s there was little sectionalisation such as had developed in other textile trades, notably cotton. Between the wars some firms carried vertical integration a stage further. An important intermediate process in hosiery manufacture is dyeing and finishing. Some garments are made from coloured yarns, but others, and particularly stockings, are dyed after they are knitted. The finishing process may be applied to fabric in the piece or to completed garments. It includes such operations as scouring, bleaching, brushing, calendering and trimming or boarding, ie shaping in a steam press or on a former. Traditionally British hosiery manufacturers relied on specialist firms for their dyeing and finishing. The plant required is fairly large and expensive and few manufacturers have a big enough output of individual lines to keep such a plant running to optimum capacity. Another circumstance favouring the separation of dyeing and finishing from manufacturing was the geographical concentration of the hosiery industry which encouraged the growth of numerous dyeing and finishing firms in the same areas. Nevertheless there was in the 1920s and 30s an increase in the amount of dyeing and finishing done by manufacturers, especially of stockings and socks.

One reason for this was the setting up of firms outside the traditional areas. In the USA where the hosiery industry is widely distributed it is customary for manufacturers to do their own dyeing and finishing, and dispersal in Britain, though far less marked, had a similar effect. But even in the hosiery districts some firms found it advantageous to develop a dyeing and finishing department. It reduced delay in the execution of orders and saved transport costs. Further, a good deal of the selling value of hosiery depends on the appearance and 'feel' of the fabric, and it is easier for the manufacturer to get the exact qualities required if he has the finishing processes under his own control. There is also the question of comparative costs. Hosiery manufacturers are apt to complain about the charges levied by dyers and finishers, most of whom are organised in trade associations, though this is countered by evidence of a highly erratic flow of orders and the demand for a multiplicity of shades, especially by stocking manufacturers. As a very rough generalisation it can be said that dyeing and finishing costs average some 10 per cent of the value of hosiery manufacturers' sales. But the prospect of reducing costs by taking over the processes is often doubtful and the desire for better control may be a stronger inducement.

Apart from these extensions into dyeing and finishing there were no significant changes in the industry's structure on the manufacturing side in the period of growth between the wars. More important were the developments in selling methods, which, in so far as they involved an extension of the manufacturer's functions are a form of vertical integration. Before 1914, perhaps nine-tenths of British hosiery goods were distributed through wholesale houses. These ordered from manufacturers in anticipation of seasonal requirements and supplied retailers from stock. The system was, and still is, common to many trades dealing in consumer goods, and it was especially appropriate in the hosiery trade with its hundreds of small manufacturers and its goods sold in great variety through thousands of independent shops. But, as we have seen, relations between manufacturers and merchants were not always happy. When trade was bad wholesalers increased the pressure on manufacturers to cut prices, often, it was alleged, by using unscrupulous tactics; when trade was slack they tended to shift marketing risks to the manufacturers by ordering only in such quantities and at such times as the goods were required by their retailer customers. As early as 1888 the feasibility of the manufacturer displacing the merchant was being discussed and in 1891 a certain amount of direct selling was carried on, wholesalers having to cut their margins to compete.[7] In 1898, again, it was declared that manufacturers would do better to deal with retailers owing to the tendency for wholesalers to order in such small quantities. The chief obstacles, however, were the 'enormous variety' of the trade and the fear of retaliation by the wholesalers where manufacturers could not afford to dispense with their services entirely.[8] It was apparently the discovery some ten years later that certain prominent jobbers, in a spell of good trade, had begun to manufacture on their own account, that finally decided a few of the larger manufacturers to retaliate by going direct to the retailer.

The divergence of interests between manufacturers and wholesalers appeared again in the two periods of depression between the wars and it was further emphasised in the safeguarding inquiries of 1926 and 1927 when the manufacturers' claim for protection was opposed by a group of wholesalers and importers. By this time, however, other developments were encouraging the adoption of direct selling by manufacturers. One was the increasing use of brands or trade marks and the advertising of goods so distinguished. In some cases the brands were introduced and publicised by wholesalers, and manufacturers worked to a specification. But many of the bigger manufacturers recognised the possibilities of branding and advertising on their own account. It is difficult for the hosiery manufacturer to make direct contact with the final consumer by having his own shops, though there are a few examples, particularly in the stocking and outerwear trade. Branding, however, enables him to identify the goods with himself and so exercise direct influence over the consumer, while selling through independent retailers. His influence will be the more powerful the better the brand is advertised; but manufacturers who have created a demand in this way, at considerable expense, will endeavour to dispense with wholesalers or to use them only where it is more convenient or cheaper to do so.

Such direct selling is confined mainly to large firms or specialised producers like stocking manufacturers and makers of high-class outerwear. It is not a cheap method of distribution. The margin of 25 to $33\frac{2}{3}$ per cent allowed to the wholesaler is retained by the manufacturer, but there are many expenses to set against it: the costs of brand promotion, sales representatives, the carrying of stocks, the receipt, despatch and invoicing of numerous and often small, orders, the allowance of credit and so on. There is also the difficulty of being able to offer a sufficient range of goods. A few very large manufacturing concerns meet this by having merchanting branches which, besides selling to retailers also buy from other manufacturers, British and foreign, if the goods come out cheaper than having them made in their own factories.

The movement towards direct selling was also influenced by the remarkable growth of large-scale retailing. In the clothing trade it started with department stores, but in recent years it is the multiple or chain-store concerns that have set the pace. According to the census of distribution the total trade of non-food shops increased by 44 per cent in value between 1950 and 1957 and by a further 20 per cent in the period 1957-61; but the corresponding figures for retailers with 10 or more branches were 69 and 34 per cent.[9] The concentration of retailing in larger units makes it easier for manufacturers to sell direct, while the larger retailing concern, buying in 'wholesale' quantities, will expect to deal direct with manufacturers, and on wholesale terms.

In dealing with big retailers manufacturers are in much the same position as when selling to wholesalers; they are not absorbing the marketing function as in the cases described earlier. On the contrary, the big retailer may come to dominate the manufacturer. The multiples' success depends on achieving economies of scale. They attract customers by offering a limited range of goods at relatively low prices. They keep down costs by bulk purchasing, rapid turnover of stocks and by reducing services to the bare essentials. But the manufacturers with whom they deal have to conform with this policy. They must work to an exact specification and at prices that allow a narrow margin of profit per article; and they lose their identity in so far as the goods carry the retailer's brand name. In return they are relieved of much of the marketing function, with its attendant risks, and so can concentrate on the business of manufacture.

A possible danger of this system is that of becoming unduly dependent on one big buyer. This might lead to monopoly exploitation, especially when a manufacturer has lost his other trade contacts. There is, however, no evidence of such exploitation as a deliberate policy. Indeed, chain store representatives have declared that they would deprecate any tendency for hosiery manufacturers to become tied houses.[10] They preferred manufacturers to retain some independence and originality and their orders would be so placed as not to take more than say 60 per cent of a manufacturer's capacity. Some manufacturers, especially small firms, do feel themselves under pressure in dealing with the big multiples, but this often stimulates them to find ways of increasing efficiency, and the assurance of an outlet that will employ a large part of their capacity for a given time helps them to plan their yarn purchases and labour requirements.

This close relationship with the chain stores is by no means confined to the smaller manufacturers. Some of the biggest firms in the industry are involved. It began in 1926 when one of these —Corahs of Leicester—responded to a proposal from Marks & Spencer who were about to extend their trade into knitted goods. The arrangement developed to the great advantage of both firms, but the change in marketing methods was marked by the closure of all Corah's wholesale warehouses over the period 1927–36. It also required the substitution of the retailer's brand for that of the manufacturer on goods supplied to Marks & Spencer.[11] There is, however, still considerable scope for the older methods of selling. Firms working under contract to the chain stores may continue with their own branded lines which they advertise and sell direct to selected retailers like department stores. Often the goods differ little in quality, though in the latter case margins will be wider, partly because of the higher distribution costs. This means higher retail prices; but many customers are willing to pay for amenity and variety of choice in shopping; they are also influenced by the belief that higher prices usually denote higher quality. Then there is the traditional method of distribution through wholesalers. When direct selling began, wholesalers were inclined to adopt a militant attitude; manufacturers must either use their services exclusively or risk being denied them altogether. Later, however, they were forced to come to terms with the changes in marketing methods. Thus a committee of the Wholesale Textile Association reporting in 1945 were of the opinion that 'if the wholesale trade is to maintain its rightful place in the national economic machine in the post-war era . . . it must adopt both individually and as a trade, a more progressive outlook'.[12] In acting on this advice, wholesalers have shown that there is still a large volume of trade, involving big as well as small manufacturers, that can best be handled through their agency.

It was estimated that in 1970 some 40 per cent of British knitwear was sold through chain stores and mail-order firms. But changes in marketing methods, though important for the organisation of trade, had little effect on the industry's structure. The chain stores did not usually seek to absorb their suppliers or to encourage the formation of larger units. On the contrary, the keenly competitive conditions associated with small-scale enterprise suited their interests. Moreover, many of the smaller firms were strengthened by their contacts with the big retailers; bulk orders relieved their marketing risks and the keen prices they were offered forced them to give closer attention to work organisation and costing, which increased their efficiency.

When the reconstruction of the industry came to be considered after its wartime contraction very little was said about its structure. Along with several other industries, hosiery was investigated by a 'working party' set up by the Board of Trade; but its only important recommendation with regard to organisation was for a hosiery and knitwear council 'to act in an advisory and consultative capacity to the government and the industry'. The report was largely concerned with the task of restoring the industry to its former condition, which was what its members most desired.

By 1951 this task had been completed, net output was nearly 50 per cent higher than in 1948 and employment, at 118,900, was slightly above the 1935 level. Three years later it was practically the same as in 1939. The structure, too, showed little change; among the larger British manufacturing industries hosiery was an outstanding example of small-scale, independent enterprise. Its traditional character of competitive individualism had been unaffected by the movement towards consolidation and the dominance of a few big firms that appeared in many industries, including textiles, between the wars; and it survived the wartime concentration schemes. There was, it is true, a growing awareness of common interests as represented particularly by the National Hosiery Manufacturers' Federation and in the organisation of co-operative research; but there was a noticeable absence of the kinds of restrictive practices that led to legal intervention in so many trades. Until about 1960 the structure of this growing industry looked very much the same as before the war; indeed it was not markedly different from that which emerged after the transition to factory production in the latter part of the nineteenth century.

The changes now to be described were partly a reflection of external influences. The rise of the chain stores as major distributors of knitwear had profound effects on marketing organisation, but it was not the policy of the big retailers to take over their suppliers or to set up their own manufacturing plants. A similar situation existed with regard to yarn suppliers, so far as traditional materials were concerned. Manufacturers generally bought in great variety from many spinners and integration between spinning and knitting was rare. But with the emergence of man-made fibres as the hosiery industry's prinicipal raw material the situation changed.

In Britain the man-made fibres industry is dominated by two concerns: Courtaulds Ltd and Imperial Chemical Industries Ltd. Courtaulds, the successor of a silk-manufacturing business established in 1816, introduced the spinning and weaving of viscose yarn in 1906 and extended into acetate yarn in 1926, in competition with British Celanese Ltd, which had developed the cellulose acetate process during the war and applied it to yarn production in 1921. Several other companies came into existence during the rayon boom of the 1920s, but most of them failed or were absorbed by the dominant firms, and finally in 1957 Courtaulds took over British Celanese. Meanwhile, the production of other man-made fibres had been developed as an offshoot of the chemical industry. In Britain, Imperial Chemical Industries entered the field by acquiring rights under the Du Pont nylon patents and in 1940 British Nylon Spinners Ltd was formed as a joint venture by ICI and Courtaulds. The partnership lasted until 1946 when Courtaulds were bought out by ICI and started making their own brand of nylon.

The development of the man-made fibres industry in all its technological and commercial complexity and its international ramifications cannot be traced here in further detail. Our interest is in its impact on the textile industries and on hosiery in particular. The manufacture of man-made fibres is capital-intensive; in 1967 Courtaulds' capital employed per employee ranged from £10,000 to £13,000 and since 1954 they had invested £100 million on buildings and plant for cellulosic fibres alone.[18] As these facts suggest, substantial economies of scale are possible in this industry, but if they are to be realised and the heavy costs of research and development are to be recouped, the demand must be on a commensurate scale. Moreover, if plants are to be kept running at optimum capacity the demand must be as steady as possible. These conditions point to the desirability of a firm relationship between yarn suppliers and users, not merely as parties in a commercial transaction but as partners with a mutual interest in the promotion of new materials.

Already in the 1920s British Celanese was experimenting with vertical integration; it installed large knitting, dyeing and finishing units in conjunction with its fibre plant at Spondon near Derby and in the 1930s it set up a number of garment-making subsidiaries and also selling subsidiaries using Celanese brand names. After the take-over in 1957, the Celanese knitting interests were combined with those developed by Courtaulds themselves in a new company, Furzebrook Knitting Co Ltd, said to have the biggest warp-knitting plant in Europe. Courtaulds then proceeded to acquire other firms in various sections of the textile trades. In the hosiery industry no fewer than 18 firms were taken over between 1963 and 1968; they included some of the biggest, with products covering the whole range of knitted goods. Some of the firms had wholesale and retailing interests and overseas branches, either for manufacture or sales, and these divisions became Courtaulds' subsidiaries.

The other main British man-made fibre producer, ICI moved in the same direction but using different methods. They had, it is true, been associated with Courtaulds in the development of British nylon and for a brief period in 1962 a much closer relationship seemed possible, for ICI made an offer for the whole of Courtauld's issued share capital. However, Courtaulds successfully resisted the bid and in the end ICI's only acquisition was Courtaulds' 50 per cent share in British Nylon Spinners. ICI now proceeded to strengthen its relations with manufacturers, not by taking them over as subsidiaries, but by giving financial assistance to selected companies likely to grow as vertically integrated units. A notable case was that of Viyella International which started in 1961 when Gainsborough Cornard, a highly successful warp-knitting firm, was joined with William Hollins, itself a vertically integrated concern with activities ranging from spinning to weaving and garment-making and including dyeing and finishing.[14] In 1963 ICI acquired a substantial shareholding in Viyella itself, which eventually became a federation of 90 companies organised in 12 trading groups. Then in 1970 Viyella was taken over by ICI together with Carrington Dewhurst, but with the intention of retaining only a minority interest in the combine.

As a result of these groupings, in which the fibre producers had been instrumental, a new conception of the textile trades began to emerge; that of a multi-fibre, multi-process textile industry with the traditional sectional distinctions obliterated. This was recognised to some extent in the creation of the Textile

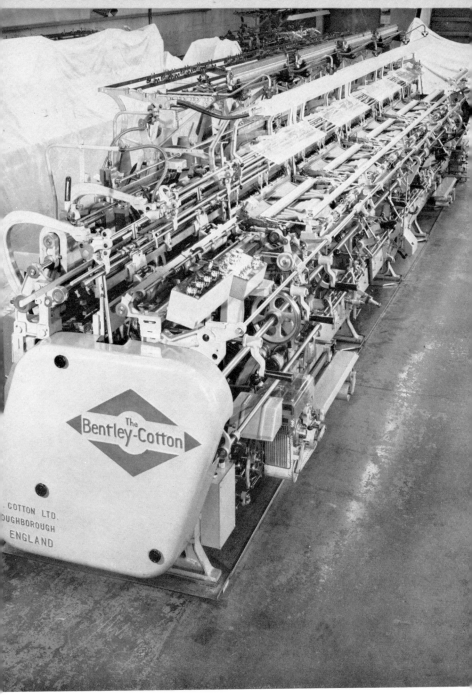

page 197　*The Bentley-Cotton Model F machine for childrenswear garments, 1970.*
The basic principle of Cotton's Patent frame remained but stocking frames were extended
to knit as many as 32 at once (see pp 172-4)

page 198 *A modern Cottons' Patent type frame. Since the decline of full-fashioned hose, these machines are used mainly on fashioned outerwear* (see pp 172-4)

Council to replace the former Cotton Board. But the new conception does not necessarily imply more vertically integrated combines. In the vertically integrated concern there is always the problem of balancing the successive stages with their differing optimum scales of production. Thus Courtaulds' numerous subsidiaries absorb only a portion of the parent company's fibre output and adding more subsidiaries would increase the difficulties of management. Moreover the subsidiaries themselves, in the interests of both technical and commercial efficiency, must be allowed some freedom in buying yarns. Then there are constraints that may be imposed by government in the public interest. In 1965 the Monopolies Commission investigated the case of cellulosic fibres, the inquiry being directed particularly at Courtaulds. The report published in 1968 acknowledged Courtaulds' contribution towards strengthening the British textile industry and agreed that, on balance, vertical integration had not acted against the public interest. It did, however, recommend that any further acquisitions should be subject to the Board of Trade's permission.

By 1970 the motivation for further acquisitions by either Courtaulds or ICI had been weakened by the somewhat disappointing results of vertical integration. There was, in fact, some movement in the opposite direction of vertical disintegration with the growth of firms specialising in knitted fabric for sale to makers-up. This was encouraged by the increasing substitution of knitted for woven fabrics by manufacturers of clothing and household textiles; warp and weft, or circular knitted fabric was sold in this way instead of being converted in the hosiery and knitwear industry. Indeed, the warp knitters, especially, were coming to regard themselves as no longer belonging to the industry in which their process had originated. Nevertheless, they share an interest with the hosiery industry in technological development and also in the market for their products, since most of their output goes into garments.

The result of the changes so far described is a certain loss of identity. On the one hand we have a section of the knitting industry linked with other branches of textiles and clothing manufacture in vertically integrated groups; on the other, specialist knitters supplying the clothing and making-up trades in the same way as weavers. But the hosiery industry as traditionally defined was still growing. Here again, however, the traditional

N

structure was changing. In the past growth had been sustained more by the entry of new firms than by the expansion of a few leading concerns. The great majority of firms, even some of the largest, were private companies, often with a strong family interest. Where nepotism restricted opportunities for promotion, able and enterprising employees would often break away and set up their own business, and it is a curious fact that the sons of hosiery manufacturers sometimes did the same.[15] However, after the 1939–45 war several factors combined to change the situation. Private companies without access to capital through a public issue of shares were handicapped by the ever-rising costs of equipment, and owners of family businesses were particularly vulnerable to the demands of taxation. But the formation of public companies and the floatation of share issues requires the services of specialised institutions and the appearance of many such institutions in this period was a notable feature of the capital market. As a result, members of the hosiery industry became more familiar with the ways of the investment market than before the war and there was also more knowledge of the industry among the investing public. The formation of public companies with bigger financial resources was undertaken, in some instances, as a means of strengthening bargaining power in dealing with the large yarn suppliers on the one hand and the chain store buyers on the other. Moreover, large manufacturers undertaking market research, design innovation and brand promotion could aspire to partnership with the big retailers in developing their trade, instead of serving as mere contractors.

In the hosiery industry, as elsewhere, growth in the scale of enterprise has usually involved the merging or grouping of firms. Although economies of scale in manufacture are limited, a concern owning several plants can rationalise both the distribution of machines and the allocation of orders. There are marketing advantages in having a varied range and a firm may find it convenient to extend its range by acquiring an existing specialised firm rather than by internal expansion. Then there is the possibility of managerial economies. Hitherto, the hosiery industry had been somewhat backward in its management methods. It was largely inbred both with regard to its supply of capital and of talent. But after the last war a change began. The increase of productivity became a matter of national concern and this directed attention to the improvement of management. New techniques and new forms of expertise were developed, sometimes inspired by American examples, and they were taken up by the more progressive firms in many industries, including hosiery. Such firms were able to attract capital and managerial ability and they sought further scope for their superior resources in taking over other businesses where assets were under-employed because of lack of capital or deficiencies in management. They found willing sellers among owners wanting to retire or wanting to reduce their responsibilities, or perhaps welcoming the chance to participate in the direction of a larger concern.

The effect of grouping in the hosiery industry is shown in the census of production returns of 1958 and 1963, which give for the first time particulars of both enterprises and establishments. Although employment continued to grow, the number of enterprises (defined as one or more firms under common ownership or control), employing more than 25 persons fell from 604 to 500. The number of establishments fell too, but only from 830 to 794, so that the average of establishments per firm increased from 1.38 to 1.59. There were still very many small separate businesses the inclusion of which brought the total number of enterprises to 924 in 1963, but five years earlier it had been 1,112. The position with regard to what are called the 'larger' firms is shown in the table below.

SIZE DISTRIBUTION OF FIRMS & ESTABLISHMENTS 1963

Average number employed by the enterprise in the industry	Number of Firms	Number of Establishments	Number Employed	Net Output £'000
25–49	134	136	4,934	4,396
50–99	151	168	10,543	10,185
100–199	94	117	13,402	14,400
200–299	42	64	9,954	8,512
300–399	14	20	4,592	4,228
400–499	8	24	3,698	3,107
500–749	25	79	14,955	14,856
750–999	7	26	6,062	5,253
1,000–1,499	15	75	18,225	17,463
1,500–1,999	5	22	8,473	7,040
2,000 and over	5	63	22,570	21,408
Total	500	794	117,408	110,845

It will be seen that large firms, which in the hosiery context may be defined as firms with 1,000 employees or more, now number 25. In 1930, when census returns were also based on firms, there were only 12 in this size group and about 21 per cent of hosiery workers were employed in them. In 1963 the large firms accounted for 42 per cent of total employment and about the same proportion of total output. They controlled altogether 160 establishments and in the largest size group there was an average of nearly 13 establishments per firm.

It is evident that in the hosiery industry the emergence of large firms does not imply any marked tendency towards concentration of manufacture in large plants. Efforts to increase the size of plant have no doubt been frustrated to some extent by local labour shortages and by the government's distribution of industry policy with its aim of taking the work to the worker. But British hosiery manufacturers are still sceptical about the advantages of mass production; they emphasise the great variety of the trade and the limitations of the British market, in contrast with the USA which offers more opportunity for specialisation. Structural change has taken the form of a merger of firms rather than the concentration of manufacture. The typical large firm is now a group of enterprises, each of which may have its branch establishments. Subsidiary members of a group often continue to trade in their own names and in their own branded lines, but they are in some degree subordinate to the parent company which determines group policy.

The extent of these structural changes must not be exaggerated; the hosiery and knitwear industry still affords scope for independent small-scale enterprise, but this is no longer so characteristic. Throughout its history the industry adapted but slowly to the changing economic environment. Its 'industrial revolution' was long delayed and the 'managerial revolution', which was already attracting attention in the 1920s, hardly affected the hosiery industry until the 1960s. The rapidity of recent changes is therefore the more impressive. They have been brought about partly by external forces and partly by pressures from within the industry and they are likely to continue. In a larger sense they are seen as belonging to a movement which is transforming the whole textile and clothing group.

CHAPTER 14

LABOUR AND MANAGEMENT

The growth of employment in the British hosiery industry, as measured by the number of insured workers, reached a peak of 120,800 in 1939. The 1969 figure was 133,700 and although not strictly comparable with the pre-war total because of administrative changes, it indicates a further growth of some 10 per cent. This is a moderate increase in relation to the expansion of production as shown in Chapter 12. One reason is the greater regularity of employment; between the wars unemployment never fell below 6 per cent and in some years was much higher, whereas between 1945 and 1970 it rarely exceeded 2 per cent. There was also less short-time working; the percentage of workers involuntarily on short-time was 2.4 at the June count in 1969; in 1924 it was 11.0 and in 1931, 10.1.[1]

The steadiness of employment in contrast with the fluctuations of earlier years is due basically to the general scarcity of suitable labour. Variations in demand are still something of a problem; a cold spring, for instance, can have serious repercussions in some sections of the trade, or a fashionable line may suddenly fall from favour. But workers threatened by unemployment or short-time can usually transfer to busier firms. On the other hand, employers have a strong motive for keeping their labour force intact by improving their business methods. Continuity of employment has also been assisted by the increasing trade with chain stores which place bulk orders, ensuring long runs. All this makes for more effective use of the available labour. But the gain is offset to some extent by a reduction in hours worked. The normal working week was 40 hours in 1969 as against 48 hours before the war, but the excess of overtime over short-time brought the average weekly hours of men to 42.8. Few women worked overtime and their average for 'full-time' workers was 37.6 hours, while part-time workers, 13.5 per cent of all female employees, averaged 23.2 hours. In 1924 the average weekly hours of both male and female employees were 44.2; there are no comparable figures for the 1930s. Paradoxical as it may seem, the shorter hours worked by women is a reflection of the scarcity of female labour. The industry is now heavily dependent on married women and hours have to be adjusted to their domestic circumstances. Moreover, the money incentive to work longer hours is likely to be weak in married women.

Judging by the number of vacancies advertised in 1970 there was still a considerable unsatisfied demand for operatives, especially women. But continuing improvement in techniques and changes in the industry's products meant that labour shortage became less of a handicap to growth. Knitting was now a capital-intensive process. Although basic to the whole industry and in some sections representing the main value of output, it employed in 1968 only 13,650 people (9,380 men and 4,270 women) or about one-tenth of the total labour force.[2] In the exclusively women's occupations, mainly sewing and other making-up processes, technical progress was less marked. But employment was affected considerably by changes in the nature of output. The simpler garments now in vogue called for less sewing and cutting out, while the substitution of seamless for full-fashioned stockings and the remarkable versatility of modern knitting machines, largely eliminated seaming, welting and linking. The effect of all this was to reduce female employment, which averaged about 80 per cent of the total in the 1930s, to 66.5 per cent by 1970. In this year the industry employed fewer women than before the war. Common to manufacturing industries generally, is the increasing proportion of administrative, technical and clerical workers. The number of men so engaged was 21 per cent of the total in 1968 and of women 10 per cent. This results from many factors: the use of more sophisticated management methods in the bigger firms, the demands of legislation, the expansion of employee services, the growth of maintenance work and the employment of specialists for tasks formerly performed by machine operatives.

A fairly high proportion of hosiery workers can be described as skilled. They include those engaged in such occupations as knitting, cutting, machining, mending, trimming and folding. But in many operations the traditional skills are less needed. Knitting machines are more automatic in action and sewing machines are equipped with various attachments making for easier control.

Making-up has also been simplified to some extent by specialisation, so that the machinist concentrates on a single simple operation. The incidence of such developments varies according to the size of firm and the nature of its products, but the general tendency is to shift the emphasis from craftsmanship to speed and concentration of effort.

These changes have affected the nature and organisation of training. The transition to factory production in the latter part of the nineteenth century was accompanied by a revival of apprenticeship after its decline in the long years of depression among the framework knitters. Trade unionism was a growing force among the power-frame operators, and its aim was to maintain the status of a skilled occupation and to strengthen the member's bargaining power by controlling entry. As more unions were formed most of them adopted rules relating to young workers. For instance, the Nottingham and District Hosiery Workers' Society, formed by an amalgamation in 1925, forbade its members to employ a boy on a frame without consent of the committee, and the boy must not work in the absence of the journeyman. The society endeavoured to limit the number of apprentices on the basis of one to every four men in a shop. No boy over the age of 16 was to be taught without permission, but a learner starting at 14 might be considered competent after five years; another two years must elapse, however, before he could take a boy himself. Where a man and a boy worked together, the latter, after a few months of time work, was to be paid so much in the pound of their joint earnings. The Leicester and Leicestershire Trimmers Association had similar rules and Hinckley and District Warehousemen's Association attempted to regulate apprenticeship to folding.[3]

The effectiveness of such rules, however, varied greatly from district to district and even from firm to firm within districts. In any case there were many occupations where apprenticeship was clearly irrelevant. This was becoming true even in knitting. There was, for instance, little restriction of entry into the seamless hose branch, where the average learner could become an efficient machine-minder after a few months' training. Many women were employed on this work; the only advantage held by men was in their ability to manage more machines and to work shifts. In trimming and folding, too, women were encroaching on what the unions regarded as a male preserve. As for the traditional women's occupations, the training period varied with firms and with individual operatives, ending when the worker went 'on her own time'. This meant a change from time work to piece work and it occurred when the worker was able to earn something like the normal wage for the occupation.

In a report of 1927 on 'Apprenticeship and Training for the Skilled Occupations in Great Britain' the Ministry of Labour showed that in the hosiery industry the great majority of boys and girls in all occupations were recruited and trained under a very indefinite system of learnership. The working party of 1946 was also critical of existing conditions and recommended the establishment of a national joint apprenticeship and training council for the industry. At that time the most urgent need was to increase the supply of skilled knitters, especially in the full-fashioned hose trade, and the working party was sceptical about the customary four-year apprenticeship. It quoted American experience, which showed that by careful selection and systematic training a competent knitter could be produced in six to twelve months. In Britain a few firms had set up training departments for knitters and for women machinists. But the general practice was for young knitters to learn the job by assisting a skilled operative, while girl machinists would be started on simple tasks under the overlooker's supervision and gradually introduced to more complicated work.

Facilities for more formal and comprehensive training were, however, available at technical colleges in Leicester, Nottingham, Loughborough, Hinckley and Hawick. In the years between the wars the hosiery departments of these institutions gave a much-needed impetus to technical education, and the more enlightened firms helped with funds, plant and materials. They also encouraged employees to attend courses by paying fees and allowing day-release. But these were a small minority; most of those attending were evening students without any sponsorship by their employers. There was no specific training for management or supervision; although the curriculum might include a course in business administration, the emphasis was on the technical aspect of the industry. This was appropriate in a scheme of basic training and some young men, often manufacturers' sons, took a full-time diploma course before embarking on their business career. But success in business demanded more than technical qualifications, and the general feeling in the hosiery industry was that the requisite qualities could best be developed through practical experience. The feeling was prevalent throughout British industry, but it was naturally strong under the conditions of small-scale enterprise characteristic of the hosiery trade.

After the 1939–45 war industrial training and training for management at all levels became matters for national concern. Economic recovery and sustained growth were seen to depend on rising productivity, and international comparisons, particularly with the USA, showed how far Britain lagged behind. The superior productivity of American industry was due to several factors, eg the size of plants and the wealth of capital equipment, but all investigators emphasised the importance given to training. This came out in the report of the team representing the hosiery and knitwear industry which visited the USA in 1950 under the auspices of the Anglo-American Council on Productivity. They found that the standard of technical knowledge was no higher than in the best British firms. But 'technical knowledge', they declared, 'needs to be backed by the highest standards of administrative practice'. It was their 'considered opinion that in this field reside major possibilities for increased production efficiency in our industry'.

The accumulation of such evidence from more and more industries and from other countries besides America had its impact on British industry and educational institutions. But in many industries systematic training was still confined to a minority of progressive firms, and eventually it was decided that government action was needed to raise the general standard. Under the Industrial Training Act of 1964 training boards were set up, whereby the provision of facilities became a collective responsibility of the industries concerned.

The Knitting, Lace and Net Training Board is equally representative of employers and employees and includes also educational members. Others are associated with its work through membership of its five sub-committees concerned, respectively, with operative, commercial, technical and management training and research. The board's resources are mostly derived from a levy of one per cent on the payroll of firms within its scope. This produced £1,108,056 in 1969–70, most of which was returned to firms with approved training schemes, eg for the training and payment of instructors, and for employees attending day-release and part-time courses and conferences. As might be expected, the greater part of the fund went to finance operative training; there were 20,712 operative trainees in 1969-70, and about three-quarters of the total grant to employers was on this account. Experience showed that substantial savings could be obtained in learning times and training costs. Progress in management training at the higher levels of technical education was somewhat disappointing and in 1970 the board set up a working party to investigate the position.[4]

Complementary to the improvement of human resources through education and training is the organisation and application of technological research. Before 1945 the hosiery industry showed little initiative in this respect. Mechanical innovation was in the hands of machine-builders while progress in the range and quality of materials and in processing methods was the responsibility of yarn suppliers, dyers and finishers. A few of the larger hosiery manufacturers had research departments but their total expenditure was probably not much over £10,000 a year.[5] However, in 1945, a Hosiery Research Council was formed by the joint action of the manufacturers' federation and that of the Midland dyers and finishers. Following the working party's strong recommendation for the development of research on a co-operative basis the council established in 1949 the present Hosiery and Allied Trades Research Association. Although operating until 1969 on a voluntary basis and largely concerned with consulting work for individual members, HATRA has always aimed at developing fundamental research for the benefit of the industry as a whole. At its Nottingham headquarters there are well-equipped laboratories and workshops, an extensive library and facilities for training. In 1969, its financial basis was strengthened by a statutory order for a compulsory levy on manufacturers and this will not only foster the development of research but will also assist the wider dissemination of the results.

HATRA is not directly concerned with economic affairs or business methods and policy. These matters are covered to some extent by the manufacturers' federation and its constituent bodies which include a large proportion of firms in the industry. Trade associations vary widely in their range of functions. In contrast with many such institutions the hosiery manufacturers' federation has made important contributions towards increasing business efficiency, eg through the improvement of accounting methods and the introduction of inter-firm comparisons. It is however a voluntary organisation, representing only one interest and that to only a limited extent. The working party had recommended a development council with employer and employee representatives and a number of government-appointed independent members. This, like similar proposals for other industries proved unacceptable at the time, but later the idea was revived. In 1962 the Conservative government, newly converted to the idea of national economic planning, set up a National Economic Development Council and this in turn gave birth to a number of Economic Development Committees for individual industries, including hosiery and knitwear.

The EDC has two declared objects: firstly, to review the industry's performance, prospects and plans; and secondly, to consider means for improving performance and adaptation to changing economic conditions. It has given particular attention to the future demand for British hosiery and knitwear as affected by social and economic conditions and by trends in marketing and in international trade. It has also been concerned with labour resources and the effects of technological developments on productivity and costs. Among its various reports the most comprehensive is 'Hosiery and Knitwear in the 1970s' based on research by a firm of consultants. It is described as 'a first attempt to equip the industry with a picture of its likely future environment'. However, at the time of writing the future of the EDC itself is uncertain, being dependent on government finance. The committee has met a need not hitherto provided for, but it could be argued that the industry is sufficiently well organised for collective action to carry on the work with its own resources.

Collective action in relations between management and labour has a long history in the hosiery industry. The first effort in the 1860s ultimately failed in circumstances already described,[6] but voluntary collective bargaining was eventually revived and gradually strengthened. In contrast with the clothing trades, which it resembles in some ways, the hosiery industry has never needed a statutory wages council.

As we have seen, the transition to factory production in the latter part of the nineteenth century stimulated trade unionism among the skilled men in the industry. Few women factory workers were attracted, however, and as late as the 1930s only about 20 per cent were trade unionists, though among men the proportion was twice as great. As might be expected, labour organisation was strongest in Leicester and Nottingham, while Hinckley and Loughborough had a fair number of union members.[7] But in the hosiery villages and in the new localities remote from the main centres organisation was still as difficult as in the early days of the factory system and the competition of low-paid country workers was as keenly felt.

One reason for the rather slow progress of trade unionism, despite the growth of employment, was in the sectional character of organisation. Some consolidation had been effected in the latter years of the nineteenth century and by 1925 the number of unions had been further reduced. There were now only six in the East Midlands as compared with 14 in 1897. An important step was the formation of the Nottingham and District Hosiery Workers' Society which, like its counterpart in Leicestershire, established 40 years earlier, united various craft unions together with an organisation catering for women hosiery workers. But the achievement of full industrial unionism was still delayed. Even the National Hosiery Federation was not fully representative owing to the aloofness of the Scottish workers, many of whom had joined the hosiery branch of the National Union of General and Municipal Workers.

The employers were similarly organised on a district basis with a National Federation which in the 1930s claimed to speak for 90 per cent of the trade in the East Midlands, but it did not include the Scottish section, whose members had their own West of Scotland Hosiery Manufacturers' Association.

In the sphere of industrial relations the great achievement of the inter-war period was the formation of the National Joint Industrial Council for the Hosiery Industry. Ever since the break-up of the old conciliation boards there had been a strong body of opinion among the workers in favour of their revival, but the employers remained sceptical. However, during the 1914–18 war, both workers and employers strengthened their organisations, and it became clear that if disputes were to be avoided a joint body was required to deal with the problems that would arise when the industry returned to peace-time conditions. An approach was made in 1917 by the Nottingham Rotary Power Framework Knitters' Society, but consideration was postponed pending the report of the Whitley Committee on relations between employers and employed.[8] Thus when the Whitley scheme for joint industrial councils appeared the ground had already been prepared and the hosiery industry was one of the first to adopt it. Unlike so many similar bodies established in the 1920s it continued to function with remarkable success.

One reason for this success is the practice of holding regular quarterly meetings; the council does not come into operation only when disputes have arisen. Much of its business concerns matters of common interest as affecting the industry's welfare and efficiency; its negotiating functions are confined to general conditions of employment such as holidays-with-pay, the guaranteed week and fall-back rates. Until 1970 wage negotiations were conducted mainly by the employers' district associations and trade union branches, and often by officials of these bodies dealing with individual firms. Such decentralisation was inevitable in an industry so varied in its output and equipment and subject to rapid technological change, with a considerable range of occupations and skills and most of its operatives on piece rates. In the 1960s, however, the big firms, which were under-represented in the district associations began to press for more say in negotiations. Further, it became evident that the employers needed a central organisation as a counterpart to the workers' national union; their existing federation, though effective as a trade association, had no power to make wage agreements. They therefore set up a separate Employers' Association, but it proved unsatisfactory since its membership was not co-extensive with that of the federation. Finally, in 1970, the Knitting Industries Federation was established to replace the two existing organisations; it acts as a trade association and, through its Industrial Relations Board, as a medium for general, as distinct from local, wage negotiations.

The council of the new federation has one-third of its members nominated by the big firms, another third nominated by the district associations, of which eight (including the Scottish federation) are recognised, and the remainder elected from the general membership. However, despite the concessions made to the interests of the large employers, the Courtaulds group, representing about one-fifth of the industry, remained outside. This weakened the representative character of the federation somewhat; but with a membership of 550 firms, employing about two-thirds of the industry's labour force, and the extension of its functions in industrial relations, the new body should prove effective.

While this reorganisation was in progress the employers were faced with a claim for a general increase in wages. Hitherto, general adjustments had been effected by the cost of living bonus introduced during the first world war, but this automatic device, which takes no account of rising productivity and the industry's capacity to pay, was abandoned in 1967 and wages were left to be determined by piecemeal negotiations influenced by pressures in the labour market. The claim now presented was for a national increase of 12½ per cent on all earnings and the employers, in return, insisted on the acceptance of four-shift working in appropriate sections of the trade. This concession was refused and a national strike, unprecedented in the industry's history, was threatened. It was averted by the intervention of the NJIC under its independent chairman, who secured agreement on a 10 per cent wage increase, the shift proposal being dropped. The settlement was influenced by the fact that the two biggest employers—the Courtaulds group and Corahs of Leicester—had already come to terms with the union: the agreement covering the rest of the industry organised for collective bargaining followed similar lines.[9]

This episode illustrates the NJIC's continuing role as conciliator. Its negotiating function is limited to what its members are prepared to allow; but it is the most widely representative organisation in the industry and its regular meetings have undoubtedly done much to foster the generally good relations between management and labour that now exist. However, the crisis of 1970 did show the need for a stronger organisation on the employers' side to match the growing power of labour, represented since 1946 by the National Union of Hosiery and Knitwear Workers.

The formation of this industrial union to replace the former federation was the culmination of a movement begun many years before. It was not quite completed in 1970; the Hinckley warehousemen, for instance, still had their own association and many Scottish workers were separately organised. But with 58,276 members—13,473 men and 44,803 women—in 1968 the national union was in a fairly strong position. The increase in female membership from about 20 per cent of total employment in the 1930s to nearly 50 per cent in 1969 is particularly impressive. The union is organised in ten districts, including Scotland, and each trade section has its own committee.

Much of the union's work is done at district level in dealings with individual firms or with employers' district associations. It is largely concerned with applying principles and standards laid down in national agreements to particular cases. Most problems arise in connection with piece rates and the related matter of work loads, the union's objective being to ensure that effort-earnings are as uniform as possible throughout the industry.

The traditional piece-rate system has been consistently upheld by the unions in the belief that it gives the worker a better chance of benefiting by improvements in machinery that might otherwise result in mere speeding-up without any increase in earnings. The system is also favoured by employers as offering the easiest means of securing a high output per operative and per machine. But in knitting, especially, rapid technical progress has created some difficult problems in wage determination. Faster machines increase productivity, perhaps with little or no extra effort on the operator's part, yet the worker expects to share in the gain. As machines become more automatic it becomes feasible to increase the number of machines per operator, or to employ semi-skilled minders, which may provoke union resistance. There is also the question of relative rates for similar work done on new and older machines.

A frequent cause of dispute is lack of care in rate fixing when a new machine, a new process or a new material is introduced. In such cases the earnings on a particular job may get seriously out of line with the normal level for the occupation. Trouble of this kind can be avoided by scientific work-study and measurement, and the use of these techniques has been encouraged by the employers' associations and also by union officials, most of whom have received appropriate training. The union is particularly insistent on consultation where work-study is applied, as a means of safeguarding the workers' interests and also as establishing confidence in the system.

Another matter for local negotiation is the conditions applying to shift working. The system is accepted in principle and many knitters are now on a three-shift basis, which involves night work and thus precludes the employment of women. The increasing cost of knitting machines and their rapid obsolescence emphasises the need for better utilisation and the extension of the system to include week-end working was an issue in the 1970 dispute. So far, the union has resisted the so-called rotating shift system involving week-end working, to which there are obvious social objections. It is also of doubtful value where women and young people are employed in ancillary operations, although there are suggestions for overcoming this difficulty by substituting men in such work. Within the present system, however, such questions as the timing of shifts, break periods and premium payments call for local negotiations.

AVERAGE EARNINGS AND HOURS IN A PARTICULAR WEEK
IN THE HOSIERY INDUSTRY

	1924		1931		1955		1969	
	M	F	M	F	M	F	M	F
Earnings	54/8	28/8	58/8	30/3	246/3	118/11	466/2	252/5
Hours	42.2	44.2	NA	NA	45.6	41.1	42.8	37.6

In interpreting the earnings figures in this table, two points must be borne in mind: firstly, the wide range of earnings among piece workers, and secondly, the effect of the cost of living bonus. This bonus was an addition of so much in the shilling to basic rates, ie the hourly earnings of an average worker. In 1930 the bonus made up 35 per cent of total earnings and it fell between 1924 and 1931 in sympathy with the cost of living index number. Yet despite this downward bias average earnings rose. Moreover 1931 was a year of trade depression when hours worked would certainly be no higher than in 1924. The indication is that the efficiency of production was rising and that labour was increasing its share of the gain. In 1955 the bonus element had increased to 66 per cent of earnings, and it exerted an upward bias, but in the following years the rise in money earnings far exceeded the effect of this automatic adjustment based on the index of retail prices. As in other industries, real wages rose in response to pressure in the labour market. However, in presenting their case for a general wage increase in 1970 the hosiery workers claimed that they had fared less well than others, and despite the fact that output per man-hour had risen 52 per cent since 1961, compared with 38 per cent for all manufacturing industries. Hosiery was no longer a labour-intensive industry, and a $12\frac{1}{2}$ per cent increase in wages would, they contended, add no more than 3 per cent to manufacturers' selling prices, which had, indeed, risen by only 8 per cent since 1961 as against 24 per cent for manufactures generally. In the light of past experience it seemed reasonable to suppose that the effect of increased wages would be offset by further improvements in productivity.[10]

It is of some interest to compare the recent trend of earnings in the hosiery industry with that in related trades. In 1931 men

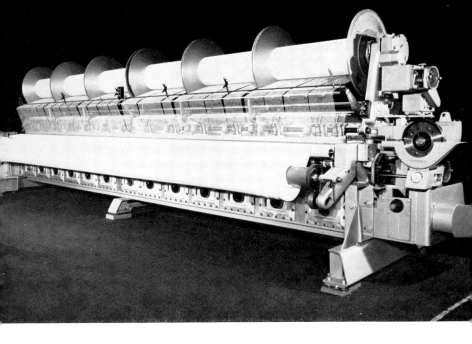

page 215 (above) *A German warp knitting machine making plain fabric. The warp threads are carried on a beam, as shown. The threads, controlled by guide-bars are looped on the needles and joined sideways. This produces a more rigid fabric than simple knitting;* (below) *a warp knitting machine making lace. Patterning effected by using a multiplicity of guide-bars for manipulating the threads. This machine has 30 guide-bars. The controlling mechanism is shown on the right (see p 181)*

page 216 (left) *A circular frame making patterned fabric. This machine, with 48 feeders, can knit 12-14 yards of three-colour fabric per hour. It has a 30 inch diameter cylinder; (below) a plant of automatic seamless-hose frames (see p 180)*

hosiery workers had the second highest earnings in the textile and clothing groups, being exceeded only by silk and artificial silk and high-class clothing. Women hosiery workers were the best paid in the textile group, but they earned less than those in certain sections of the clothing group, eg mantles and costumes, millinery and fur. By 1955 men hosiery workers had become by far the best paid in textiles and clothing. The women's earnings exceeded those in all the clothing trades, though women did better in cotton, woollen and worsted and man-made fibres. In 1969 man-made fibres headed the list for male textile workers, followed by the small narrow fabrics industry; but among the rest, and in comparison with the entire clothing group, hosiery was well ahead. This was also true of women in comparison with the clothing group, and in the textile trades hosiery earnings were exceeeded only by those in the narrow fabrics industry.

These relative movements in earnings are due to various influences. Women hosiery workers have benefited from the acute scarcity of labour, particularly sewing-machinists, in the main centres of the industry where newer trades like light engineering are strong competitors for female labour. Conditions for men became somewhat less favourable in the 1960s because of the decline in the full-fashioned hose trade in which very high wages could be earned. But the union was able to take advantage of the continuous improvement of machines to force up earnings in other branches.

The economic position of both men and women workers is also strengthened by the fact that direct labour accounts for only a relatively small proportion of total costs, including manufacturer's profit margin. In 1968 it was estimated at 20.6 per cent for full-fashioned knitwear and 18 per cent for seamless stockings. The overall figure in 1924 was 21.5 per cent. Wage increases will however increase the proportion and raise selling prices unless offset by further improvements in machines and in work organisation. Hitherto, such improvements have helped to contain the effects of rising wages. The consumer has also benefited by the comparative cheapness of man-made fibres and by the reduction of selling costs effected by Marks and Spencer and other large distributors. However, a continuing rise in wages can hardly fail to raise selling prices, and the industry's prospects will depend on the proportion of consumers' income spent on knitwear. For the British industry in particular there is also the question of

o

imports and exports. At the cheaper end of the trade the cost disadvantage of British manufacturers seems likely to increase; but there appears to be a growing demand, both at home and abroad, for goods in which quality in design compensates for expensive labour and high selling price.

REFERENCES

Chapter 1 (p 15)

1 Cunningham, *Growth of English Industry and Commerce: Modern Times*, 26. In Elizabeth's reign it was complained that people had left off wearing caps, and for the encouragement of the trade an Act was passed (13 Eliz c 19) requiring every person, with a few exceptions, to wear one on Sundays and Holy Days.

2 Quoted in *Wealth of Nations*, 245 (Cannan's edition).

3 Ibid.

4 *VCH Surrey*, Vol 2, 365.

5 Heaton, *Yorkshire Woollen and Worsted Industries*, 265.

6 Postlethwayte, *Dictionary of Trade and Commerce* (1774).

7 *Giving Alms No Charity* (1704), 19.

8 Postlethwayte, op cit.

9 Bremner, *The Industries of Scotland* (1869), 173. See also article by Thos Henderson, 'The Scottish Hosiery Trade', in *Scottish Banker's Magazine*, October 1910.

10 Brand, *A Brief Description of Orkney, Zetland, etc.* (1701), 132.

11 Pennant, *Tour of Scotland* (1769), 137.

12 Postlethwayte, op cit.

13 *Truck Commission, Second Report*, 1872, XXXV, 45.

14 *Committee on Truck Acts*, 1908, LIX, 118 et seq. The fact that the knitters were not employees made it difficult to check the practice of the merchants who compelled them to take goods in payment for their products.

15 'At present worsted stockings are sold as high as 8s. or 9s. a pair.' *SPD*, CCXXXI, 1590, 652.

16 *History of Notts* (1677), Vol 1, 42.

17 Notts County Record Office.

18 Gravenor Henson, *History of the Framework Knitters* (1831, reprinted Newton Abbot 1970), 39 et seq.

19 Price, *The English Patents of Monopoly*, 8.

20 Hunsdon was himself engaged in the woollen trade; in 1589 he was granted a licence 'to transport 20,000 broadcloths for the space of six years'. Ibid, 142.

21   The Carey family maintained their connection with the trade for many years. A record preserved by the Framework Knitters' Company states that 'Lord Rd. Carey, Earl of Hunsdon, was admitted a member on 25th June, 1666 and in 1677 was admitted a workhouse keeper and bound Wm. Pope apprentice'.

22   A letter in *SPD*, 1611, 4 July, Vol LXV, 54, suggests that the frame was actually prohibited. The writer begs the favour of Sir Dudley Carleton 'for Mr. Joiner who is going to Venice to practise the silk loom stocking weaving which is not permitted in England for fear of ruining the knitters'. In a letter dated 20 August, it is reported that 'the English stocking weavers, after fruitless experiments here, have gone over to Venice'.

23   Deering, *Nottinghamia Vetuset Nova* (1715), 100

24   The contract is reproduced from the original document in *Stockings for a Queen* by Milton and Anna Grass (1967). Some of its provisions are rather obscure and I offer my own interpretation.

25   These events are recounted in the framework knitters' petition to Cromwell, 1655, see below

26   *SPD*, 1611, Vol LXV.

27   Henson, op cit, 53.

28   Petition to Cromwell.

29   Henson, op cit, 57.

30   *Tour Through England and Wales*, Vol II, 89 (Everyman edition).

31   Op cit, 60.

32   *Acts of Scottish Parliament*, 1661, Vol VII, 261.

33   Scott, *Records of a Scottish Cloth Manufactory* (1905).

34   This amounts to about £56 each in English money.

35   Chapman, 'The Genesis of the British Hosiery Industry', *Textile History* (forthcoming).

36   Bremner, op cit, 177.

37   Adam Smith, *Wealth of Nations* (1776), Vol I, 119.

Chapter 2 (p 28)

1   See Unwin, *Industrial Organization in the VIth and VIIth Centuries*.

2   Ibid, 104.

3   At Beverley in 1492 express permission was granted to the drapers to 'make hose and keep apprentices and servants sewing in their shops without hindrance or any payment to the Tailors' craft'; and a sixteenth-century ordinance for Worcester declared 'hyte shall be lawful to the saide drapers and their

apprentices to make women's hoses as they heretofore have used'. Westerfield, *Middlemen in English Business*, 307-8.

4 Op cit, 96.

5 Even in the later eighteenth century the maker of a speciality might sell it direct to the public. For instance, the frame-knitted velvet which Ross patented in 1767 was in such demand that he never employed agents to sell it. Ibid, 327. The first master stockingers were probably in a similar position.

6 *FWKs' Charter*, 1657.

7 Deering, op cit, 301-8, gives the full text. There is a summary in *SPD* (Letters and Papers) 1655, Vol 102, 156.

8 See Cunningham, op cit, 205.

9 *SPD*, 1655, Vol CII, 77.

10 J. D. Chambers, in his article 'The Worshipful Company of Framework Knitters' (*Economica*, November 1929), states that the contents of this charter are unknown as no copy has been preserved. In this he is mistaken, for there is a copy among the records kept by the company's clerk.

11 *SPD*, 1658, Vol CLXXXIV, 215.

12 Ibid, 1660, Vol XXII, 373; 1661, Vol XXXII, 532.

13 Colonial Entry Book, No 1, 1660.

14 The charter did not extend to Scotland. Framework knitting had not yet been established in that country, but Parliament had already made provision for the regulation, among other trades, of cloth and stocking manufacture. The Act of 1661 empowers 'the Masters, erectors or interteaners of manufactories to meit of themselves for the makeing of ordinances for the good and advancement of their trade, for the right ordering of their servants and for the sufficiency of their stuffs'. *Acts of Scottish Parliament*, 1661, Vol VII, 261.

15 Op cit, 84.

16 *SPD* (Petitions), 1660, Vol 22, Nos 20, 22.

17 Colonial Entry Book, No 1, 1660.

18 Henson, op cit, 87.

19 Any member of the company who had not already served in this capacity was liable to be elected as steward. It was his duty, according to the bylaws, to provide the officials with a dinner on Lord Mayor's day or on other occasions, failing which he must pay a fine varying from £6 to £10. In 1696 the company brought an action against a defaulting steward who refused to pay his penalty of £10. A verdict was given for the plaintiffs, but judgement was arrested on the ground that it was unreasonable to compel a man to make dinner only for the luxury of others; if, however, it had been to make the dinner to the end

that the company might assemble to choose officers or any other thing for the benefit of the corporation it had been reasonable enough. (King's Bench, 1696; Master and Company of FWKs *v* Green). Despite this verdict the practice was continued until near the end of the eighteenth century; the company's minute book contains numerous cases of fines being exacted from members who refused to serve as stewards.

20 *HCJ*, Vol 11, 27 and 51.

21 Ibid, Vol 13, 1699, 316.

22 Op cit, 95.

23 Henson, op cit, 96.

24 The Admittance Book (1713-24) shows regular admittances at Nottingham and a number at Leicester and Hinckley each year; Derby entries appear in 1724.

25 The serving of two writs brought twenty-two masters to the Nottingham court to bind their apprentices on one occasion. Letter Book, November 2, 1725.

26 Letter Book, 26 July 1725.

27 Ibid, 7 December.

28 Ibid, 19 July 1725. The attorneys managing the case declared that they expected to obtain an injunction against the company.

29 Ibid, 1 March 1726.

30 Letter Book. In informing the Nottingham deputies of the result the master and wardens declare their intention of bringing another case after having the mistake rectified.

31 The Admittance Book has only three entires for 1727, five for 1728, eight for 1729, and six for 1730.

32 Letter Book, 28 August 1729.

33 Ibid, 30 January 1730.

34 Letter Book, 14 October 1730.

35 Letter Book, 4 December 1831.

36 Ibid, 1 December 1731.

37 Ibid, 5 April 1732.

38 This is important as showing that a charter granted by the Crown but without the confirmation of Parliament would not necessarily be upheld in the courts. The charter expressly required all framework knitters to become members of the company and in that case the bylaws would automatically apply throughout the trade.

39 Letter Book, 20 May 1732.

40 A list of 190 promotions including that of the framework knitters is given by W. R. Scott, *Joint Stock Companies*, Vol III, 445-58.

41 The account of the joint stock scheme is based on extracts from the company's records quoted in *HCJ* as part of the evidence collected for the inquiry of 1753. There is no material relating to it among the existing records.

42 This seems a fantastic sum, but the framework knitters followed the prevailing fashion. Most of the projects described by Professor Scott were floated with a nominal capital of a million or more.

43 The Bubble Act, repealed 1825.

44 The highest price touched by the shares in 1720 was $12\frac{1}{2}$ times their par value. Scott, op cit, Vol I, 421.

45 Op cit, 147. Henson's verdict is that there was 'much to condemn and much to admire' in the scheme.

46 Court Book, 23 October 1746.

47 Ibid, 5 October 1742.

48 Op cit, 175.

49 Op cit, 216.

50 The full list is given in *HCJ*, Vol 26, 788-94.

51 The mention of male children suggests a desire to exclude women from the trade. In the earlier records there are several instances of apprentices being bound to women.

52 The Admittance Book records the first meeting on 29 October 1750.

53 The Account Book records the receipt of £24 7s in 1749 for 195 apprentices bound in London; but admittances do not reappear until 1754 and then only one or two at each court.

54 Court Book, 9 October 1750.

55 Admittance Book shows four admittances, 28 September 1751.

56 Henson, op cit, 184.

57 *HCJ*, Vol 26, 785.

58 Quoted in *HCJ*, Vol 26, 794. 'Colt' signified a framework knitter who had not served a regular apprenticeship.

59 *HCJ*, Vol 26, 781.

60 Ibid, Vol 26, 593-615.

61 The account published in the *Commons Journals* is, for this period, unusually full, and suggests the importance attached to the inquiry.

62 Evidence of John Page, fwk, Nottingham, and Thomas Eaton, fwk, Derby. *Commons Journal*, 781.

Chapter 3 (p 47)

1 Eden, *State of the Poor* (1797), 558-9.

2 It was stated in evidence before the Commons Committee of 1753 that hose were being made for $1\frac{1}{2}$d a pair at Nottingham.

Manufacturers could only secure the cheap trade by being able to employ women and children. *HCJ*, Vol 26, 781.

3 Throsby, *History of Leicester* (1791), 403. A descendant of Iliffe was still engaged in the hosiery manufacture at Hinckley in 1791.

4 Throsby gives the date of Alsop's settlement in Leicester as 1680, but Gardiner (*Music and Friends* [1835], Vol II, 810) puts it ten years earlier. The latter is probably nearer the mark, for, as the *Register of Freemen* (ed H. Hartopp, 1927) shows, there were two or three hosiers in Leicester by 1680, and in 1693 a former apprentice of Nicholas Alsop was made a freeman.

5 Thorsby, op cit, 403.

6 *Tour through England and Wales*, Vol II, 88.

7 Gardiner, op cit, 810.

8 Deering, op cit, 99.

9 Op cit, 106.

10 Henson, op cit, 170.

11 *HCJ*, 1753, Vol 26, 781.

12 Op cit, 100.

13 Hutton's *History of Derby* (1791), contains a full description of the mill and its machinery.

14 Warner, *The Silk Industry*, 201.

15 Op cit, 165. They had been worn much earlier, however. Pepys tells how he 'went up to the 'Change to buy a pair of cotton stockings'. *Diary*, 4 April 1665. These were probably imported, perhaps from India.

16 G. W. Daniels, *The Early English Cotton Industry*, 9.

17 Henson, op cit, 165.

18 This was an old complaint in the woollen branch. In 1703, for instance, the Irish House of Commons resolved 'that the making of worsted stockings of less than three threads or woollen stockings of less than two threads is a deceit and greatly prejudicial to the publick'. The masters and wardens of trade corporations were requested to test all goods and cause offenders to be prosecuted. *IHCJ*, 1703, Vol II, 410.

19 Henson, op cit, 130. For petition and summary of evidence, see *HCJ*, 1766, Vol 30, 545 and 697.

20 6 Geo III, c 29. Usually referred to as the Tewkesbury Act.

21 Mantoux, *Industrial Revolution in the Eighteenth Century*, 216.

22 Henson, op cit, 364.

23 Baines, *History of the Cotton Manufacture*, 134.

24 Henson, op cit, 364.

25 Baines, op cit, 158. Henson says one jenny had eighty-four spindles.

26 Many of the jennies were made by George Whitaker, a Nottingham framesmith, who also built the early carding machines used by hosiers. 'Trial of a cause to repeal a patent granted to Rd. Arkwright,' 1785.

27 Henson, op cit, 364.

28 Blackner, *History of Nottingham* (1815), 247, contends that Arkwright was also 'fearful that Hayes should hear what he was about and find friends to push his previous claim at the Patent Office'.

29 Ure, *Cotton Manufacture*, Vol I, 251.

30 Henson, op cit, 368.

31 *Beauties of England and Wales* (1802), Vol III, 519. The frequent flooding of the river at Nottingham made it impossible to employ water power; silk mills in the town were still driven by horses in 1813. Ibid, Vol XII, 37. There were, however, several watermills in the north of the county, some of which were later converted to steam power.

32 Felkin, op cit, 88-101.

33 *Beauties of England and Wales*, Vol III, 530.

34 Arkwright's case in *Trial of a Cause*.

35 Ure, op cit, 274.

36 Blackner, op cit, 247.

37 *Beauties of England and Wales*, Vol XII, 26.

38 Baines, op cit, 392.

39 Macpherson, *Annals of Commerce* (1785), Vol IV, 80.

40 Baines, op cit, 344.

41 Cunningham, op cit, 644. The price of wool doubled between 1780 and 1791.

42 Baines, op cit, 357. Fine cotton yarn was still worth 35s a pound in 1788, by 1793 it had fallen to 15s, and by 1804 to 7s 10d.

43 Blackner, op cit, 235.

44 Op cit, 114.

45 An indication of their temper had been given some years earlier when a crowd of country workers smashed a new frame, said to be capable of making a dozen pairs of hose at once, which was exhibited in the Leicester Exchange. On this occasion the hosiers were made to promise not to introduce any machine that might reduce employment. Thompson, *History of Leicester* (1871), 147, quoting account in *Leicester Journal*, 20 March 1773.

46 Gardiner, op cit, 82, 83.

47 Felkin, op cit, 230.

48 Throsby, *Memoirs of Leicester* (1777), Vol VI, 26.

49 Op cit, 235.

50 Framework knitting appears finally to have died out in Surrey about the middle of the nineteenth century. *VCH Surrey*, Vol 2,352.

51 O'Brien, *Economic History of Ireland from the Union to the Famine*, 434.

52 Felkin has a description of a hosier, the last example of this old school, who died in 1808 leaving £20,000. The business was owned by two brothers, one of whom superintended the manufacture, while the other performed the part of salesman. 'The latter made his journeys on foot to the London market, and might be seen in town with his samples strapped under his belt and cloak, visiting his customers.' Op cit, 437.

53 Throsby, *Memoirs*, Vol VI, 27.

54 Gardiner, op cit, 92.

55 Thomas, *I & R. Morley: a Record of a Hundred Years* (1900).

56 Jopp, *Corah of Leicester 1815–1965*.

Chapter 4 (p 60)

1   Unwin, op cit, App A 11.

2   *Early English Cotton Industry*, 36.

3   *HCJ*, 1779, Vol 37, 370.

4   Deering, op cit, 101.

5   *Report of Factory Commissioners*, 1833, Vol XX, 535.

6   This practice became so common that severe penalties were imposed. In 1836 a bagman at Leicester was fined £20, the lowest penalty, for receiving 2s 5d worth of stolen worsted. *Leicester Chronicle*, 16 September 1836. In 1839 a hosier's apprentice at Nottingham was sentenced to seven years' transportation for stealing silk. *Nottingham Journal*, 5 April 1839.

7   'Humanus', who is criticised by Cobbett in his *Weekly Register*, 14 April 1821.

8   An Act Touching Weavers, 2 and 3 Phil and Mary, c 11.

9   *Commission on FWKs*, 1845, 257.

10 *HCJ*, 1753, Vol 26, 593.

11 *HCJ*, 1779, Vol 37, 370. In 1770 a registry office for the hiring of frames was opened in Nottingham. *Nottingham Journal*, 8 September 1770.

12 Advertisements in the Nottingham press show that auctions of frames became increasingly frequent after about 1770; in the early nineteenth century almost every issue contains a sale announcement.

13 *Report of Commission on FWKs*, 1845, XV, 417, 512.

14 Evidence before House of Commons committee, 1779.

15 In 1780 an Alfreton hosier employing fifty frames stated that a number of these were hired at 20s to 26s a year; they were let to workers at the comparatively low rents of 1s for fine frames and 9d for coarse, but even this left a comfortable margin since presumably the owner would be responsible for repairs. *FWKs' Bill*, Reprint of Evidence, 1780. Derby Public Library.

   In 1845 frames were being let by framesmiths to middlemen and manufacturers by the year at the rate of 5d a week. *Commission on FWKs*, 48. Evidence at Leicester.

16 *Select Committee on FWKs' Petitions*, 1812, 18 and 28.

17 Ibid, 17.

18 *Commission on FWKs Report*, 1845, 45.

19 *Commission on FWKs*, 1845, 130.

20 Ibid, 17. A manufacturer owning some 2,000 frames estimated the net return at $7\frac{1}{2}$ per cent on capital.

21 *Committee on Stoppage of Wages in Hosiery Manufacture*, 1845-55, Vol XIV, 19.

22 *Leicester Chronicle*, 19 September 1836.

23 *Commission on FWKs' Petitions*, 1812, 61.

24 *Committee on FWKs' Petitions*, 1812.

25 Ibid, 20.

26 *Leicester Chronicle*, 27 August 1836.

27 Ibid, 13 February 1836.

28 See Dunlop, *English Apprenticeship and Child Labour*.

29 *Committee on FWKs' Petitions*, 1812, 35.

30 Op cit, 227.

31 *HCJ*, Vol 26, 781, 783.

32 *Committee on FWKs' Petitions*, 16, and *Second Report*, 75, 80.

33 Op cit, 455.

34 *Commission on FWKs*, 386.

35 Glover, *History of Derby* (1831), 208.

Chapter 5 (p 72)

1 See, for instance, *SPD*, 1678.

2 Collection of Proclamations, 1657-91. *BMG* 5302.

3 *HCJ*, Vol 11, 27, 533.

4 This is Henson's opinion, op cit, 87.

5 This was on the report of a committee appointed in 1695 to consider a petition of the Dublin stocking weavers. The petitioners, who were Protestants, freemen of the city, and had served their apprenticeship, complained that the charter, which had been procured by a popish attorney, was full of oppressions and grievances. According to their statement, it declared that 'no person should presume to keep any instrument or engine for

weaving stockings within the City of Dublin or within fifteen miles of the same'. *Irish HCJ*, Vol II, 64, 136. This wording, however, is misleading; what is meant, surely, is that the use of the frame was prohibited to anyone not a member of the company. It seems likely, especially in view of the reference to the 'popish attorney' who was clerk to the guild, that the petitioners were excluded because they were Protestants.

Although framework knitting was never very important in Ireland, records show that the company continued through the eighteenth century to play an active part in the civic life of Dublin as one of the twenty-four corporations.

6　Letter Book, 4 October 1726, 21 January and 11 April 1727.

7　On one occasion information was sent from Nottingham that eight worsted frames were about to be transported thence, and the London court replied that they would take steps to prevent it. Ibid, 18 August 1726.

8　Henson, op cit, 88.

9　*HCJ*, 1713, Vol 17, 366, 397.

10　The small export to France—5,820 dozens in 1668 and only 8,638 in 1685—is significant of the strained relations between that country and England. Again, in 1745, petitions from the manufacturers and traders in woollen hose at Worcester and Evesham showed they were apprehensive that the increased duties on linen would be prejudicial to their extensive trade with Germany, Holland, and Russia. *HCJ*, Vol 24, 830.

11　Henson, op cit, 105.

12　*HCJ*, 1738, Vol 23, 288. Also a petition from gentlemen, freeholders, farmers, and manufacturers of the town and country of Nottingham. Ibid, 1741, Vol 24, 91.

13　Ibid, 1744, Vol 24, 825.

14　Henson, op cit, 172.

15　*HCJ*, Vol 30, 1765, 87.

16　'Report of Committee on Import of Foreign Silks,' ibid, Vol 30, 1766, 724.

17　Op cit, 376.

18　Campbell, *London Tradesmen* (1747), 215, says that a youth of tolerable genius might acquire all the necessary knowledge to make him a decent workman in three years' time.

19　When trade was good apprentices might make 8s or more as their weekly task; since they could often be boarded for 2s 6d they were distinctly profitable to their employers. Henson, op cit, 98.

20　Ibid, 100.

21　*HCJ*, Vol 26, 783.

22　Campbell, op cit, 215.

23 *Music and Friends,* Vol III, 1853, 112.

24 *HCJ,* Vol 36, 1778, 740; Vol 37, 1779, 370.

25 A London hosier stated that the cheap work was usually sent abroad. *HCJ,* Vol 36, 740.

26 Eg., marking goods as of finer gauge than they actually were, and paying the worker at the rate for, say, 24 gauge when the goods he had made were 26 gauge.

27 The case of the woollen weavers twenty years earlier shows that Parliament was already wavering in its attitude towards wage regulation. The Woollen Cloth Weavers' Act was passed in 1756 but was quickly repealed on petitions from the employers. S. and B. Webb, *History of Trade Unionism,* 44.

28 The Leicester glove trade, for instance, was largely for export, and was badly hit by the troubles in America. *HCJ,* Vol 36, 740.

29 England, however, still prohibited the importation of silk goods, and France that of mixtures of cotton and wool.

30 Felkin, op cit, 117. Also a statement dated 26 November 1811, published in *The Nottingham Review* giving average weekly earnings on cotton stockings for 1794-1803 inclusive.

31 The inventions are described in detail by Henson, 256-355, and Felkin, chs vii, ix.

32 Felkin, op cit, 435.

33 *Committee on FWKs' Petitions,* 1812, II, 16, 19.

34 Ibid.

35 *Evidence,* 32.

36 Ibid, 31.

37 Coldham, town clerk of Nottingham, in a letter to the Home Office, dated 2 June 1812, alleges that the employers are 'terrorized' by their workmen. Parliament must not infer their acquiescence from their silence. *HO,* 42, 123.

38 *Committee on FWKs' Petitions, Second Report,* 76.

39 Ibid, 78.

40 *Committee on FWKs' Petitions, Second Report,* 78.

41 *First Report,* 48.

42 *Parliamentary Debates,* 22 July 1812, 1162.

43 Eg, the reference to Arkwright's improvements in spinning; his single thread cotton yarn was said to be uniformly excellent.

44 'If it should be more convenient or profitable for a workman to receive payment for his labour partly or wholly in goods, why should he be prevented from doing so? For if such a practice were inconvenient or injurious to any man he would not work a second time for the master who paid him in that manner.'

45 *Parliamentary Debates,* 25 July 1812, 1250.

46 Felkin, op cit, 440.

47   Ibid, 138.
48   *Committee on FWKs' Petitions,* 1819, V.
49   *Evidence,* 41.
50   *Evidence,* 18.
51   Ibid, 48.

Chapter 6 (p 88)

1   'So long as Companies continued to exercise any jurisdiction over
     their trade,' say the Webbs, 'we find them supported by any
     workmen's combinations that existed.' The case of the Dublin
     silk weavers is cited besides that of the framework knitters.
     History of Trade Unionism, 14.
2   The account of events during 1778 and 1779 is based on Henson
     (383-415), and on contemporary records in the *Nottingham
     Journal.*
3   *Nottingham Date Book,* 1750–1879, ed H. Field.
4   Published in *Nottingham Journal,* 1 August 1778.
5   Admittance Book, 1724–86.
6   Minute Book. The list is ten years later, but there is no reason
     to suppose that the composition of the livery had changed very
     much in the interval.
7   Tradesmen had their own grievance against the hosiers who, it
     was alleged, paid their workers in bad coin.
8   Announcement in *Nottingham Journal,* 15 May 1779.
9   *Nottingham Journal,* 8 May 1779.
10   Ibid, 18 September 1779.
11   Op cit, 53.
12   Minute Book.
13   Ibid, 21 October 1805.
14   Ibid, 14 November 1806.
15   Ibid, 16 January, 21 March, 15 April 1807.
16   *Nottingham Date Book,* 26 December 1805.
17   Minute Book, 24 June 1807.
18   Minute Book, 18 October 1808.
19   See *Report of London Livery Companies Commission,* 1884,
     XXXIX, Part III, 420.
20   By 1845 the company began to languish, the livery having fallen
     to twenty; in 1861 the plate was sold to help to pay for the
     repair of almshouses; but the year 1879 saw a distinct revival
     and the company was restored to its former position among
     the City guilds. Merchants and hosiery manufacturers with
     agencies in London applied for admission, and I am informed
     that at the present time the proportion of trade members is
     greater than in almost any similar body.

21 Minute Book, 14 June 1809.
22 This point is brought out in the report of the Nottingham police magistrates, 6 February 1812, *HO*, 42, 120.
23 'A Declaration' from 'Ned Ludd's Office,' dated 1 January 1812. A reward is offered for the detection of 'various banditti going about robbing under the pretence of framebreaking'. *HO*, 42, 119.
24 See especially *The Skilled Labourer* by J. L. and B. Hammond.
25 Information was usually obtained through spies. 'It is inconceivable the difficulty there is in getting framework knitters upon whom you can rely to obtain information, and no other person can be of the smallest use,' says the Nottingham town clerk in his letter to the Home Office, 10 May 1814. *HO*, 42, 138.
26 Op cit, 240.
27 Letter from Nottingham magistrate, *HO*, 42, 163.
28 See *Evidence before Committee on Artisans and Machinery* (1824), 282, and his letter to Sidmouth while imprisoned in London. The more desperate Luddites, he said, had threatened to shoot him for frustrating their designs. *HO*, 42, 166, 1817.
29 *HO*, 42, 139.
30 Ibid, 42, 163.
31 Ibid, 42, 160, 162. No doubt it was on this evidence that Henson was arrested during his visit to London on behalf of the condemned Luddites in 1817; the Habeas Corpus Act was suspended at the time.
32 Felkin, op cit, 240, quoting Henson's manuscript account.
33 Ibid, 231.
34 This did not please the Nottingham magistrates who were averse to any negotiations until the men gave up all appearance of riot. Coldham's report, 8 December, *HO*, 42, 118.
35 Op cit, 233.
36 Felkin, op cit, 235.
37 Letter to Sidmouth, 5 February. *HO*, 42, 119.
38 *HO*, 42, 126.
39 Copy of constitution sent to the Home Office by a Leicester spy, 14 December 1812, also a copy dated 1813, in Nottingham Public Library.
40 *HO*, 42, 139.
41 *HO*, 42, 137.
42 Letter from Rev J. L. Becher of Southwell, *HO*, 42, 139.
43 *HO*, 42, 139.
44 Ibid, 42, 140.
45 Ibid, 42, 139.

46 This account is based on Coldham's reports to the Home Office during June and July 1814. *HO*, 42, 139, 140.

47 The progress of the scheme is given week by week in *The Stocking Makers' Monitor or Commercial Magazine*, 25 October 1817, to 5 March 1818.

48 *Committee on Artisans and Machinery*, 1824, V, Fifth Report, 363.

49 *Committee on Artisans and Machinery*, 365.

50 On this occasion the Nottingham masters had been publishing their resolutions to reduce wages in the newspaper week by week. Henson went to the magistrates, but was informed that he had not sufficient evidence; when they eventually decided to grant a warrant it was refused by the town clerk because Henson could not say which parish they had met in. Ibid, Fourth Report, 280.

51 *Committee on Artisans and Machinery*, 1824, Fourth Report, 366.

52 *Committee on Artisans and Machinery*, 1824, Fourth Report, 365.

53 Felkin, op cit, 237, 241.

54 *Committee on Artisans and Machinery*, 268.

55 *Leicester Chronicle*, February 1817.

56 Pamphlet in Leicester Public Library.

57 This and a similar statement by 'Humanus' are ridiculed by Cobbett, who is a man of a single idea; all ills are the result of high taxation and mismanagement of the currency, and parliamentary reform is the only cure. *Weekly Register*, 14 April 1821.

58 'The Turnout, or an inquiry into the present state of the hosiery business.' Derby Public Library.

59 One man who was summoned in 1817 said he owed it more to the leniency of the magistrates than to the inefficiency of the law that he was not put in prison. *Committee on Artisans and Machinery*, 266.

60 *Leicester Journal*, 3 June 1817.

61 *Committee on Artisans and Machinery*, 266.

62 Ibid, 268, 270.

63 Op cit, 445.

64 'Report of proceedings on the conviction of Benjamin Taylor, John Ball, William Rutherford, and James Snow, part of the Framework Knitters' Committee, Nottingham, April 30, 1821.' Nottingham Public Library.

65 Pamphlet in Leicester Public Library.

66 Felkin, op cit, 443, and *Commission on FWKs*, 1845, 95.

67 'Reply to principal objections advanced by Mr. Cobbett and others,' 1821. Leicester Public Library.

68 Some were still in existence in 1824. *Committee on Artisans and Machinery*, 270.
69 'Case of Hosiers and F.W.Ks. impartially considered,' 1824. Derby Public Library.

Chapter 7 (p 106)

1   *Commission on FWKs*, 1845, XV, 64.
2   The bitter hatred of the system, 'which destroys every species of independence', is revealed in a leading article of the *Nottingham Journal*, 16 January 1846.
3   *Commission on FWKs*, 77.
4   *Commission on FWKs*, 64.
5   Ibid, 17.
6   *Weekly Register*, 14 April 1821. Reply to 'The Question at Issue between the Framework Knitters and their Employers', by 'Humanus'.
7   Loc cit, 26.
8   *Commission on FWKs*, 54.
9   Ibid, 17.
10 *Factory Commission*, 1833, XX, 557.
11 *Commission on FWKs*, 108.
12 Loc cit, 540.
13 Op cit, 455.
14 *Select Committee on Import Duties*, 1840, V, 246-7.
15 *Leicestershire Mercury*, 1 April 1837.
16 *Committee on Import Duties*, 250.
17 *Nottingham Journal*, 25 January 1839.
18 *Commission on FWKs*, 14.
19 Loc cit, 83.
20 *Committee on Import Duties*, 247.
21 Felkin in evidence before *FWKs' Commission*, 87.
22 *Nottingham Journal*, 25 January 1839.
23 Op cit, 455.
24 Op cit, 453.
25 There were 8,951 wide as against 34,991 narrow frames in 1844. Felkin's estimate, *Commission on FWKs*, 14.
26 Ibid, *Commissioner's Report*.
27 Ibid, 205, 286.
28 Op cit, 459.
29 *Factory Commission*, 538.
30 *Commission on FWKs*, 209.
31 The petition which led to the appointment of the commission was signed by over 25,000 framework knitters in the three counties and presented to the House of Commons in 1843.

P

32 Op cit, 472.
33 *Nottingham Journal*, 7 June 1839.
34 *Factory Commission*, 1833, 539.
35 *Leicester Chronicle*, 12 March 1836.
36 *Leicester Journal*, 20 May 1836.
37 *Commission on FWKs*, 75.
38 'The sock employers encourage their hands and even lecture them if they do not subscribe to their trade fund.' FWKs' Appeal, *Leicester Chronicle*, 12 March 1836.
39 *Leicestershire Mercury*, 25 April 1838.
40 *Leicestershire Mercury*, 9 June 1838.
41 Ibid, 23 June 1838.
42 *Leicestershire Mercury*, 25 June 1838.
43 *Commission on FWKs*, 238.
44 Ibid, 87.
45 Ibid, 65, 135, 236, 373.
46 Gardiner, *Music and Friends*, Vol II, 573.
47 Beamish, *Life of Brunel*, 1862, 143. Also Felkin, op cit, 496.
48 Catalogue of the Exhibition of Arts, Manufactures, etc, at the Exchange Rooms, Nottingham, 1840. Nottingham Public Library. The machine was said to be extensively used on the Continent for making knitted caps and other articles.
49 Felkin, op cit, 489.
50 *Commission on FWKs*, 262. Even at the present day the leg and foot of a fashioned stocking are made on different frames.

Chapter 8 (p 118)

1 *Select Committee on Stoppage of Wages in Hosiery Manufacture*, 1854–5, XIV, 131, 204.
2 Felkin, op cit, 490.
3 Ibid, 500.
4 This firm claimed to be the first to produce stockings, shirts, pants, and other articles by steam power. *Knitters' Circular*, June 1897.
5 The account of William Cotton is based on an article in the *Knitters' Circular*, February 1898.
6 See Erickson, *British Industrialists: Steel & Hosiery 1850–1950*.
7 *Commission on Children's Employment*, 291.
8 Select Committee on Home Work, 1908.
9 *Report of Nottingham Chamber of Commerce*.
10 *Commission on Children's Employment*, 279. All these are employers' estimates.
11 *Reports of Factory Inspectors*, 1862.
12 *Commission on Children's Employment*, 289.

13 *Commission on Children's Employment*, 269.
14 *Trade Union Commission*, 1867–8, XXXIX, 10th Report, 81. Evidence of A. J. Mundella.
15 Loc cit, 274. Evidence of Mary Thorpe, Bulwell, Nottingham. Other witnesses said it was not usual for children to begin before six years of age.
16 Ibid, 287.
17 It was said that men were more irregular when trade was good, knowing that they could 'make enough anyhow'. Ibid, 285.
18 There were exceptions, however. One witness, a Nottingham manufacturer, declared: 'He would often be put to inconvenience if prevented from keeping young persons at work as long as he had occasion. He had formerly had occasion to keep the hands till eleven and twelve at night. More harm was caused by young females leaving their employment early than by their staying later.' *Children's Employment Commission*, 270.
19 Ibid, 290.
20 There were about 2,000 hosiery workshops in Nottingham and district. No adequate statistics were available for Leicester, but the number of workshops in the district was estimated at about 5,000, of which two-thirds were used for the manufacture of hand-made boots and hosiery. *Commission on Factory Acts, 1876*, XXIX. *Reports of Factory Inspectors*.
21 *Report*, XXIX, Appendix E.
22 Evidence of Hosiery Manufacturers' Association of Leicester, ibid, XXX, 378.
23 Loc cit, 386.
24 There were half a dozen seaming schools at Hinckley. 'If you drive through any of the villages about here,' said a witness before the Factory Commission, 'you will see all the children sitting at the doors seaming stockings.' Loc cit, XXX, 385.
25 *Commission on Children's Employment*, 287. Report of schoolmaster at Hinckley. The report of the headmaster of Great Meeting Day School, Leicester, shows that 742 boys attended during the year 1862. Of this number 341 attended 100 days and over, and 337 left during the year. The attendance did not average more than 17 months. Ibid, 293.
26 Although there was some shortage of juvenile labour in Leicester, the Hosiery Manufacturers' Association considered that it would be best to prohibit the employment of children under thirteen. *Commission on Factory Acts*, XXX, 378.
27 'When either Government or private members dangled before the eyes of the men Bills which destroyed their feeling of self-

reliance it could only prolong that state of things which the House desired to put an end to, and leave the employees more defenceless than ever. If the House were going to take charge and cognisance of such industrial questions, then trade organizations were a mere pretence.' Debate on second reading of Bill, *Hansard*, 1872, CCXIII, 212.

28   Bindley, *History of Struggle for Abolition of Frame Rents and Charges* (1875). Pamphlet in Leicester Public Library.
29   *Truck Commission*, 1871, XXXVI, 840.
30   Hosiery Manufacture (Wages) Act, 1874.

Chapter 9 (p 133)

1   *TU Commission*, 1867-8, XXXIX, 10th Report, evidence of A. J. Mundella, 74.
2   Felkin, op cit, 344.
3   Included in *An Account of the Machine-Wrought Hosiery Trade and Condition of the Framework Knitters* (1845).
4   Felkin, *Account of Machine-Wrought Hosiery Trade,* etc.
5   *Industrial Democracy*, 226.
6   A copy of the rules is preserved in the Webb Collection.
7   E. Renals, 'Arbitration in the Hosiery Trades of the Midland Counties,' *Journal of the Royal Statistical Society*, 1867, Vol 30, 548-56.
8   *TU Commission*, 74.
9   'Arbitration as a Means of Preventing Strikes' (Bradford, 1868), quoted by S. & B. Webb, *Industrial Democracy*, 223.
10   *TU Commission*, 77.
11   Renals, loc cit.
12   *TU Commission*, 75.
13   *TU Commission*, 77.
14   Ibid, 80.
15   Quoted by Felkin, op cit, 486-7.
16   Bremner, op cit, 180.
17   *TU Commission*, 80.
18   Felkin, op cit, 488.

Chapter 10 (p 141)

1   *Hosiery Review*, January 1888.
2   This subject is discussed in an article on 'Competition in our Trade: some of its causes and effects,' *Hosiery and Lace Trades Review*, December 1891.
3   *Knitters' Circular*, February 1897.
4   Statistics collected by the Rev M. Anstey of Leicester, quoted in *Hosiery and Lace Trades Review*, May 1891.

5 *Wright's Directory* gives the numbers of hosiery manufacturers in Nottingham at various dates as follows: 1854, 48; 1862, 53; 1870, 54; 1881, 64; 1891, 80; 1900, 73. This does not include 'bag hosiers' who declined from 32 in 1881 to 8 in 1900.

6 Select Committee on Exportation of Machinery, 1841, VII.

7 *Evidence*, 150.

8 Report on French Hosiery Trade, Felkin, op cit, 549. Felkin puts the English output for 1865 at £7,795,000, though this figure is inflated by the high price of cotton in that year.

9 Abstract of Table of Hosiery Machinery in District of Chemnitz given in *Report of Nottingham Chamber of Commerce*, 1863.

10 Article on Growth of Hosiery Trade in Saxony in last thirty years, *Hosiery Review*, December 1894.

11 *Hosiery Review*, June 1888. The cheapening of transport was also a factor favouring the foreigner in the home market. A warehouseman who was now buying the whole of his wool knitted goods from Germany stated that they could be brought from Berlin to London almost as cheaply as from Leicester. Commission on Depression of Trade, 1886, XXI, *Evidence*, 137, 142.

12 The Continental Trade suffered even worse depressions than the English, however. It was stated in evidence before the Labour Commission in 1892 that half the machinery in Germany, France, and Belgium was idle, the depression having been caused by the introduction of power machinery.

Conditions in the Saxon hosiery trade were again reported to be very bad in 1897. During the past decade the value of the export to the United States had fallen from $11 million to $3½ million, and over forty factories were closed. *Knitters' Circular*, June 1897.

13 The growth of the wool and cashmere trade was stimulated by the increasing supplies of wool from Australia. *Hosiery Review*, February 1890.

14 *Hosiery Review*, November 1891.

15 It was reported in 1886 that Nottingham manufacturers were now able to compete with Chemnitz, having turned to new lines and introduced improved machinery. *Commission on Depression of Trade*, 234.

16 Trade unions were blamed for their 'utter incapacity to recognize the signs of the times and to moderate their demands for wages'. It was admitted, however, that in the prosperous years 1880, 1881, and 1882, the men acted better than the manufacturers; they did not ask for an advance but some manufacturers put up prices. Ibid, 244.

17 Minutes of Nottingham Chamber of Commerce, 1867.

18 Article on Foreign Competition in the Hosiery Trade, *Hosiery Review*, October 1887.

Chapter 11 (p 152)

1 *Labour Commission*, 1892, XXXVI, Vol II, 77-9. The estimate of 5,000 framework knitters in the Midlands refers to men only, the union having 'no cognisance of the great number of women who are employed'.

2 *Labour Commission*, 1892, XXXVI, Vol II, 77.

3 The Nottingham Chamber of Commerce considered the Bill 'wholly impracticable and mischievous, interfering as it does with the whole trade of the country'. Minutes, 11 April 1890.

4 *Labour Commission*, 1892, XXXVI, Vol II, 80.

5 As late as 1908 there were still a thousand old men in Leicestershire and Nottinghamshire making army pants on the hand frame. They made three or four pairs a week, which meant a wage of 6s or 7s. *Fair Wages Committee*, 1908, XXXIV, 71.

6 *Labour Commission*, 1892, XXXV, Vol II, 78, 87.

7 *Labour Commission*, 1892, XXXVI, Vol II, 87.

8 Safeguarding Inquiry, 1926, *Evidence*.

9 *Labour Commission*, 1892, XXXVI, vol II, 65.

10 *Hosiery Review*, February 1888.

11 *Knitters' Circular*, January 1896.

12 *Nottingham Rotary Power Framework Knitters' Society, Annual Report* (undated).

13 A Leicester manufacturer stated that about one-fifth of those employed by his firm were men. The Union had objected to the employment of women on frames, but they could do the work as well as men, he declared, and were paid less. *Labour Commission*, 1892, XXXVI, Vol II, 94.

14 *Factory Return*, 1890, LXVII.

15 *Commission on Factory Acts*, 1876.

16 *Labour Commission*, 1892, XXXVI, Vol II, 66. The workers' representatives favoured the revival of the boards, but the employers showed little enthusiasm. In 1891 one of the union secretaries circularised fifty manufacturers in Nottingham and Derby on the subject; only nine replied, of whom five were favourable.

The impossibility of enforcing the board's decisions was one of the main reasons for the employers' lack of faith in the system. This point was brought out, and the recent dissolution of the Hosiery Board cited as an example, when the Nottingham Chamber of Commerce was discussing a proposal of the

Associated Chambers of Commerce for statutory boards of conciliation and arbitration. Minutes, December 1889.

17 *Hosiery Review*, November 1889.

18 *Labour Commission*, 1892, XXXVI, Vol II, 64.

19 Ibid, 61.

20 Mention is made of extremely low rates for hand seaming, working out at about five hundred stitches a farthing. *Hosiery Review*, June 1888.

21 This is commented upon in the *Knitters' Circular*, March 1898.

22 *Hosiery Review*, June 1890.

23 Ibid, November 1889. 'Within the last fifteen years there has been one firm a year leaving Leicester for the rural districts.' *Fair Wages Committee*, 71.

24 *Fair Wages Committee*, 1908, evidence of representative of Midland Counties Hosiery Manufacturers' Association, 241.

25 *Knitters' Circular*, December 1895, March 1898, 71.

26 *Report on Standard Piece Rates and Sliding Scales*, 1900.

27 Despite its title the federation had no members outside the three Midland counties. *Fair Wages Committee, Evidence*, 66,

28 Statistics of membership are not very reliable. There were probably less than 6,000 unionists in 1892.

29 *Labour Commission*, 1892, XXXVI, Vol II, 54.

30 *Hosiery Review*, October 1888.

31 *Labour Commission*, 1892, XXXVI, Vol II, 97.

32 Ibid, 241.

33 *Fair Wages Committee*, 1908, 68. In 1892 there were many women working obsolete sewing machines on which they could earn no more than 9s or 10s a week full-time, yet the average for that occupation was over 14s. *Labour Commission*, 1892, XXXVI, Vol II, 61.
   There were also men on twenty-year-old frames who made as little as 15s to 20s a week; these were members of the Midland Counties Hosiery Federation.

34 *Wages in Minor Textile Trades*, 1890, LXVIII. It is doubtful how far the returns were representative since only 8 per cent of the manufacturers furnished them. In Scotland, many workers were paid on a time basis and earnings were generally much lower than in the Midlands.

35 There was a fear that the Patent branch might become overcrowded through 'teaching too many lads who only compete with us for a job when they get grown up'. The Nottingham Rotary Power FWKs' Society requested the Patent hands who were wanting youths to take on the rotary men whose machines

were being superseded by the improved type. *Annual Report,* 1892.

36 Reports of Nottingham Rotary Power FWKs' Society and L. & L. Amalgamated Hosiery Union.

37 Report of National Amalgamated Hosiery Federation, 1892, and trade union evidence before Labour Commission.

38 *Hosiery Review,* July 1891, and *Nottingham Rotary Power FWKs' Society, Annual Report,* 1892.

Chapter 12 (p 169)

1 A detailed account with numerous illustrations is given in Quilter & Chamberlain, *Framework Knitting & Hosiery Manufacture* (1911).

2 The committee issued two reports, 1926 and 1927. Minutes of Evidence were circulated privately. See also *Survey of Textile Industries: Committee on Industry & Trade* (1928).

3 Silverman, *Studies in Industrial Organisation: the Hosiery Industry,* 31-5.

4 *Hosiery Working Party Report,* 10.

5 See NEDO report, 'Hosiery & Knitwear in the 1970s', for details. It was estimated that in 1970 about half of all apparel in the world was made from knitted fabric.

6 Census of Production. A more recent development is the switch from stockings to tights and panty-hose.

7 Henson, op cit, 326-7.

8 The story will appear in a forthcoming book, *Three generations in a Family Textile Firm* by Jocelyn Morton. An extract was printed in *The Hosiery Trade Journal,* April 1971.

9 Textile Council, Annual Reports.

10 'Hosiery & Knitwear in the 1970s'.

11 'Hosiery & Knitwear in the 1970s'.

Chapter 13 (p 184)

1 Census of Production.

2 Ministry of Labour Returns.

3 The British Hosiery Industry, First Report.

4 Board of Trade, Survey of Industrial Development.

5 Pool and Llewellyn, op cit, 17.

6 Dun & Bradstreets, *Guide to Key British Enterprises.*

7 *Hosiery Review,* Dec 1888 and Dec 1891.

8 *Knitters' Circular,* Nov 1898. As illustrating the variety of the trade, one wholesaler was reported to stock no fewer than 750 different numbers of goods, 726 British and 24 of foreign manufacture.

9   'Hosiery & Knitwear in the 1970s' estimates that by 1973 53 per cent of clothing sales will be through multiple and variety chains. It also refers to the significant growth of mail-order trading and of 'rack merchandising'. The latter development is due to the advent of the one-size stocking made of stretch yarn. Racks of such articles are displayed not only in chain stores but in small grocers, newsagents etc.

10   Hosiery Working Party Report.

11   Jopp, op cit.

12   Hosiery Working Party Report.

13   Monopolies Commission, *Report on the supply of man-made cellulosic fibres* (1968).

14   Wells, *Hollins & Viyella,* Newton Abbot (1968).

15   Erickson, op cit, 124.

Chapter 14 (p 203)

1   Ministry of Labour returns.

2   Ministry of Labour occupation returns.

3   Trade union rule books.

4   Knitting Lace & Net Training Board Annual Reports.

5   Hosiery Working Party Report.

6   Part 1, chapter eleven.

7   Trade union annual reports.

8   Minutes of Nottingham Chamber of Commerce, 3 July 1917.

9   National Union of Hosiery & Knitwear Workers, Report of 24th Annual Conference, 1970.

10   National Union of Hosiery & Knitwear Workers, Report of 24th Annual Conference, 1970.

Q

BIBLIOGRAPHY

MANUSCRIPT SOURCES

Records of the Framework Knitters' Company

Charters, 1657, 1664.
Lists of Bylaws, 1664, 1745.
Account Books, 1694–1809.
Admittance Books, 1713–86.
Letter Book, 1725–45.
Minute Books, 1745–1809.

State Papers

Domestic Letters and Papers, Petitions, etc, 1655–61.
Home Office Papers, 1811–17.

Miscellaneous

Minutes of the Nottingham Chamber of Commerce, from 1860.
Memoranda submitted by the National Joint Industrial Council of the Hosiery Industry to the Board of Trade in connection with the applications for a Safeguarding Duty, 1926, 1927.
Minutes of Evidence taken by the Board of Trade Committee on the applications for a Safeguarding Duty, 1926, 1927.

CONTEMPORARY AUTHORITIES

BAINES, E. *History of the Cotton Manufacture in Great Britain* (1835).
BEAMISH, R. *A Memoir of the Life of Brunel* (1862).
BEAMISH, R. *Beauties of England and Wales* (1802, 1813).
BLACKNER, J. *History of Nottingham* (1815).
BRAND, M. *A Brief Description of Orkney, Zetland, etc* (1701).
BREMNER, D. *The Industries of Scotland: their Rise, Progress, and Present Condition* (1869).

CAMPBELL, R. *The London Tradesman: being a compendious view of all the trades, professions, and arts now practised in the Cities of London and Westminster* (1747).

DEERING, C. *Nottinghamia Vetus et Nova* (1751).

DEFOE, D. *A Tour Through England and Wales* (1724).

DEFOE, D. *Giving Alms No Charity and Employing the Poor a Grievance to the Nation* (1704).

EDEN, F. M. *State of the Poor* (1797).

FELKIN, W. *A History of the Machine-wrought Hosiery and Lace Manufactures* (1867).

FELKIN, W. *An Account of the Machine-wrought Hosiery Trade and the Condition of the Framework Knitters* (1845).

FIELD, H. (ed) *The Nottingham Date Book, 1750–1879*.

GARDINER, W. *Music and Friends* (vols I and II, 1838, vol III, 1853).

GLOVER, S. *History of Derby* (1831).

HENSON, G. *The Civil, Political, and Mechanical History of the Framework Knitters* (1831).

HODDER, E. *The Life of Samuel Morley* (1887).

HUTTON, W. *The History of Derby from the Remote Ages of Antiquity to the Year 1791* (1791).

MACPHERSON, D. *The Annals of Commerce* (1805).

PENNANT, T. *A Tour of Scotland* (1769).

POSTLETHWAYTE, M. *Dictionary of Trade and Commerce* (1774).

RENALS, E. 'Arbitration in the Hosiery Trades of the Midland Counties', *Journal of the Royal Statistical Society*, 1867.

SMITH, A. *An Inquiry into the Nature and Causes of the Wealth of Nations* (1776).

THOMPSON, J. *History of Leicester in the Eighteenth Century* (1871).

THOMPSON, J. *History of Leicester to the End of the Seventeenth Century* (1849).

THOROTON, R. *Antiquities of Nottinghamshire* (1677).

THROSBY, J. *Memoirs of the Town and County of Leicester* (1777).

THROSBY, J. *History and Antiquities of Leicester* (1791).

URE, A. *The Cotton Manufacture of Great Britain* (1861).

PAMPHLETS, ETC

Evidence given before the House of Commons Committee on the Framework Knitters' Bill (Reprint, 1780). Derby Library.

The Trial of a Cause to Repeal a Patent Granted to Richard Arkwright (1785). British Museum.

Articles and General Regulations of the Society for Obtaining Parliamentary Relief and the Encouragement of Mechanics in the Improvement of Mechanism (1813). Nottingham Library.

An Appeal on behalf of the Framework Knitters' Fund. Rev Robert Hall (1819). Leicester Library.

A Reply to the Principal Objections advanced by Mr Cobbett and Others against the Framework Knitters' Friendly Relief Society. Rev Robert Hall (1821). Leicester Library.

Report of the Proceedings on the Conviction of Benjamin Taylor, John Ball, William Rutherford, and James Snow, part of the Framework Knitters' Committee, at Nottingham on April 30, 1821. Nottingham Library.

The Turnout, or an Inquiry into the present state of the Hosiery Business (1821). Derby Library.

The Case of the Hosiers and Framework Knitters impartially considered (1824). Derby Library.

Catalogue of the Exhibition of Arts, Manufactures, etc., at the Exchange Rooms, Nottingham, 1840. Nottingham Library.

The History of the Struggle for the Abolition of Frame Rents and Charges. R. Bindley (1875). Leicester Library.

Trade Union Rules and Reports. Webb Collection, London School of Economics.

NEWSPAPERS AND PERIODICALS

The Nottingham Journal. Various issues, 1767–1850.

The Nottingham Review, 1811–18.

The Leicester Journal, 1836–40.

The Leicester Chronicle, 1836–40.

The Leicestershire Mercury, 1837–40.

The Stocking Makers' Monitor, 1817–18.

The Hosiery and Lace Trades Review, 1888–92.

The Knitters' Circular and Monthly Record, 1897, continued as *The Hosiery Trade Jornal,* 1900 to date.

PARLIAMENTARY PAPERS, OFFICIAL DOCUMENTS AND PUBLICATIONS

Calendar of State Papers, Domestic, 1582, 1590, 1592, 1611, 1624, 1655, 1658, 1659, 1660, 1661, 1678.

House of Commons Journals. 1693, 1696, 1699, 1713, 1738, 1741, 1744, 1745, 1753, 1765, 1766, 1778, 1779.

Irish House of Commons Journals. 1695, 1703.

Acts of the Parliament of Scotland. 1647, 1661, 1663.

Proclamations, 1657–91.

Parliamentary Debates. 1812, 1819, 1853, 1854, 1872.

Reports from the Committee on the Framework Knitters' Petition, With Minutes of Evidence. 1812, II.

Reports from the Committee on the Framework Knitters' Petition, with Minutes of Evidence. 1819, V.

Reports from the Committee on the Laws relating to Emigration, Combinations, and Export of Machinery, with Minutes of Evidence. 1824, V.

Report of the Commissioners on the Employment of Children in Factories, with Minutes of Evidence. 1833, XX.

Report from the Select Committee on Import Duties, with Minutes of Evidence. 1840, V.

Report from the Select Committee on the Exportation of Machinery, with Minutes of Evidence. 1841, VII.

Report of the Commissioner appointed to inquire into the Condition of the Framework Knitters, with Minutes of Evidence. 1845, XV.

Report of the Select Committee on the Stoppage of Wages in the Hosiery Manufacture, with Minutes of Evidence. 1854–5, XIV.

Factory Returns. 1862, LV; 1875, LXXI; 1890, LXVII.

Report of the Commissioners on the Employment of Children and Young Persons in Trades not already regulated by Law, with Minutes of Evidence. 1863, XVII.

Tenth Report of the Commission on Trade Unions. 1867, XXXIX.

Reports of the Commissioners on the Truck Acts. 1871, XXXVI; 1872, XXXV.

Report of the Commissioners appointed to inquire into the working of the Factory and Workshops Acts, with Minutes of Evidence. 1876, XXIX, XXX.

Report of the Royal Commission on the City of London Livery Companies. 1884, XXXIX, Part 3.

Report of the Royal Commission on the Depression of Trade and Industry. 1886, XXI.

Returns of Rates of Wages in the Minor Textile Trades. 1890, LXVIII.

Report on Standard Piece Rates and Sliding Scales. 1900.

Report on Earnings and Hours of Labour. Textile Trades. 1906.

Report of the Committee on the Fair Wages Clause. 1908, XXXIV.

Reports of the Select Committee on Home Work. 1907, VI; 1908, VIII.

Report of the Committee on the Position of the Textile Trades after the War. 1918, XIII.

Report of the Ministry of Labour on Apprenticeship and Training for the Skilled Occupations in Great Britain and Northern Ireland. 1925–6.

Report of the Board of Trade Committee on the Application for a Safeguarding Duty on Hosiery, 1926, XV.

Reports of the Committee on Industry and Trade:
Survey of Industrial Relations, 1926.
Survey of Overseas Markets, 1927.
Factors in Industrial and Commercial Efficiency, 1927–8.
Survey of the Textile Industries, 1928.

Memorandum on the Marketing of Hosiery in England. USA Bureau of Foreign and Domestic Commerce. 1927.

Census of Population Returns, 1851–1921.

Census of Production Returns, 1907, 1912, 1924, 1930, 1954, 1963.

Survey of Industrial Development, 1933.

Working Party Reports: Hosiery. 1946.

Hosiery and Knitwear: Productivity Team Report. 1951.

Man-made Cellulosic Fibres: Monopolies Commission. 1968.

Hosiery and Knitwear in the 1970s. National Economic Development Office, 1970.

MODERN BOOKS AND ARTICLES

CHAMBERS, J. D. *Nottinghamshire in the Eighteenth Century* (1932).

CHAMBERS, J. D. 'The Worshipful Company of Framework Knitters', *Economica*, November 1929.

CHAPMAN, S. D. 'The Genesis of the Hosiery Industry', forthcoming work.

CHAPMAN, S. J. *The Lancashire Cotton Industry* (1904).

CLAPHAM, J. H. *An Economic History of Modern Britain: The Early Railway Age* (1927).

CUNNINGHAM, W. *The Growth of English Industry and Commerce in Modern Times* (1925).

DANIELS, G. W. *The Early English Cotton Industry* (1920).

DUNLOP, J. *English Apprenticeship and Child Labour* (1912).

ERICKSON, C. *British Industrialists, Steel and Hosiery 1850–1950* (1958).

GRASS, M. & A. *Stockings for a Queen* (1967).

HAMMOND, J. L. and B. *The Town Labourer (1760–1832)*, (1917).

HAMMOND, J. L. and B. *The Skilled Labourer (1760–1832)*, (1920).

HARTOPP, H. *Register of the Freemen of Leicester, 1196–1770, including the Apprentices sworn before successive Mayors for certain periods, 1646–1770*, (1927).

HEATON, H. *The Yorkshire Woollen and Worsted Industries from the Earliest Times up to the Industrial Revolution* (1920).

HENDERSON, T. 'The Scottish Hosiery Trade', *Scottish Bankers' Magazine*, October 1910.

HUTCHINS, B. L., and HARRISON, A. *A History of Factory Legislation* (1926).

JOPP, K. *Corah of Leicester 1815–1965.*

MANTOUX, P. *The Industrial Revolution in the Eighteenth Century* (revised edition, 1927).

O'BRIEN, G. *The Economic History of Ireland from the Union to the Famine* (1921).

PINCHBECK, I. *Women Workers and the Industrial Revolution* (1930).

POOL, A. G. & LLEWELLYN, G. *The British Hosiery Industry: a Study in Competition, 1955–58.*

PORTER, G. R. *The Progress of the Nation* (revised edition, F. W. Hurst, 1912).

PRICE, W. H. *The English Patents of Monopoly* (1906).

QUILTER, J. H. & CHAMBERLAIN, J. *Framework Knitting and Hosiery Manufacture* (1911).

SCOTT, W. R. *Records of a Scottish Cloth Manufactory* (1905).

SCOTT, W. R. *The Constitution and Finance of English, Scottish, and Irish Joint Stock Companies to 1720*, (1912).

SMITH, D. *Industrial Archaeology in the East Midlands* (1965).

THOMAS, F. M. *I & R Morley: a Record of a Hundred Years* (1900).

UNWIN, G. *Industrial Organization in the Sixteenth and Seventeenth Centuries* (1904).

Victoria Histories of the Counties of England: Nottinghamshire, Derbyshire, Surrey.

WEBB, S. and B. *History of Trade Unionism* (1911 edition).

WEBB, S. and B. *Industrial Democracy* (1920 edition).

WELLS, F. A. *Hollins and Viyella* (1968).

WESTERFIELD, R. B. *Middlemen in English Business* (1915).

INDEX

Plates and diagrams are indicated by numbers in italic